We, the Anarchists

A Study of the Iberian Anarchist Federation (FAI) 1927–1937

Stuart Christie

AK Press
Edinburgh, Oakland, West Virginia

We, the Anarchists: A Study of the Ibrian Anarchist Federation (FAI)
1927–1937
by Stuart Christie

© Stuart Christie

ISBN 9781904859758
Library of Congress Control Number 2007939202

AK Press
674-A 23rd St.
Oakland, CA 94612
USA
akpress@akpress.org
www.akpress.org

AK Press
PO Box 12766
Edinburgh EH8 9YE
Scotland
ak@akedin.demon.co.uk
www.akuk.com

The addresses above would be delighted to provide you with the latest complete AK catalog, featuring several thousand books, pamphlets, zines, audio and video products, and stylish apparel published and distributed by AK Press. Alternately, please visit our websites for the complete catalog, latest news and updates, events, and secure ordering.

Cover Design: John Yates | www.stealworks.com
Design and layout : JR

Printed in Canada on acid-free, 100% recycled paper with union labor.

Table of Contents

Introduction

"With the crowd of commonplace chatterers, we are already past praying for: no reproach is too bitter for us, no epithet too insulting. Public speakers on social and political subjects find that abuse of anarchists is an unfailing passport to popular favour. Every conceivable crime is laid to our charge, and opinion, too indolent to learn the truth, is easily persuaded that anarchy is but another name for wickedness and chaos. Overwhelmed with opprobrium and held up to hatred, we are treated on the principle that the surest way of hanging a dog is to give it a bad name."

Elisée Reclus

Since the official birth of organized anarchism at the Saint Imier Congress of 1872, no anarchist organization has been held up to greater opprobrium or subjected to such gross misrepresentation than the Federación Anarquista Iberica, better known by its initials—FAI. Although the above lines by anarchist geographer Elisée Reclus predated the FAI by almost fifty years, they might well have been written as that organization's epitaph.

The hostility of extreme right-wing commentators to revolutionary working-class movements is hardly surprising and need not detain us long. The following quote is included merely as an example of how authoritarian commentators attempted to calibrate popular attitudes in such a way as to present the FAI, the rallying point for the defenders of the anarchist constitution of the Confederación Nacional del Trabajo (CNT), the Spanish anarcho-syndicalist union, as the agent of disharmony and the conspiratorial epicenter of mindless violence.

"The other (great corporation) unites the men who profess anarcho-syndicalist doctrines, styling itself on the Confederación Nacional de Trabajadores (National Confederation of Workers)

[sic]. It is for brevity's sake designated as CNT. Its ruling committee, the FAI (Federación Anarquista Ibérica—Iberian Anarchist Federation) bears a name which strikes terror into the heart of most Spaniards. If 'ruthless' be the qualification fitted for the UGT, 'bloodthirsty' does not sufficiently describe the FAI. The members of both of these associations are recruited by methods most closely resembling coercion than persuasion, the flourish of a pistol being one of the most frequent. They are inscribed on the rolls without the slightest regard to their trade. One and the other furnish gunmen for social crimes, voters for the elections and militiamen for the front. These three seem the only activities of the UGT, the CNT and the FAI. To belong to any of these three justify vehement suspicion of criminality: membership of the last makes it certain."[1]

Present day attitudes toward the FAI have been and continue to be formed, in the main, by the works of Liberal and Marxist historians. More sophisticated than Arnold Lunn, these views, as the American commentator Noam Chomsky has noted, continue to be supported "by ideological conviction rather than history or investigation of the phenomena of social life."[2]

This study developed out of a sense of irritation that the same myths and distortions about the millenarian or manipulative role of the FAI in its symbiotic relationship with the CNT continue to circulate unchallenged. I was equally concerned to establish that indolent and intelligent commentators alike have sought to demonize the FAI—and Spanish anarchism, in general—by cynically or unintentionally distorting the available historical evidence. Whether to reinforce their own political prejudices, refute their enemies, or because of plain ignorance or malice is immaterial; what is intriguing is that apparently diligent historians should adapt and perpetuate wild hearsay assertions such as those propagated by Arnold Lunn—making no attempt to distinguish between fact and fantasy—is more than a simple infraction of the rules of historical hypothesis. Their failure to apply the rules of evidence in the case against the FAI not only undermines that case, but it also raises serious questions as to their intellectual and moral honesty.

In order to fully comprehend the role and function of the FAI it is first of all essential to understand three things:

1. That anarchism caught the imagination of a substantial section of the Spanish working classes because it reflected and articulated the values, lifestyles, and social relationships that existed at the base of Spanish society.

2. That the predominant ideological influence within the major Spanish labor organizations between 1869 and 1939 was anarchism.

3. That the "conscious minority" of rank and file militants who built up and sustained their unions through lengthy periods of relentless and often bloody repression were anarchists who sought, as an immediate objective through social revolution and the introduction of Libertarian Communism, a just and equitable classless and stateless society, moral objectives which brought them into conflict, not only with the state and employers, but also with their own union leadership whose immediate objectives were material.

There are two dimensions to this book. The first is descriptive and historical. It outlines the evolution of the organized anarchist movement in Spain and its relationship with the wider labor movement. At the same time it provides some insight into the main ideas that made the Spanish labor movement one of the most revolutionary of modern times. The second is analytical and tries to address, from an anarchist perspective, what for me is the particularly relevant problem of understanding change in the contemporary world: How can ideals survive the process of institutionalization? If this is not feasible, at least to be able to identify the turning points so that we may be able to counter the process.

In tracing the history of the CNT and the FAI it is clear that anarchist organizations, like all other organizations and civilizations before them, are subject to a process of rise and fall. Once they achieve their specific objectives, even the most committed libertarian and directly democratic organizations quickly degenerate. From being social instruments set up to meet real social needs they become transformed into self-perpetuating institutions with lives and purposes of their own, distinct to and in tension with the objectives that called them into being in the first place.

My main contention is simple: briefly, it is that, as the Primo de Rivera dictatorship began to founder in 1927, a struggle broke out between the non-anarchist leadership and anarchist base of the anarcho-syndicalist Confederación Nacional del Trabajo (CNT). The leaders, that is, the members of the Regional and National Committees of the CNT, having become intermediaries between labor and capital, openly challenged the ideological objectives of the "conscious minority" by seeking to overturn the federally structured anti-capitalist and anti-statist constitution of the CNT in order to compete with the socialist Union General de Trabajadores (UGT) for hegemony over the Spanish working class. In their view, the workers' cause would only be advanced when all workers belonged to their union, something that could only be achieved by operating within the legal parameters of the capitalist and statist system.

To the "conscious minority" of anarchists, this threatened to transform the CNT from a revolutionary weapon that could eliminate the misery of everyday life into a reformist labor union that served only to perpetuate and legitimize the exploitation of man by man. The anarchist militants who constituted the base of the CNT responded by founding the Federación Anarquista Ibérica, an ad hoc federally-structured association, whose function was to reaffirm the revolutionary nature of anarchism and to provide a rallying point for the defense of the anti-political principles and immediate Libertarian Communist objectives of the CNT. By 1932 the reformist threat had been eliminated—democratically!—and the working class anarchists who had spoken in the name of the FAI (although many of these, like Garcia Oliver and Durruti, had never been affiliated to the FAI) reverted to everyday union activity at Local Federation level or to conspiratorial revolutionary activity in the Confederal Defense Committee.

Instead of disbanding, however, or confining itself to acting as a liaison secretariat between autonomous agitational or propaganda groups, the FAI was taken over in mid-1933 by a group of rootless intellectuals and economic planners under the leadership of Diego Abad de Santillán, a man for whom abstract theories took precedence over workers' practical experiences. With the coming of the Spanish Civil War three years later, the FAI had abandoned all pretense of being a revolutionary organ. Like the institutionalized CNT leadership it had helped oust in 1930–1932, the FAI had become, in its turn, a structure of vested interests serving to apply the brakes to the spontaneous revolutionary activity of the rank and file and repress the new generation of revolutionary activists among the Libertarian Youth and the "Friends of Durruti" group. "Anti-fascist unity" and state power were promoted at the expense of anarchist principles, while the hegemony of the CNT-FAI leadership was imposed over the local revolutionary committees and the general assemblies. Its principal aim had become to perpetuate itself, even at the expense of the revolutionary anarchist principles that had inspired it: the instrumental means had become the organizational end.

Stuart Christie

1

Roots: 1872–1910
The First International

Anarchism in Spain has its roots in the so-called Bourgeois revolutionary period of Spanish history between 1868 and 1873, when the pillars of the old semi-feudal regime finally collapsed and the State became transformed into an organ of bourgeois government. This new dominant bourgeois class did not spring from the still small and weak industrial bourgeoisie, but from an agrarian-based mercantile bourgeoisie, whose political and economic objectives were liberal agrarian capitalism. The tension between a State-supported agrarian capitalism, on the one hand, and the growing economic power of industrial capitalism that came to a head at this time set the stage for the political and economic struggles of the period.

The break up of Church lands and the entailed estates in the middle of the 19th century was not simply an anti-clerical measure implemented by a Liberal government. It was, in fact, an attempt to force the pace of the liberal revolution and lay the foundations for growth by shifting the economy away from the land to exchange, commerce, and speculation. In 1869, there was an estimated active population of around 6.5 million, of whom some 2.5 million were thought to be farm laborers and a further 1.5 million wage laborers working either in still fairly small scale industries such as textiles, mining, steel, and construction or artisanal workshops. This remained fairly stable for the rest of the century. In the period between 1860 and 1900, "The sector normally described as the primary one (i.e. agriculture) accounted for 65–60 per cent of the total active population; the secondary (industrial) sector accounted for 15–14 per cent; the tertiary (services) sector for 20–18 per cent."[1] This implies a population of 4.5 million involved in farming, an industrial population of one million, and a services sector of 1.25 million.

An important consequence of the *desamortizacion*, as the break up of the estates was called, was the rapid and steady influx of large numbers of farm workers into the towns and cities of industrial Spain, particularly around Barcelona. According to Pere Gabriel, if we take urban residents to cover those who live in townships with upwards of 10,000 inhabitants, the urban population of Spain would have grown as follows: "from 14 per cent of the total population in 1820, to 16 per cent in 1857, to 30 per cent in 1887 and 32 per cent in 1900."[2] This rapid urbanization coupled with the equally rapid political changes within a system in which the political and economic contradictions were becoming more apparent, forced the pace of mass radicalization and was to exert a powerful stimulus to the growth of the Spanish labor movement.

Libertarian ideas concerning freedom, and its related critique of power and arbitrary authority had been circulating in different regions of Spain in one form or other since the French Revolution: Saint Simonism in Catalonia, Fourierism in Cadiz, etc. Above all, however, it was the influence of the federalist and anti-statist ideas of the French anarchist Pierre-Joseph Proudhon on Spanish radicals such as Ramón de la Sagra and Francesc Pi i Margall in the 1850s that set the federalist seal on the Spanish labor movement. It was not until 1868, however, with the introduction of Michael Bakunin's International Alliance of Socialist Democracy into Spain by the Italian Giuseppe Fanelli and others, that anarchism developed from being a doctrine of abstract philosophical speculation on the use and abuse of political power to a theory of practical action.

The heart of Bakunin's criticism of capitalism and statism, which was so enthusiastically received by Spanish radicals, was that in society the existing order was maintained by three forces: the State, religion, and property. Because the State had always

---

1 Pere Gabriel, *Anarquismo en España*, in G. Woodicut.
2 Ibid.

been the means by which the ruling elite had safeguarded their interests and privileges, it could not, therefore, be used as a means of overthrowing capitalism, as the authoritarian socialists claimed. The State, therefore, was the principal area of opposition. Representative democracy was also, Bakunin argued, a massive fraud through which the ruling elite successfully persuaded the masses to build their own prison. Bakunin's most critical condemnation, however, was reserved for Marxist state socialism which, he prophesied, would be the most tyrannical regime of all. Power concentrated in the State, he maintained, would inaugurate "the rule of scientific men, the most aristocratic, the most despotic, the most arrogant" of rulers. Anarchism was the only means by which a free society could exist, the State being replaced by free federations, based on local communes, through provinces, nations, continents, and, ultimately, a world federation representing all humanity. These ideas articulated the values, aspirations, and traditions of the Spanish people, and were enthusiastically received in the federalist atmosphere of the time. It was the only acceptable alternative to the interventionist state sought by the agrarian-based mercantile bourgeoisie, to allow them to establish an efficient transportation and communications system that would allow them to break into the growing continental and world markets, and the centralized and bureaucratic structure demanded by the dominant Marxist faction within the International.

The program of Bakunin's Alliance of Socialist Democracy was received with enthusiasm by working class radicals and, particularly, by landless peasants. Bakunin's program held that capitalism was the worst of all economic systems because it upheld property both as a natural right and as the main legitimizer of the social order. The consequence of this had been a class-divided society in which poverty, ignorance, toil, and insecurity had been the lot of the majority, with abundance, satisfaction, power, and security for the few. Bakunin's answer to capitalism was to replace it with a system based on the voluntary association of producers who owned their enterprises in common, the output being divided among the members of the association, not equally, but fairly.

The revolutionary role of anarchists within the nascent Spanish labor movement was first spelled out clearly in the statutes of the Spanish section of the First International, the International Working Men's Association (IWMA/AIT), formed on 2 May 1869 under the aegis of the Alliance. The program, statutes, and structure of this organization were to lay the foundations and set the pattern for the anarchist movement in Spain for many years to come. The Alliance, the first organizational instrument of Spanish anarchism, was the progenitor and inspiration for a long line of mass workers' organizations whose main distinguishing and characteristic features were its anti-statism and collectivism, which encouraged them to resist the taking or exercise of power by any political factions and all groups that threatened their anti-authoritarian integrity.

The Alliance declared itself atheist, collectivist, federalist and anarchist: "Inimical to all despotism, the Alliance acknowledges no form of state and rejects all forms of revolutionary action whose immediate, direct objective is not the triumph over capital of the workers' cause."[3]

Its program called for the complete reconstruction of society by means as different to those proposed by State socialism as the means to the respective ends: the federation of self-governing communes based on workers' ownership and control of the means of production. The anarchists of the Alliance firmly believed that workers and the oppressed generally must generate and control their own struggles. "No saviour from on high delivers"—neither on the picket line nor at the barricades.

The first mass-organized Labor movement in Spain, the Federación Regional Española (FRE), was conceived and delivered by the Alliance, which endowed it with the revolutionary spirit of anarchism. This Congress, held in Barcelona in June 1870, was attended by eighty-nine delegates (seventy-four of whom were Catalan; fifty of them from Barcelona). Among the statutes of the Spanish section of the Alliance was the following explicit statement of anarchist aims in relation to organized labor: "The Alliance shall bring whatever influence it can to

---

3   For full text of the Preamble and Program of the Alliance see *Bakunin on Anarchism*, Sam Dolgoff (ed.), Montreal, 1980, pp. 426–428.

bear inside the local labor federation to prevent it developing in a reactionary or anti-revolutionary manner."[4]

The attitude of the FRE itself toward political activity was spelled out in the following resolution:

"It being our opinion… That the hopes for well-being placed by the people in the conservation of the state has, in fact, taken a toll in lives.

"That authority and privilege are the firmest supports underpinning this society of injustice, a society whose reconstitution upon the basis of equality and liberty is a right incumbent on us all.

"That the system of exploitation by capital favored by the government or the political state is nothing more than the same old, ever-increasing exploitation and forcible subjection to the whim of the bourgeoisie in the name of legal or juridical right, signifying its obligatory nature."

Following their expulsion by the Marxist faction from the International at the rigged Hague Congress of 2–7 September 1872, the Libertarian Communists and Federalists held their own Congress just over a week later, on 15 September, at Saint Imier. This Congress, with which the FRE associated itself, laid down the basic principles of organized anarchism, principles which were to provide a guideline for future generations of anarchist activists. In them we can clearly see what had inspired and guided anarchist militants through to the present day. They were to have particular influence on the anarchist unionists who, half a century later, were to found the Federación Anarquista Ibérica—the Iberian Anarchist Federation.

The resolutions passed at the Saint Imier Congress were federalist, anti-political and anti-statist. These were not the fruit of abstract philosophical speculation but the distilled essence of earlier hard-won revolutionary experiences.

"And being persuaded—

"That any political organization cannot be anything other than the organization of power to the advantage of one class and to the detriment of the masses, and that should the proletariat seize power, it would wind up as a ruling, exploitative class;

---

4   Diego Abad de Santillán, *Contribución a la historia del movimiento obrero español*, Mexico, 1962, Vol 1. p. 116.

"This Congress, meeting at Saint Imier, declares:

1. That the demolition of all political power is the primary duty of the proletariat.

2. That any form of political power—even one that is supposedly temporary and revolutionary—destined to effect this demolition cannot be anything other than a trick and would be every bit as dangerous to the proletariat as any of the governments in existence today.

3. That proletarians the world over should fight shy of all compromise along the road of social revolution and must establish an immense solidarity campaign of revolutionary activity outside the parameters of bourgeois politics."

Another approved resolution read:

"Every state, which is to say, every government, and every administration of the masses of the people which comes down from above, being of necessity rooted in bureaucracy, and reliant upon armies, espionage and the clergy, will never be able to establish a society organized on the basis of labor and justice, since they are, by their very essence, naturally impelled to oppress the laborer and deny justice... As we see it, the worker will never be able to free himself from oppression in this world unless he substitutes for that absorbent, demoralizing body, the free federation of all producers; groups, a federation founded upon solidarity and equality."

2

The Confederación Nacional del Trabajo (CNT) 1910–23

The founding of the Confederación Nacional del Trabajo in Barcelona in 1910 was, for many, the most significant date in the history of organized labor in Spain after 1869. Anarchist workers, inspired by the anti-authoritarian, anti-state, and federalist principles of syndicalism as outlined in the 1906 Charter of Amiens and, in particular, the writings of French syndicalist Fernando Pelloutier, saw in the direct action and anti-parliamentarism of industrial unionism an ideal vehicle for introducing anarchist ideas to the workers and the means for overthrowing the State.

"The school for the intellectual training of the workers to make them acquainted with the technical management of production and economic life in general, so that when a revolutionary situation arises they will be capable of taking the socio-economic organism into their own hands and remaking it according to Socialist principles."[1]

The revolutionary syndicalists, on the other hand, saw the industrial unions, not as a means to an end, but the end itself.

The Charter of Amiens was, however, an exclusive program which asserted that syndicalism was sufficient unto itself. It called on anarchist workers not to form specifically anarchist unions, but, instead, to collaborate in a politically neutral and broad-based working-class unionism. It laid down specific, immediate economic demands aimed at improving working

---

1 Rudolf Rocker, *Anarcho-Syndicalism*, London, 1938, p. 86.

class conditions, but, at the same time, reaffirmed that the principal objective of revolutionary syndicalism was to prepare the working class for complete emancipation through expropriation by means of the general strike.

The anarchists agreed that they should play an active role in the unions, but they did have considerable differences with the revolutionary syndicalists. Their main argument (apart from what they felt was syndicalism's unduly optimistic reliance on the general strike as a revolutionary panacea and that post-revolutionary society should be based on the community, not just through the organs of production) was that unions were essentially reformist, conservative, and self-seeking organs that helped sustain capitalism. It was in the nature of union organizations to stimulate elitism and encourage a utilitarian and hierarchical mentality in the interests of the greater good of the working classes.

"Each time a group is formed," wrote Emile Pouget in 1904 in *Les bases du syndicalisme,* "wherein conscious men come into contact with one another, they should disregard the apathy of the mass... The un-unionized, the unconscious ones, have thus no reason to object to the sort of moral tutelage which the 'conscious' assume for themselves... Anyway, the dull-witted were in no position to offer recrimination, for they profit by the results achieved by conscious and activist comrades, and they enjoy them without having had to endure the struggle."

The danger, foreseen by anarchists, was that the "conscious men" would be tempted to accept positions of responsibility within the union. Once an anarchist accepted permanent office in a union or any similar legalitarian body, he or she would be under obligation to defend the corporate economic interests of their membership, most of whom would not be anarchists, even against their own moral principles. Faced with a choice between overthrowing or negotiating with capitalism, thereby perpetuating the status quo, the "conscious men" would be obliged either to follow their conscience and resign, or abandon anarchism to become accessories of capitalism and statism.

In Spain, the CNT, which had grown out of the anarchist and socialist-inspired Solidaridad Obrera federation, founded in 1907, was to develop along different lines to the other major revolutionary syndicalist unions of the period. Although inspired by anarchists, the CNT was not yet avowedly anarcho-syndicalist, although it was heavily influenced by the French revolutionary syndicalists. At its first proper Congress in Barcelona in October 1911, after the Socialists had withdrawn, the representatives of 26,585 workers adopted the revolutionary slogan that the goal of the new union (which could only be joined by the workers) would be the emancipation of the workers themselves.[2] Committed to direct action and class war, and opposed to political and class collaboration, the stated objective of the CNT was to attain sufficient numerical strength to permit it to mount the revolutionary general strike.

Following the collapse of a general solidarity strike in support of striking workers in Bilbao and in protest against the flare-up of the war in Morocco, the CNT was declared illegal by the Canalejas government and forced into clandestinity within a matter of weeks of its founding Congress. It managed to regain its legal status in Catalonia in July 1914, on the eve of World War I, but it was not until October 1915 when a new National Committee was elected, with its base in Catalonia, that the CNT began to re-emerge as a genuinely national union. The CNT remained, however, Catalancentric with some 15,000 Catalan workers out of a national membership of around 30,000.[3]

The war provided a massive stimulus to industrial growth and the export market. The expansion of the export market meant, however, a surge of price rises at home and from 1916 onwards, as inflation and unemployment increased, the CNT began to attract more and more workers. The economic crisis caused by the ending of the war, which led to the collapse of the lucrative foreign markets for Spanish goods, gave the anarcho-syndicalist labor movement an even greater boost. The political climate was further radicalized by heightened tension between the industrial bourgeoisie and the agrarian power elite who proposed taxing excess war profits in order to regenerate the failing agricultural industry.

By late 1917, horrified by the course events had taken in Russia with the overthrow of the Kerensky government, the

---

2 Pere Gabriel, *Anarquismo en España*, p. 364. "Out of a total membership of 26,585 in 1911, some 12,000 were from Catalonia, some 6,000 were Andalucians and a little more than 1,000 Valencians."
3 Ibid.

bourgeoisie, in spite of the enormous leverage war profits had brought them, lost their taste for reform and their nerve in the struggle for political power. The threat of social revolution from a combative working class under anarchist leadership had displaced the landed interest as the main threat to the financial and political interests of the industrial bourgeoisie. The situation was described by Spanish historian Díaz del Moral as: "The imminence of a political revolution which worried even the most optimistic... The clear vision of these events and the examples of eastern Europe pointed all of the proletarian strata with hopes of victory. It was at this point that the most potent labor agitation in the history of the country was initiated."[4]

The Socialist Unión General de Trabajadores led by Largo Caballero was, at this time, far larger than the CNT. In February 1916 it had 76,304 members, rising to 99,530 by March 1917. Following the disastrous collapse of a political general strike in support of the middle class Assembly Movement in August 1917 and the subsequent vicious repression, the Socialists had been traumatized and formally abandoned all pretense at radical political aspirations. By the end of 1917, it had become an unashamedly reformist social democratic union committed to working within the legal parameters laid down by the State. To the workers and peasants of Spain, the liberal bourgeoisie, parliamentary socialists, and class collaborative unionists had lost all credibility. They had shown themselves incapable of resolving the social and economic problems that faced the Spanish people, particularly the crucial land question. The anarchist argument that these problems could not be resolved within the framework of the system acquired greater credibility. In such a polarized situation, the only force capable of opposing such a cohesive and intransigent ruling class were the workers and peasants organized in the revolutionary anarcho-syndicalist CNT. The dispossessed masses began to flock to its red and black banners in large numbers.

In the winter of 1918 a National Conference of Anarchist Groups was organized in Barcelona to discuss their relationship with the CNT. Delegates attended from every region of Spain. The conference, addressed by a delegate from the National

4 Juan Diaz del Moral, *Historia de las agitaciones campesinas andaluzas,* Madrid, 1967, p. 277.

Committee of the CNT, stressed the need for greater anarchist involvement in the labor movement, particularly in the committees. Until that time, many anarchists had remained outside the CNT, and those who were active in the union deliberately avoided positions of responsibility within it. After considerable debate, the anarchist groups decided upon massive entry into the CNT, a decision that was to have a tremendous impact on the political development of the CNT.

The thrust toward anarcho-syndicalism had received a massive boost earlier that summer with the Regional Congress of the powerful Catalan CNT in Sants (28 June–1 July, 1918). It was here that the CNT began to come of age as an anarcho-syndicalist union. Congress, representing almost 74,000 workers (around 30 per cent of the Catalan workforce) decided to replace its traditional craft union structure with the Sindicato Unico, the industrial union that brought together all the different trades within the same industry. These industrial unions were organized in local, district, and regional federations. By organizing industrially, they planned to build the foundations of the new society within the shell of the old. CNT committee rooms were not confined to union matters; they became community social and cultural centers where Ferrer-type free schools were set up to teach subjects as diverse as Esperanto, vegetarianism, herbal medicine, birth control, and female emancipation.

The Sants Congress also resolved to abolish union dues on the grounds that it encouraged bureaucracy, caution, and an overriding concern for minor matters. The only paid official of the Catalan Regional Committee of Labor, as the Catalan CNT was known, was to be the full-time secretary. It was also agreed to organize a nationwide anarcho-syndicalist propaganda and recruitment drive, which, given the revolutionary atmosphere of the time, was electrifyingly successful. In the agrarian south, industrial worker and peasant associations affiliated en bloc. By the end of the year, the CNT boasted 345,000 members. The State responded by jailing the CNT propagandists and driving the union underground again.

It was, however, an important strike early in 1919 that provided the CNT with the industrial victory it needed to consolidate its reputation as the biggest and most combative union in Spain. In January 1919 the management of the Canadian-controlled electrical power company reduced the wages of a group of workers without notice. When eight workers who protested against this arbitrary action by the management were summarily dismissed, the CNT called its members out on strike on 4 February. The *"La Canadiense"* strike, as the dispute became known, rapidly escalated from a series of sporadic solidarity strikes into an impressive city-wide general strike by 21 February. With Barcelona without electricity the authorities declared a state of siege and called in the army. Many union leaders were arrested. The dispute finally ended in victory for the union, on 19 March, when the employers relented and reinstated the sacked workers and agreed to pay a portion of lost wages. The Romanones government, for its part, released some of the CNT prisoners and, on April 3, introduced the eight-hour day. Sensing weakness, the CNT re-launched its strike to force the government to release the remaining prisoners. The authorities replied by forcing Romanones to resign and embarking on a massive campaign of repression against the CNT in Barcelona, a campaign that was to last from April until August 1919. The poisonous tension in the city was not to abate until 1923–1924.

It was in the wake of the bloody repression in Barcelona that the CNT held its second National Congress at the La Comedia theater in Madrid in December 1919. Membership of the CNT stood at around 715,000, approximately three times the size of the UGT.[5] This figure broke down into 427,000 Catalan-based industrial workers; 132,000 from the Levante; 90,000 from Andalucia and Extremadura; 28,000 from Galicia; 24,000 from the Basque country; 26,000 from the two Castiles; and 15,000 from Aragón. It is possible that it was the influence of such large numbers of Andalucians and Extremadurans—workers who experienced the raw power of capitalism every day of their lives, living and working as they did in conditions of abject poverty, subject to the arbitrary class justice of the landlords and their agents—who swung the balance of influence within the CNT to the revolutionary anarchist position.

Whatever the source or the cause, the revolutionary and intransigent mood of the CNT rank and file in 1919, particularly

5 Gabriel, op.cit., *Historia del Sindicalismo Español,* Paris, 1973, p. 16 gives a total membership of 750,000 and a Catalan membership of 450,000.

that of the southern agricultural workers, was reflected in the key resolutions approved by the Congress. Resolutions that confirmed the CNT was a revolutionary anarcho-syndicalist union imbued with the spirit of the Alliance and that echoed the objectives of the Saint Imïer and Cordoba Congresses of the First International forty-seven years earlier in 1872— Libertarian Communism!

"To Congress:—The undersigned delegates, bearing in mind that the tendency most strongly manifested in the workers' organizations in every country is the one aiming at the complete, utter and absolute liberation of mankind in moral, economic and political terms, and considering that this goal cannot be attained until such tome as the land, means of production and exchange have been socialized and the overweening power of the State has vanished, suggest to Congress that, in accordance with the essential postulates of the First Workers' International, it declares that the desired end of the CNT in Spain is Anarchist Communism."[6]

The La Comedia National Congress also decided to adopt the structural reforms introduced by the Catalan CNT the previous year. As in Catalonia, sensitivity to the dangers of oligarchization and a wish to ensure the minimum of tension between the leadership and the base of the organization, Congress resolved that only Secretaries of Regional Federations and the Secretary of the National Committee would receive salaries. All other members of the National and Regional Committees and those who held positions of responsibility within the movement would be obliged to continue to work at their trades in order to earn a living. To facilitate this, Congress decided that the entire National Committee should be recruited from among the confederal membership of one particular region. Invariably, with the exception of the early years of the Primo de Rivera dictatorship, the National Committee was Barcelona-based.[7]

6 José Peirats, *La CNT en la revolución española,* Toulouse, 1952, Vol.I, Ch.1.
7 With the exception of the following names marked * all CNT National Committee Secretaries belonged to Barcelona based National Committees: José Negre (last secretary of Solidaridad Obrera and first of the CNT in 1910. The almost immediate outlawing of the Confederation makes it unclear whether, when the CNT was reconstituted in 1914, Negre became secretary again.) Manuel Andreu (November 1915 to August 1916); Francisco Jordán (until February 1917 when he resigned the post from his prison cell);

Ironically, the rapid growth of the CNT from 1919 onwards placed an enormous strain on it, calling into question its hostility to the State and constitutional commitment to class war and direct action. Could anarchists, enemies of all coercive power, compromise with capitalism and the State, maintain their principles within a mass labor union that was developing its own goals and vested interests? How could an instrument of anarchist revolution seek immediate short term economic gains for its members through tactical alliances and accommodations with whichever groups circumstances happened to dictate, without seeing its principles distorted, its traditions abused, and its ultimate objectives compromised out of all recognition?

Although the anarchist workers in the CNT were as enthusiastically committed to the struggle for immediate economic improvements and social justice as Socialists or enlightened Conservative Republicans were, they were equally convinced that any improvements won by the union would be illusory and short-lived so long as capitalism and the State remained. Because they were willing to accept that other political parties and unions might serve a useful purpose and were prepared to cooperate with them in those aims which they shared in common, it did not mean that they ceased to be anarchists. Where they parted company with the Socialists was over the question of negotiating with the enemy, diverting class struggle into class collaboration by participating in the leadership functions of capitalism and the illusory representative functions of the bourgeois state.

Francisco Miranda (until July 1919; he was replaced for a time by Manuel Buenacasa between August and November 1917); Manuel Buenacasa (until December 1918); Evelino Boal (murdered March 1921); Andreu Nin (until May 1921); Joaquín Maurín (until February 1922); Joan Peiró (until July 1923); * Paulino Díez (until March 1924) (Seville); * Garcia Galán (until June 1924) (Zaragoza). (It is not known if there was a secretary from June 1924 to September 1925). * Gonzalez Mallanda (September 1925 to June 1926) (Gijón); * Segundo Blanco (until November 1926) (Gijón); Juan Peiró (until mid-1929); Ángel Pestaña (1929); Progreso Alfarache (1930. Temporarily replaced either by Manuel Sirvent or Arín); Angel Pestaña (until March 1932); Manuel Rivas (1933); Miguel Yoldi (1934); * Horacio Martínez Prieto (1935-1936) (Zaragoza. Temporarily replaced by David Antona and Antonio Moreno until September 1936); * Mariano Rodríguez Vázquez (November 1936 until February 1939) (Madrid-Valencia). Source: Cuadernos ...amendment No.22, May 184, entry 336.

Although the CNT was founded and, in the main, influenced by a minority of rank and file anarchist activists who were less concerned with economic demands than defending the union's ideological position, the bulk of the members who came into the CNT between 1917 and 1923 would probably not have described themselves as anarchists in the sense that they were committed to an idea. The workers and peasants who flocked to the CNT during this period were, however, almost certainly heavily influenced by the polarized and radical political climate of the period and identified with the union's anti-authoritarian, libertarian, and revolutionary ethos. Their choice of union reflected the mood of the period and their individual views on the key issues that affected them in a brutal and unashamedly class-ridden society.

The leadership, on the other hand, were either not anarchists or merely paid lip service to anarchism as an abstract principle. For the conscious minority of militants this was an important reason to maintain their agitational pressure to ensure the union continued to express anarchist policies and that the reformist and administrative-minded leadership did not lapse too far from the anarchist-inspired constitution. The leaders, for their part, needed the support of this "conscious minority" of activists to retain their positions of responsibility, and found themselves obliged to adopt artificially revolutionary positions that they never intended or believed possible to implement, and felt to be a hindrance to their negotiating position with employers and State functionaries. Attempts to change the revolutionary constitution of the CNT and neutralize the influence of the "conscious minority" of anarchists inevitably met with the defeat of the leadership.

Apart from countering the class-collaborationist tendencies of the leadership, which was constantly attempting to turn the Confederation into a mirror image of the UGT, and attempts by Marxist and pro-Bolshevik infiltrators such as Andreu Nin and Joaquín Maurín to suborn the union to the Moscow-based Third International, the "conscious minority" of anarchists did not see themselves as seeking to impose ideological hegemony over the membership. It was, rather, to provide moral leadership to their fellow workers by example and inspiration, not the command and obey relationship that normally operated within authoritarian party and union structures; to protect and advance working class interests; to educate the rank and file in the unity between the theory and practice of anarchism; and to stress the difference between what is and what could be.

To the reformist leaders of the higher committees, the anarchist militants at the base were undoubtedly nuisances, particularly because they understood the realities of the world too well and knew precisely what the reformists were trying to do. To this latter group, the revolutionary objectives of the CNT were visions on the horizon of a far distant future—visions which menaced their careerism—not something that could or should be on the daily agenda of a major union. If the unions were able to introduce Libertarian Communism, which after all was only the application of anarchist principles to the reconstruction of society, that made the unions organs of genuine democracy, with no place in them for a leadership structure. Which, of course, is why the reformists incessantly sought to play down the goals of anarchism and constantly emphasized the lack of interest in anarchism by the rank and file. Writing in 1922, Soledad Gustavo observes in the anarchist paper *Redención*, "...the organized masses which we have called syndicalist is not libertarian."[8]

"The great triumphs achieved by means of organization and collective actions," observed Díaz del Moral, "the spread of the syndicalist press, which, though still directed in large measure by libertarians, cultivated mainly through union themes; the habits of discipline with which conviviality in workers' organizations and the heat of the battle infused the members; the structuring of the new 'Sindicatos Únicos,' which subordinated individual activity to that of the sections...to collective ends, restricting the liberty so sedulously defended by anarchism: [all] were slowly modifying the convictions of the leadership groups, who, without being aware of it, unconsciously moved toward pure unionism, radically opposed, at bottom, to fundamental anarchist principles."[9]

The rapid (but short-lived) growth in union membership accelerated the contradictions inherent in a revolutionary labor movement attempting to perform all the functions of a reformist labor movement. It proved to be an increasing source

8   *Redención*, Alcoy, August, 1922.
9   Diaz del Moral, op.cit.

of tension creating conflict between the anarchist militants with their immediate revolutionary objectives and the equally influential union-oriented elements with their immediate economic demands and work-based claims. For the anarchists, morals—i.e. principles—and reality were inseparable. If the principles were the right ones for dealing with reality then clearly they were the right ones for formulating goals.

For the reformists, on the other hand, although they praised anarchist militancy and upheld anarchism as a positive moral influence, they deplored its revolutionary goal of Libertarian Communism and sought to dissociate it from the struggle. As an ideal, anarchism was commendable, but naive, an ideal which was incapable of coping with the political and social realities of contemporary capitalist society. It was an abstract moral yardstick that could be discarded as and when circumstances demanded. The unionists felt it to be an embarrassment and an obstacle in their pursuit of realizable objectives, much as Clause 4 has been to the British Labour Party.

Inside the Catalan CNT, new leaders began to emerge who had had little to do with the earlier working class anarchist movement and whose main priority was the union struggle. CNT leaders like Salvador Seguí, Marti Barrera, Salvador Quemades, Josep Viadiu, Joan Peiró, Sebastian Clara, and Ángel Pestaña began to displace the anarchist activists who played a dominant role in the Solidaridad Obrera federation and in the early years of the CNT—men like Negre, Herreros, Andreu, Miranda, and so on.

In November 1916, CNT leader Salvador Seguí and Ángel Pestaña (a watchmaker by trade, whose organizational career had taken him fairly rapidly from revolutionary to philosophical anarchism) had successfully engineered the first socialist-anarcho-syndicalist union agreement to coordinate a joint protest strike against the rising cost of living. Earlier, the CNT membership had baulked at the proposal, but finally the rank and file at the 1916 National Congress agreed to the alliance to force political concessions out of the Romanones government. The so-called "Pact of Zaragoza," inspired mainly by Seguí and Pestaña, had been signed in November 1916.

Much of the membership of the CNT showed little enthusiasm for collaborating with authoritarian socialists to replace the government of Count Romanones with a bourgeoisie liberal republic. The disastrous experiences with self-styled radical and bourgeois politicians during the Cantonalist movement in 1873 had shown the anarchist militants that political leaders of all hues, prompted by their urge to conquer power, only collaborate out of self interest. Their distrust of the socialist union and the republicans proved well-founded, as we have seen, but although the pact was short-lived, with unfortunate consequences for the Labor movement, it did serve to highlight the unbridgeable differences between revolutionary and reformist unionism. (Although there is no proof that the leaders were reformists and the base revolutionary.)

In 1920, in direct defiance of the decisions of the 1919 Congress and without any attempt to consult with the membership, Salvador Seguí demonstrated further disregard for the democratic process by negotiating another pact with the UGT. This arbitrary and undemocratic move by the CNT leader was condemned by a CNT plenum later that same year. Faced with a *fait accompli*, however, the decision was made to give the Socialist union the benefit of the doubt. They tested the bona fides of their allies by declaring a general strike in solidarity with the miners of the Rio Tinto company. The socialists, whether fearful of a confrontation with the State or unwilling to concede the initiative to the CNT, reneged on the agreement and the Rio Tinto strike collapsed after four months of struggle.

Pistolerismo, the shooting down of militant unionists by gangsters hired by the Employers' Federation and right wing killers of the "Sindicato Libre," the so-called free union, first emerged on a small scale during World War I.[10] By 1920, the individual kills had escalated into the institutionalized slaughter of CNT militants. One estimate places the number of assassination attempts between 1917 and 1922 at 1,012, of which 753 were workers, 112 policemen, 95 employers, and 52 foremen. The CNT Pro-Prisoners Committee in 1923 lists the number of CNT members killed as 104 with 33 wounded.[11] This strategy of tension was orchestrated by Barcelona police chief Arlegui. He was supported by the highest authorities in

---

10 Ángel Pestaña, *Terrorismo en Barcelona*, Barcelona, 1979.
11 Miguel Sastre, *La esclavitud moderna*. (Quoted in Peirats, *Anarchists in the Spanish Revolution*, Toronto, 1977, p. 32.)

the region, including the Captain General, Milans del Bosch, and Civil Governor Martínez Anido.

This parallel state terror was given the judicial seal of approval in December 1920 with the introduction of the notorious *ley de fugas*, a law that permitted the security forces to shoot dead any alleged suspect who attempted to "evade" capture. The CNT again appealed to their pact allies, the UGT, to declare a revolutionary general strike in Catalonia in order to halt the cycle of violence, but the Socialist union refused to lend its support and Seguí's pact finally collapsed in ignominy. Frightened by the revolutionary threat to the fundamental institutions of their society—tradition, property, and privilege—the ruling elite turned to the only weapon it understood: violence.

The anarchist militants within the CNT unions were left with no alternative but to respond in kind. They organized defense committees to identify, locate, and assassinate those responsible for the wave of semi-official terrorism. These action-oriented defense committees became, understandably, the central focus for the younger, more dynamic, and revolutionary elements who began to rise to prominence within the CNT, while the collaborationists such as Salvador Seguí, who sought to restore the emphasis to purely union matters, suffered a corresponding decrease in influence.

In October 1922, the Los Solidarios anarchist affinity group was formed in Barcelona (see Ricardo Sanz: *Los Solidarios*). It consisted of young, working-class CNT defense group militants whose ideas and attitudes had been forged during the murderous period of governmental and employers' terrorism. The group had particularly close links with the woodworkers' union. It had evolved from the Zaragoza-based Crisol group, who were, in turn, linked to the earlier Los Justicieros group. Its members included some of the most famous names in the history of Spanish anarchism—Buenaventura Durruti, a mechanic from Leon; Francisco Ascaso, a waiter from Zaragoza; and García Oliver, an apprentice chef, waiter, and later French polisher from Tarragona—and its influence was to prove crucial in the development of the Spanish anarchist movement in the first half of the 1930s.[12]

---

12 The core of the group consisted of: Francisco Ascaso, waiter; Buenaventura Durruti, machinist; Rafael Torres Escartín, pastry cook; Juan

According to Aurelio Fernández, a founder of Los Solidarios, the declared aims of the group were to resist *pistolerismo*, defend the anarchist objectives of the CNT, and set up a "nationwide anarchist federation, which would unite all the groups that were close to each other ideologically, but were scattered throughout the peninsula." Having successfully turned the tables on the most prominent leaders and organizers of the anti-CNT terror campaign, they used the columns of their influential journal *Crisol* to press for a national anarchist conference. Their appeal was successful, and both the CNT and the Federation of Anarchist Groups were represented. Durruti, Ascaso, and Aurelio Fernández were elected on to the National Liaison Commission, a body that was to be the forerunner of the Iberian Anarchist Federation—the FAI.

Among the fifty delegates present at the conference was Seguí's protege, Ángel Pestaña, ex-editor of *Solidaridad Obrera*, now a union organizer of considerable standing within the CNT. Pestaña had been released from prison in April 1922, after having been arrested on his return to Spain from Russia in 1921. It had been his report to the Zaragoza Conference earlier that same year that led to the CNT revoking its provisional adherence to the Communist Third International.

The disastrous handling of the Moroccan War and scandals affecting the highest authorities in the land—including the king—led many anarchists to believe that the only remaining solution for the ruling elite was a military coup. One of the main tasks of the National Liaison Commission was, therefore, to discuss plans of how to prevent this occurring. Defense Committee activists García Oliver, Gregorio Suberviela, and others outlined proposals for an insurrection to preempt the expected military coup and speed up the revolutionary process throughout Spain.

García Oliver, waiter; Aurelio Fernández, machinist; Ricardo Sanz, textile worker; Alfonso Miguel, cabinet maker; Gregorio Suberviela, machinist; Eusebio Brau, foundry worker; Marcelino Manuel Campos (Tomas Arrate), carpenter; Miguel García Vivancos, driver; Antonio del Toto, laborer. Over the years the membership changed; some died, some left while others joined. A number of anarchist women were associated with the Los Solidarios group, including Julia López, Maria Luisa Tejedor, Pepita Not, Ramóna Berni and Maria Rius. Other names linked with this influential group were: Mas, A. Martín, Palau, Flores, Ballano, Boada, H. Esteban, P. Martín, J. Blanco, Pérez Combina, Batlle, Sosa. Antonio Ortiz and Francisco Jover also joined the group during the dictatorship.

Ángel Pestaña, recently appointed Regional Secretary of the CNT, was firmly against the proposed insurrectionary general strike. His direct experience of the revolutionary process in Russia led him to the view that the reason for the Bolshevik success was the fact that the masses had not been adequately educated or prepared for revolution beforehand. Pestaña was convinced that a successful revolution depended on organization rather than spontaneity. He argued that, because the union was weak and disorganized and the UGT was unlikely to resist a military coup, they would be out on a limb; a revolutionary general strike at that time would only end in catastrophe.

Pestaña's opposition to armed resistance led to his expulsion from the Commission. Although he no longer belonged to the Commission, Pestaña was arrested and imprisoned by the dictatorship authorities for alleged involvement in the disastrous military invasion organized by the Commission in 1924 at Vera de Bidasoa in the Basque Navarese Pyrenees, and the unsuccessful rising at the Ataranzas barracks in Barcelona. He was to remain in jail until the end of 1926. According to his biographer Antonio Elerza:

"Although he never ceased to be an anarchist, the strategy of armed resistance proposed by Oliver led to a marked widening of the gulf between himself and militant anarchism: From now on all his energies became concentrated on union activity exclusively. He filled the position of Seguí. He began to reflect on the experiences of his life, revise tactics and objectives, and, as a consequence, to search for a new course to achieve his ends."[13]

With the murder of Salvador Seguí and his companion Francesc Comes on 10 March 1923, the credibility of the legalist unionists within the CNT collapsed completely. Even the most orthodox union members were outraged; how could they argue the case for peaceful negotiation with employers and officials who employed gunmen and terrorists to murder such firm opponents of revolutionary confrontation and

---

13 Angel Mariá de Lera, *Ángel Pestaña—Retrato de un anarquista*, Barcelona, 1978, p. 225.

champions of the negotiated settlement as Salvador Seguí, "*El Noi de Sucrè*" (Sugar Boy)?

The murders of Seguí and Comes proved the final straw for the Catalan Regional Committee of the CNT. Determined to confront and eliminate *pistolerismo*, a meeting of militants was convened to coordinate and fund the anarcho-syndicalist defense groups. The safe houses and meeting places of the *pistoleros* and the most reactionary employers, their paymasters, were located and raided by CNT defense groups, and the killers and their employers shot.

The CNT militants of groups such as the Los Solidarios—one of many confederal defense groups—targeted key counter-revolutionary figures such as General Severiano Martínez Anido, Colonel Arlegui, ex-ministers such as the "Conde de Coello," José Reguerel, the former Governor of Bilbao, and the Cardinal Archbishop of Zaragoza. Their first victim was Laguía, the most notorious of the *pistoleros*. The death of such a well-protected gangster frightened off many of the other gunmen, a number of whom fled to Zaragoza to seek the protection of their patron, Cardinal Soldevilla.

As the actions of the defense group began to bite—the assassination of prime minister Eduardo Dato earlier that year by three anarchists had brought the battle into the streets of Madrid itself—the central government quickly stepped in to remove the instigators of the Catalan terrorism from office. An uneasy peace was restored to the northern capital, but it proved short-lived.

In September 1923, General Primo de Rivera issued a "Manifesto to the Country" informing them that he had seized power "to free Spain from the professional politicians, misfortunes, and immoralities that began in 1889 and threaten Spain with a tragic, dishonorable, and speedy demise." It was an ill-concealed move to protect the reputation of King Alfonso XIII from the consequences of an imminent Parliamentary report on responsibilities for the disaster at Anual in the Spanish Moroccan War in 1921.

The CNT responded to the coup by calling a general strike. It met with little response. The political atmosphere was one of general despondency, and the CNT was in a state of complete disarray. Although no figures exist for the Catalan CNT in this period of membership shrinkage, it must have been similar to that undergone by the Levante Regional, which dropped from 130,000 at the end of 1919, to around 40,000 by December 1922. The Andalucians, for their part, had shrunk to around 30,000.[14]

The UGT and Socialist Party, Seguí's former allies, had thrown in their lot with the new regime. Largo Caballero, the Socialist leader, was appointed a Councillor of State and immediately ordered the party not to make any verbal or written act of protest against the new regime. The CNT, although not declared illegal, prepared for the worst. Many anarcho-syndicalist militants, particularly the members of the defense groups, either went underground or into exile to continue the struggle. The members of the Los Solidarios group, for example, played important parts in establishing the Committee for Revolutionary Co-ordination in France. This body organized the unsuccessful anti-Dictatorship operations at Vera de Bidasoa and the Ataranzas barracks in Barcelona on 6 November 1924, but could also take credit for the spectacular release of Francisco Ascaso from Zaragoza prison. With the death of many of its members in armed confrontations with the police and the army, the arrest of many others, and the dispersal of others into exile, the Los Solidarios ceased to exist as a cohesive group until 1931, when those comrades who survived were reunited under the Republic.

---

14 Pere Gabriel, op.cit.

3

The Dictatorship 1923–27

The attitude of the new regime towards the CNT was made clear within ten days of the *coup d'état*. On 24 September 1923, Martínez Anido was appointed Under-Secretary of the Ministry of the Interior. General Arlegui, Anido's ex-chief of police in Barcelona, the architect of governmental terrorism, was made Director General of Public Order. Government strategy, however, proved not to be the brutal onslaught on militants or the outlawing of the anarcho-syndicalist union that was expected. The method of attack was an oblique one. By selective use of the law, the authorities made it impossible for the CNT to continue functioning as a union: delegates collecting union dues were arrested on charges of embezzlement, records and membership lists were seized in government audits of accounts. In Barcelona, the nerve center of the CNT, police pressure was intense. Finally, on October 3, the anarchist activists in the union decided they had no option but to go underground and suspend publication of *Solidaridad Obrera*. This decision, coming as it did in a period in which the Spanish Communist Party was attempting to seize control of the union, caused considerable ill-feeling inside the CNT, particularly within the Catalan Regional Committee, which had lost some of its most prominent leaders, such as Salvador Seguí, during 1923. A plenum in Mataro on December 8, 1923, overturned this decision and *Solidaridad Obrera* resumed publication. Meanwhile, the Socialist UGT, now fully incorporated into the State apparatus, was being promoted at the expense of the CNT. The objective of this strategy was to neutralize and displace the Confederation as the predominant voice of organized labor in Spain.

The assassination of the new Barcelona executioner on 4 May 1924 ended the phoney peace between the CNT and the dictatorship. At an extraordinary conference of the CNT in Granollers later that month, the union reaffirmed Libertarian Communism as its prime objective. This resolution was ratified by a majority vote of 236 to 1 against—the Sabadell unions, who supported Pestaña's view of unions fulfilling purely economic functions. The conference ended in confusion when the police surrounded the building. García Oliver was one of the few delegates who failed to escape. He was arrested and spent a year in prison. The Granollers conference was the last semi-public act of the CNT under the dictatorship. It had failed to submit to the new social legislation drafted by the dictatorship's new Minister of Labor, UGT leader Largo Caballero, and was proscribed a few days later. *Solidaridad Obrera* was suspended once again, not to reappear again until 1930, and it was soon followed by most of the other anarchist and CNT papers.

The climate of uncertainty and exhaustion left in the wake of the murders of so many of the CNT's most capable militants had badly impaired its organizational and agitational ability. The clandestine National Committee set up in Seville in September 1924 was arrested in December that same year. The National Committee that replaced it in Zaragoza lasted only until May 1924. From then on it became impossible to keep the CNT functioning as a genuinely national body. According to Julián Casanova, the confederation was "a conglomeration of regional federations without any collective discipline."[1]

The repressive situation in Spain led to the forced exile and the disappearance into clandestinity of most of the more resolute and combative elements within the CNT. France and Argentina were the two main centers of emigration from which the anarchist activists began to plot the overthrow of the regime, while others sought to reassess the question of anarchist organization.

---

1 Julián Casanova, *Anarquismo y revolucion en la sociedad rural aragonese, 1936–1938*, Madrid, 1985, p. 15.

The exile of the revolutionaries left an ideological vacuum within the CNT. This was soon filled by the more legally-minded and union-oriented elements in the union, a situation that exacerbated the friction between the main contending tendencies within the union.

Apart from the broad base of the CNT who could probably be described as traditional anarcho-syndicalists, generally sympathetic to the union's anarchist principles and statutes, there were, arguably, three main trains of thought within the union, plus a fourth group of "philosophical" anarchists, represented by the Urales family with their influential magazine *La Revista Blanca*, who, seeing themselves as the jealous guardians of anarchist orthodoxy, distanced themselves totally from union involvement in order to ensure ideological purity.

The first group, represented by leaders like Pestaña, were mainly to be found within the National and Regional Committees of the CNT, and included reformist union members, Republicans, Socialists, and Catalanists. This group stressed the economic approach, with the union offering an alternative form of organization for specific, defined relations of production. Far from being spontaneous, it was extremely rigid in its views and placed no trust in revolutionary spontaneity, and little, if any, trust in the workers. Their main objective was the immediate legislation of the CNT no matter what conditions the dictatorship may lay down. To them, anarchism was an abstract moral ideal, an unattainable aspiration within the real world.

They argued that the foundation of workers' power required a methodical approach and, for this reason, they wished to turn the CNT into an "effective" labor union. This objective could only be achieved through class collaboration and distancing the union from the "ideological" influence of the anarchists and by attracting workers of all political persuasions and beliefs. The *pestanistas* wanted to relegate and confine anarchist militants to an educational and "idealist" role within the union, rather than encourage them to exert leadership by example—the only true type of revolutionary leadership. This would permit the *pestanistas* to build and control a permanent command structure within the CNT.

Pestaña and his union-minded colleagues in the Solidaridad group were firm believers in the ultimately improving effects on the workers of class harmony and of incorporating the middle classes, "the fountain of culture," into the labor movement. This view was shared, albeit for different reasons, by the more traditional political elements who hoped to ensure the stability of capitalism by absorbing the workers into the system by offering a token amount of the surplus produced.

The distortion of the revolutionary process under the Bolsheviks appears to have triggered Pestaña's final collapse of faith in the creative capacity of the workers to organize and run their own lives. Although he continued to describe himself as an anarchist, he had, since his return from Russia, come to believe that revolution was impossible while the broad mass of the workers remained "unprepared" and "uneducated." Disillusioned, Pestaña had adjusted his anarchism, like many "self-confessed" anarchists before and since, to cope with the "expediencies" and "practicalities" of an imperfect world. In doing so, his anarchism became transformed from a unity of theory and action into a mere code of subjective ethics and abstract values, which had little, if anything, to do with his actual behavior. Gradualism and class collaboration were the means by which Pestaña and his colleagues came to deny the possibility of mass revolution and, hence, the revolutionary mission of the CNT!

Pestaña and other members of his Solidaridad group openly began to argue the case for a legally recognized (i.e. State recognized) CNT. In March 1925, he made his first thinly veiled attack on anarchist influence within the union through the columns of his paper *Solidaridad Proletaria*. Intended to rally the Socialists and Syndicalists in the CNT, the article, entitled "THE ANARCHIST GROUPS AND THE UNIONS," broached his theory of the confederation as a "container" rather than "contents": "To begin with, the union is only an instrument of economic demands, subordinated to the class struggle and lacking any ideological description. Its objectives are class, economic, materialistic, and have nothing to do with questions of collective ethics or morals, of sects or party, which are those defined by the group." He continued, "We repeat, what the unions and the CNT need is not the ornately designed ticket of anarchy, but the moral, spiritual, and intellectual influence of the anarchists."[2]

The second group was represented by Joan Peiró, another member of the reformist Solidaridad group. His position was not much different from that of Pestaña, but he believed himself to be occupying a sort of middle ground between "pure" reformism, on the one hand, and "pure" revolutionary anarchism on the other. Peiró saw the unions in an independent role, but one in which he claimed he hoped the ethical influence of anarchism would predominate. This was equally reformist since it misrepresented the nature and role of anarchism.

Peiró's subsequent history confirms him as a reformist. Anarchism he took to be a kind of social theory, a set of beliefs to which he hoped the workers would some day be won; whereas in fact it is the expression of revolutionary consciousness in the working class. The anarcho-syndicalist movement was, in fact, the attempt to give organizational expression to that revolutionary consciousness. The "direct action" and "anti-parliamentarianism" that Peiró upheld were not principles for the successful defense of jobs and working conditions—nor even their enhancement—but basic principles of working class activity: "The emancipation of the workers is the task of the workers themselves," the slogan of the First International. Peiró's position was anti class war, a term that conveys, not just the intensity of feeling and scale of conflict, which the class struggle occasionally promoted, but the need to see the class struggle as one that would never be resolved until the final triumph of the workers, i.e. the social revolution.

Peiró tried to adapt the organization to cope with the constantly shifting problems posed by the rapid changes taking place within Spanish capitalism. He defined and defended his position against Pestaña in the columns of *Acción Social Obrera*: "We aspire to the unions being influenced by the anarchists, that union activity should have a determined end, in conformity with the economic concept of the anarchist communists; but all this without the anarchists acting in the unions as agents of distant groups and collectives...with no other objective than that of bringing to unionism...clarification and revolutionary

---

2   *Solidaridad Proletaria*, 21.3.1925.

efficiency... if the unions ever had this it was due to the anarchists." Peiró went on to emphasise what he saw as the proper and correct role of anarchists in the unions: "We want the anarchization of the unions and proletarian attitudes, but not through the previous voluntary consent of these while maintaining the independent and collective personality of unionism."[3]

The third group, the "conscious minority" of anarchist workers, represented by exiles such as the Los Treinta affinity group (a group which had grown up around Durruti and Ascaso of the now defunct Los Solidarios group), coordinated through the Anarchist Liaison Committee, were the anarchist heart of the Confederation. Enemies of all power, they firmly opposed establishing any relationship with employers and the State other than overt hostility. For this group of union activists, their practical opposition to the State was in perfect harmony with their theory; it was this harmony between theory and practice that set them apart from all other political groupings.

To the anarchists, the legalistic arguments sustained by unionists such as Pestaña, who sought successful negotiations with the employers and the State, involved compromising fundamental principles, surrendering greater future opportunities for all of mankind to illusory short-term sectional benefits—to say nothing of perpetuating the misery and exploitation of the dispossessed.

It was not the job of the anarchists to resolve the problems of capitalism or to negotiate mutually acceptable solutions between boss and worker, but to keep alive the gulf between oppressed and oppressor and to nourish the spirit of revolt against exploitation and all coercive authority.

Pestaña's adaptation to an unjust world was wrong, they argued, if only because it is impossible to foresee what direction events will take. To choose a course that seems morally wrong, on the basis of suspect forecasts about the future, would inevitably lead to disaster—one for which they would be responsible because they knew in advance the fundamental mistake they were accepting.

An influential voice within the Spanish-speaking movement at this time was the Buenos Aires based paper *La Protesta*, edited

---

3   "Sentido de Independencia," 25.9.1925.

by Diego Abad de Santillán and López Arangó, two anarchists who had experience within the Argentinian anarcho-syndicalist union FORA—the Federación Obrera Regional Argentina.

Unlike most Spanish anarchists, de Santillán was a bohemian rather than a worker. A philosophy student in Madrid, he had become caught up in the revolutionary events of the autumn of 1917 and anarchism. Amnestied in 1918, he returned to his adopted homeland, Argentina, where he became involved in *La Protesta* and the Argentinian anarcho-syndicalist union FORA, which he represented at the founding Congress of the AIT in Berlin in 1921. Describing himself as a Kropokinist at the time, de Santillán argued vociferously against reformist unionism in the columns of the bi-weekly *Suplemento*, which he edited, encouraging the idea of a specifically anarchist national organization. From 1926 on, de Santillán threw in his lot with Manuel Buenacasa, editor of the influential confederal paper *El Productor*, published in Blanes, who advocated setting up a specifically anarchist labor movement based on the Argentinian FORA.

In an important study published in 1925, de Santillán and López Arangó outlined what they felt the anarchist position should be: "We do not whimsically confuse the labor movement with syndicalism: for us syndicalism is but one revolutionary theory out of many which pop up along the path of the revolution to thwart its ends or clip the wings of the masses' combative idealism. And clearly faced with a choice between that theory and anarchism, we cannot hesitate for a single instance in our choice, for we maintain that freedom is attained only through freedom and that the revolution will be anarchistic, which is to say libertarian, or will not be at all...

"The anarchist revolution will redeem men from the cardinal sin of abdication of the personality, but the anarchist revolution is not a revolution made according to this or that program, whatever the degree of libertarianism of the latter, but rather the revolution made by means of the destruction of the whole of State power and of all authority. It matters very little to us whether the coming revolution will be based upon the family, on the social group, on the branch of industry, on the commune, or on the individual: what matters to us is that the construction of the social order be a collective endeavor in which men do not place their freedom in pawn, whether willingly or under coercion. The anarchist revolution is today the natural revolution, the one which does not let itself be sidetracked or confiscated by groups, parties, or classes of authority."[4]

---

4 *El anarquismo en el movimiento obrero*, E. López Arango with Diego Abad de Santillán, Barcelona, 1925, pp. 10, 37, 38, 47, 57, and 136.

4

The Federación Anarquista Ibérica (FAI) 1927

On 27 July 1927, at the height of the summer fiesta, roughly twenty delegates from local, regionally federated, and exiled Spanish and Portuguese groups met in the house of Aurora López in Patraix, in the suburbs of Valencia.

This assembly was the founding conference of what was to become the most misrepresented anarchist organization in history—the Federación Anarquista Ibérica, better known by its initials FAI, the Iberian Anarchist Federation.

The Valencia Conference was to last two days. To ensure security it was held in two separate locations. The second session took place under cover of a picnic in a pine forest that bordered a beach to the south of the city, in the area known as the Grao de Valencia.[1]

Progreso Fernández, a Valencian anarchist who, until recently, had been living in France, was one of the organizers of the founding conference:

"Early in 1927 I came down to Valencia to make contacts throughout the region; this I agreed to do on condition that I found employment... I began by going to Burriana, Puerto de Sagunto, Liria, Jativa, Sueca, Villena, Elda, Alicante,

---

1 A number of sites have been given as the location for the second session. Peirats places it on the beach at Cabanel (*Los anarquistas y la crisis política española*, p. 276); Tomás Cano Ruiz cites Malvarrosa (*Confederación*, 8.8.1937, p. 1); José Llop claims it was Tremolar (*El movimiento libertario español*, p. 289); Progreso Fernández names El Saler. All these beaches are in the vicinity of the Grao de Valencia.

Murcia... I met with people who had been in the CNT and who sympathized with anarchism."[2]

"Since there were anarchists in Portugal as well, it was decided to give (the new body) an all embracing nature. Hence the name. Invitations were issued to the Portuguese CGT and to the CNT, but only the Levante and Catalan Regionals of the latter showed up."

For some time, most of the organized groups throughout the peninsula had been pressing for a peninsular organization that would establish closer links between the regional and exiled Spanish and Portuguese groups. The Portuguese Anarchist Union (UAP), founded in Alanquer in 1923, had played a prominent role in laying the groundwork for the FAI. In May 1926 the organ of the Portuguese Anarchist Union, *O Anarquista* had published a proposed agenda for an anarchist congress to be held on 1 July in Marseilles. Among the items listed was the heading "Iberian Anarchist Federation" (FAI).[3]

Two months later, in July 1926, the Federation of Spanish Speaking Anarchist Groups, formed in Lyon the previous year, convened what proved to be a major anarchist conference in Marseilles. The Spanish-speaking groups alone sent thirty delegates from all corners of the peninsula and exile. Among the main topics on the agenda were the problems of international anarchism and those peculiar to anarchist groups in exile.

A topic high on the agenda was the position of the Spanish anarchist movement in relation to the CNT. There is considerable confusion as to what actually was agreed on this question; some believe an agreement was reached to intervene directly in the CNT, a decision which others are adamant was not taken.

What is certain is that the delegates agreed that an Iberian Anarchist Federation should be formed without delay and it was proposed that a Liaison Committee for this purpose should be set up in Lisbon. The Committee was commissioned with the task of convening an Iberian Congress to give "definite shape" to the proposed federation.

---

2 Interview with Progreso Fernández, "Anarquismo en el mundo," *Bicicleta*, No. 11, Barcelona, 1977.
3 *A resistencia anarco-sindicalista a dittadura: Portugal 1922—1939*, Edgar Rodrígues, Lisbon, 1981, p. 238.

Perhaps the biggest argument at the Marseilles Congress revolved around the question of hastening the downfall of the Primo de Rivera regime. Two main tendencies emerged to clash violently. One side, led by García Oliver, supported close collaboration with all other groups—political parties and dissident army officers—willing to oppose the dictatorship irrespective of their political beliefs. (Oliver and the National Revolutionary Committee were working closely at this time with Francesc Macià's Catalan Esquerra party.) The other group, led by Manuel Pérez, opposed collaboration on the grounds that it was contrary to the anarchist ideal. Although the latter group carried the day at the Marseilles Congress, it made little difference to the degree of collaboration between the anarchists, the CNT, and the anti-dictatorship parties that continued until the advent of the Republic in 1931.

In Lisbon on 3 January 1927, a UAP congress had urged that the agreements of the Marseilles Congress to establish the FAI be implemented as soon as possible. For the Portuguese, the revolutionary nature of the proposed organization was never in doubt. Item 3 on the agenda spelled out one of the FAI's chief tasks as: "the Spanish revolution and the aid that the Portuguese, as well as others, will be able to give to it."[4]

The speed with which the peninsular organization was set up indicates it was now obviously a matter of some priority for the anarchist militants. This may have been due to the decision by the dictatorship in November 1926 to set up arbitration committees in the hope of establishing a "harmonious" corporate society. The function of the *comités paritarios* was to negotiate wages and working conditions, and when Primo de Rivera's Minister of Labor invited the Socialist UGT to collaborate in the scheme, they had jumped at the opportunity "on the grounds that there were immediate material benefits to be obtained."[5] Pestaña's response to this had been to call for the legalization of the CNT in order to compete with the UGT. Other members of the now re-organized and parallel-structured CNT, the union-dominated CNT National Committee in Mataro, and the anarchist-dominated National Revolutionary Committee, firmly opposed these proposals,

---

4   Ibid: p. 242.
5   *The Coming of the Spanish Civil War,* Paul Preston, London, 1978, p. 9.

giving rise to further serious dissension within unionist ranks and widening the split between unionists and anarchists.

On 20 March 1927, within two months of the Lisbon meeting and Pestaña's call for legalization, a Regional Plenum of the Federation of Anarchist Groups in Catalonia drew up the agenda for the first conference of the FAI. Valencia and June were chosen as the date and place for the venue. The large number of tourists in June would provide perfect cover for the proposed clandestine gathering. A provisional National Secretariat was set up to organize the founding conference and circularize all interested groups. The Anarchist Liaison Committee of Catalonia issued a public manifesto. It was the closest thing to a statement of the aims and principles of the proposed FAI:

The Federation of Anarchist Groups of Spain—To everyone:

"Who are we? We are the eternal anarchists. Those eternal foes of bourgeois or capitalist 'order,' now and always. The enemies of property, wage slavery, laws, religions, militarism, the stupidity of men, and the iniquity of society.

"We are the ones who pop up, always unconfounded in the wake of any event, however serious and momentous.

"An effort has been made to implicate us in the vilest offenses, the most repugnant of crimes. Even so, we will not deny that some wretches have styled themselves anarchists even in the throes of their execrable felonies. Nonetheless, the anarchist has no truck either with theft or with systematic murder.

"While violence is accepted as a revolutionary necessity and tyrannicide justified when spontaneous, as is exceptional, occasional expropriation whenever the individual has exhausted all of the lawful means of existence and finds himself confronted by the ineluctable necessity of ensuring his right to life, this does not condone theft as condemned in contemporary society, nor violence deployed as a weapon in individual struggle, let alone as an instrument of propaganda.

"What do we want? We have spelled out a thousand times. We seek the establishment of a new society wherein all of its members may have their material, moral, and intellectual needs catered for in full. 'To each according to his needs, from each according to his strength and capabilities.' We want that society to be without bosses, without government, without coercion of any sort. No slaves, no victims of their fellow men. A free society of free men.

"Boundless progress and infinite perfection also, with ever-increasing well-being.

"We seek the emancipation of men, women, both the sexes, all the races. We seek complete emancipation within the context of a fundamentally transfigured society.

"Ourselves at present: If, desiring all this, we were to await its arrival by means of improved social machinery, we would be deluded.

"Daily we propagate our ideals and seek to imbue individuals and groups with them. Daily we strive to be more anarchist and to conform a little more with anarchism, which in turn is imperceptibly filling new horizons.

"We do not want to be aloof from any events that may contribute to the advance of progress, but out commitment will never make us lose sight of our goal and our principles. Our contribution to forward movement is never intended to favour some at the expense of others, but rather to propel society in the direction of our views. We are not shy of new political and social forms that may bring us some slight easing of our onerous and tragic lot, but we will never abandon our views.

"Communism, the state, politics, and us: We are anti-politics and anti-Statists, and when we say anti-politics we mean that we are against all politicians whether they be called Marxists, Socialists, or Communists. We are against the State, whether it be aristocratic, bourgeois, or 'proletarian.' We are against all organized violence.

"We are absolutely sure that states have but one mission: to watch over iniquity or privilege. Upon abolition of both of these, what use is the State?

"Orchestration? Direction? Very well. But not from the top down. From the bottom up. With the power to orchestrate, appoint, and dismiss being wholly invested in collectivities.

"Syndicalism and us: The revolutionary syndicalism affiliated to the AIT in Berlin we find attractive. As workers, we are almost all active in the ranks of the National Confederation of Labor

(CNT). But our mission is not wholly consumed by being active in trade unionism. We are men and some are not subject to the yoke of bourgeois exploitation. Consequently, it is not enough to be active inside the union. Our mission has a more significant complement. Outside of the unions, absolutely independently, we disseminate our theories, form our groups, organize rallies, publish anarchist reading materials, and sow the seed of anarchism in very direction.

"We seek the utter emancipation of all human beings without distinctions of any sort, not even class distinctions. Our struggle is more comprehensive, more global. There is a place among us for all who aspire to a society without government, whatever their conception of how post revolutionary society should be organized (be it communist or individualistic). In revolutions to come, we want, if possible, to avoid what happened in Russia. What always has happened. When anarchists instigate and inspire the revolution, it almost always proceeds along the proper lines; but when anarchist activity dies down, the revolution deviates from its course and anarchists—as in Russia—are the favorite victims of the inevitable exploiters of revolutions.

"Conclusions: It is, then, necessary and urgent that we organize ourselves in anarchist groupings in order to impregnate the anarchist revolution.

"We have spoken of the approaching revolution. We harbour no doubts that the social revolution is drawing nearer by giant steps. The gangrenous old politicking is cornered, in disarray and absolutely beaten, but not in the eyes of those who are now in government. We have to ensure it does not make a recovery.

"The men of 13 September, the ones who were to have cured the nation's ills within ninety days, have devastated it completely. Behind the scenes, Maura and the reaction govern. The Directory is only the fig leaf for Maurism and the most degenerate and venal politicking. Out of an instinct for survival, the country must remove these folk from power.

"We have never imagined that the main authors of the *coup d'état* are prompted by bona fides, but are, rather, swollen with ambition and presumption. But even if that were the case, they can offer a solution to nothing. Less even than the politicians.

"Consequently, revolution draws near. Let us anarchists strive to acquit ourselves well in it and to propel it as far forward as we may.

Salud y revolución
The Anarchist Liaison Committee,
The Anarchist Liaison Committee of Catalonia."[6]

---

6   *El moviemiento libertario español,* Paris, 1974, p. 295.

5

Founding Aims

The *raison d'être* of the meeting was: to aggregate,
formally, into one peninsular association, the
anarchist affinity groups of the three parent organizations,
the exiled and dispersed anarchist groups of the Iberian
peninsula—Spain's National Federation of Anarchist
Groups, the Federation of Spanish Speaking Anarchist
Groups in France, and the Portuguese Anarchist Union;
to propagate anarchist ideas among the people. But most
important of all, for the majority of those present, was the
need to promote the Libertarian Communist vision of
society through the CNT, the parent body to which most
of those present belonged, and defend its anti-political
and direct actionist principles from the reformist threat
presented by union leaders such as Pestaña.

Although it was never referred to directly in the minutes
of the Valencia Conference, the haste with which the FAI was
established within little over a year of the initial discussions
reflects the unease with which the CNT activists who founded
the FAI viewed the public and private statements, and,
ultimately, the intentions of the reformists, particularly those
in the Catalan Regional Committee of the CNT. In January the
previous year, twenty-two well-known Catalan CNT leaders, led
by Angel Pestaña, issued a statement in the paper *Vida Sindical*
calling for the legislation and re-organization of the CNT.

The thesis that the FAI was a conspiracy by an anarchist elite
to dominate and control the CNT, as some historians have
suggested, does not stand up to analysis.[1] The chronology of

---

1   Broué and Temime, *The Revolution and the Civil War in Spain*, London,
1971, p. 57; James Joll, *The Anarchists*, London, 1979, p. 245; Frank Jellinek,

events leading up to July 1927 indicate, rather, that the FAI developed as a direct response by rank and file militants to maneuvers by the national leadership of the CNT to overturn the revolutionary objectives and constitution of the CNT, approved by the 1919 National Congress and reaffirmed at the 1922 Zaragoza Conference. The CNT militants who set up the FAI in 1927, had no need to "penetrate" or seize power within the still clandestine and dispersed union; they were the heart and spirit of the Confederation.[2] It was their views that held sway among most, if not all, of the confederal cadres who had sustained the organization throughout the years of clandestinity. Their sole objective in relation to the Confederation was to prevent it being hijacked by any party political grouping, corporatist, socialist or communist, and transformed into a purely economic union committed to working within the legally defined parameters laid down by the State and capitalism.

The allegation that the FAI had been set up to "provide a nucleus of dedicated and determined revolutionaries to inspire and control the whole movement," was dismissed as totally false by founder member Progreso Fernández, who felt there was never any real danger of the CNT falling into the trap of revisionism.[3] "The only problem was that attempts were being made to legalize the CNT to compete with the UGT." He added, "Nor is it true to say that the FAI was created to maintain the CNT's ideological purity. It is, of course, possible that, in certain regions like Catalonia, the FAI's role was conceived like that, but it was not the case in Valencia."[4] Despite Fernandez's assertions to the contrary, there seems to be little doubt that the FAI hoped to succeed in revitalizing the CNT, a strategy that had to mean combating reformism.

The Civil War in Spain, London, 1938, pp. 92–93; Gabriel Jackson, *The Spanish Republic and the Civil War 1931-1939*, Princeton, 1965, p. 20; Raymond Carr, *The Spanish Tragedy*, London, 1977, p. 15; George Woodcock, *Anarchism*, London, 1963, p. 358; Franz Borkenau, *The Spanish Cockpit*, London, 1937, p. 37; Hugh Thomas, *The Spanish Civil War*, London, 1977, p. 68; Arthur H. Landis, *Spain The Unfinished Revolution*, New York, 1972, p. 26; Gerald Brenan, *The Spanish Labyrinth*, Cambridge, 1976, p. 184; César M. Lorenzo, *Les Anarchistes Espagnoles et le Pouvoir*, Paris, 1969, pp. 66–68; Felix Morrow, *Revolution and Counter-Revolution in Spain*, New York, 1974, p.100.
2   Brenan, op.cit., p. 184.
3   Joll, op.cit., p. 245.
4   Ronald Fraser, *Blood of Spain*, London, 1979. p. 548.

Another indicator that the FAI did not set out to create a homogenous and cohesive organization to control the CNT, or . even its own affiliates, is reflected in the fact that the closest it came to publishing a statement of aims and principles was the manifesto "To Everyone" published by The Anarchist Liaison Committee prior to its formal foundation. Coordinating opposition to the dictatorship and providing a focus for anarchist propaganda were obvious matters to be discussed, but the different groups in each region remained free to pursue their own priorities in the manner they felt best suited to their capabilities.

In Progreso Fernández's view, the aims of the FAI were: "To combat the dictatorship, whenever this might be possible. With an eye to the short- or long-term future, to engage in propaganda to make anarchism more widely known—through newspapers and rationalist schools. We supported a labor movement of anarchist inclinations, what is now known as anarcho-syndicalism. As we saw it, class collaboration had failed: what we had to work for was anarchist unity."[5]

The minutes of the Valencia Conference show clearly that the prime concern of most of the delegates was to ensure that the libertarian principles laid down at the 1872 Saint Imier Congress predominated as the guiding spirit of organized labor in Spain. This view of the role of the unions was totally at odds with the gradualist concept of the improving effects on working class values and conditions of labor through inter-class harmony:

"It being understood that class harmony is an impossibility, that syndicalism, in pursuing it, has fracassed; we must seek anarchist unity. The labor organization is not only to improve the class, it has to work for its emancipation. As this is only possible in Acracy, it should be done by means of anarchism. The working class organization should return to what it was prior to the dissolution of the FRE."[6]

Much of the first session of the Valencian conference was taken up in establishing which groups would be eligible for affiliation to the FAI. Could, for example, special interest

---

5   *Bicicleta*, op.cit.
6   *El Movimiento Libertario español*, op.cit., p. 287.

groups such as naturists, vegetarians, Esperantists, etc., be considered for membership? The consensus was that all that could reasonably be asked of any group wishing to affiliate to the FAI was a commitment to seek unity of action with the other groups in the struggle for social liberation.

As to the role of the anarchists in their symbiotic relationship with the CNT, the delegates were unanimously agreed in the need to resuscitate the union, put into cold storage as a national body in 1924 by a somewhat arbitrary decision of the National Committee, and to re-affirm anarchism as the inspiration and organizing spirit of the Confederation.

According to José Llop, a delegate of the National Federation of the Anarchist Groups of Spain at the Valencia gathering, the sole function of the FAI, for him, at least, was to ensure an anarchist presence within the unions. "In conference, the groups organized themselves in such a way that trade union problems were dealt with by amalgamating the different views of the anarchists who were also members of the trade union organization or the co-operatives, etc. The union question predominated in the activities of the groups. That is, the group was set up for the sole purpose of being active within the union ranks."[7]

How were the anarchists to ensure the anarchist content of the CNT, an autonomous and sovereign organization? The FAI delegates, described by Progreso Fernández as "CNT working-class militants," who had sustained the union during its years of clandestinity, resolved the thorny problem of how to bypass the reformist or potentially reformist National and Regional Committees and, at the same time, ensure the autonomy of both bodies. The solution was the creation of an organic bond, or "dovetailing" through joint CNT-FAI Defense and Prisoners' Aid Committees at local federation level. These local committees were to provide the anarchist militants with a voice and influence within the Confederation in the revolutionary areas of solidarity and direct action.

This special relationship between the specifically anarchist and unions organizations was known as the *trabazón*. Its purpose was to defend the CNT's commitment to solidarity and direct action, thereby safeguarding the union from being

---

7   Ibid., p. 290.

manipulated by State communist or collaborationist influences. It was to become the cause of much controversy and ill-feeling among the reformists and gradualists within the CNT.

6
Secret Society—Revolutionary Elite?

It has often been affirmed by Marxist and liberal historians that the FAI was a secret and elitist organization. In fact, the FAI never constituted a secret organization, nor did its militants operate in any covert way in relation to the CNT, nor did they attempt to keep their affiliation secret from non-members. Certainly, under the conditions imposed by the dictatorship or in periods of repression, membership of the FAI was not something to broadcast widely, but this is a far cry from the "mysterious and powerful...clandestine organization... made up of kindred groups similar to Masonic Lodges under the authority of a secret Mainland Committee," as claimed by Trotskyist historians Broué and Temime.[1]

An indication of the lack of secrecy and poor security that surrounded the FAI can be seen in the fact that Primo de Rivera's police and intelligence services appear to have been fully aware of the nature and object of the Valencia meeting. Shortly after it had taken place, the homes of the members of the Sol y Vida group, hosts to the founding conference and whose members constituted the first Peninsular Secretariat, were raided and members arrested. Fortunately, the minutes of the meeting were destroyed before the arrival of the police by a quick-witted member of the Seville based secretariat.[2]

Neither did FAI meetings follow the closely guarded masonic model as Francisco Carrasquer, a noted anarchist militant, observed:

1 Broué and Temime, op.cit., p. 57.
2 *El Movimiento Libertario Español*, op.cit., pp. 293–298.

"If it was secret, how come I was able to attend FAI meetings without ever having joined or paid dues to the 'specific' organization? Because they were specific groups, affinity groups, and nothing more... It was perspective opened up for the formation of discussion groups to keep on the boil the topics that really mattered...the liberation of man and of woman, the social revolution."[3]

As an organization publicly committed to the overthrow of the dictatorship, the FAI functioned, from 1927 to 1931, as an illegal, rather than a secret, organization. From the birth of the Republic in 1931 onwards, the FAI was simply an organization that, until 1937, refused to register as required by Republican Law. In fact, the final crisis that led to the FAI's demise as a federally-structured anarchist organization was triggered by the decision to register.

Another common belief is that the FAI constituted a political elite within the CNT. Frank Jellinek, a Communist writer, drew a parallel between the FAI and the Russian Communist Party:

"By no means are all members of the CNT members of the FAI. It is as much an honour for a CNT member to be co-opted into the FAI as for a Russian worker to be accepted as a member of the Communist Party. The qualifications are an undeviating belief in the doctrines of anarchism, useful and reliable service to the cause, above all, capacity for 'direct action.'"[4]

Franz Borkenau added further confusion when he stated, quite wrongly, that "only members of the FAI could hold positions of trust in the CNT."[5]

In fact, there was no individual membership of the FAI, militants were not co-opted into the organization, and for the most part deliberately avoided "positions of trust" in the union. José Llop describes the process of recruitment thus: "As for individual entry, most of those who already enjoyed some standing in anarchist or trade union circles did not belong to the organization of the groups, or did so indirectly.

3 Francisco Carrasquer, "¿Ha habido una ideologia politica en el anarquismo español?," *Cuadernos de Ruedo Iberico*, Nos. 35–57, Jan–June, Paris, 1977, p. 163.
4 Jellinek, op.cit., pp. 92–93.
5 Borkenau, op.cit., p. 37.

For instance, take [Joan] Peiró: he had no need to intervene directly in his group in Mataro. Whenever a comrade came along who was not affiliated to a group and who sympathized with us, he would join the group. The group was formed on the basis of comrades who had an affinity."[6]

"Although all wage earning FAI affiliates were expected to be members of the CNT, it must be emphasized that only a small number of anarchists belonged to the specific organization. During the dictatorship it is unlikely its national membership exceeded 1,000. Fidel Miró claims that although no one knows for certain the total number of FAI affiliates in Barcelona, generally considered to be the heart of the specific organization, 'at no time, prior to July 1936, was it in excess of 300.'"[7]

In the early phase, 1927–1933, the FAI fell far short of providing what Gerald Brenan called "a nucleus of thinkers whose mission it would be to keep the movement ideologically pure." Nor was it "a council of action for organizing revolutionary movements,"[8] or César M. Lorenzo's "state inside the CNT."[9] Progreso Fernández, a member of the Ni Dios Ni Amo affinity group gives a less sinister, insider's account of FAI activities in its early phase, a period he described as being "of very limited activity. In point of fact, we did not manage to get one anarchist publication off the ground." He claims their main activity revolved "primarily in receiving and distributing newspapers like *Tierra y Libertad* and *La Voz del Campesino*," reading and discussing books, "above all Kropotkin" and in "atheistic propaganda." He described his FAI comrades as having "a minimum of anarchist convictions in relation to their way of thinking and acting."[10]

José Peirats, anarchist historian and secretary of the Federation of Anarchist Groups of Barcelona had this to say:

"The militants of the FAI came from the CNT and felt themselves more *cenetistas* than *faistas*. This was the root of the

6   *El Movimiento Libertario Español*, op.cit., p. 288.
7   Fidel Miró, *Catalonia: los trabajadores y el problema de las nacionalidades*, Mexico, 1967, pp. 45–50.
8   Brenan, op.cit., p. 249.
9   Lorenzo, op.cit., pp .66–68.
10 *Bicicleta*, op.cit.

problem. The FAI was more revolutionary than anarchist... It did not stand out as a school of philosophy and this damaged it enormously; the only attenuating circumstances was the corrosive atmosphere in which it was born and lived."

On the question of forming a state within a state, he added:

"The discovery of the minutes reveals that the FAI did not propose to manipulate the CNT, but to collaborate closely with it. Things only became more complicated later, after the split of 1931."[11]

Francisco Carrasquer also refutes the charge that the FAI formed a "state within a state." "It was never its aim to act as a leadership or anything of the sort. To begin with, they had no slogans, nor was any line laid down, let alone any adherence to any hierarchical structure... This is what outside historians ought to grasp once and for all: that neither Durruti, nor Ascaso, nor García Oliver—to name only the great CNT spokesmen—issued any watchwords to the 'masses,' let alone delivered any operational plan or conspiratorial scheme to the bulk of the CNT membership. For one thing, each FAI group thought and acted as it deemed fit, without bothering about what the others might be thinking or deciding."[12]

11 *El Movimiento Libertario Español*, op.cit., p. 231.
12 Carrasquer, ibid., p. 177.

7

"Dirty Tricks Department?"

F AI members have also been accused of being "other worldly," criminals, or psychopaths. On closer examination, these charges prove to be nothing more than highly subjective untestable conjectures intended to suit the author's prejudices. In the few cases where "proof" is adduced, it turns out to be hearsay evidence from hostile witnesses. The criminal pathology of Spanish anarchism can only be refuted by empirical study rather than the abstract theories of indolent or malevolent historians.

George Woodcock, for example, apparently unaware that the FAI consisted in the main of rank and file *cenetistas*, states that, apart from "hard working trade union leaders and the theoreticians of Spanish anarchism" (most of whom didn't join the FAI until 1934 by which time it had ceased to be a revolutionary instrument), it also contained a "dubious contingent from the Barcelona underworld." The latter allegation was an idea picked up and repeated from Borkenau. This unholy alliance, he claims, proves the Bakuninist connection.

"It was he (Bakunin) who laid most stress on the alliance between idealists and the marginal social elements necessary to overthrow the state and prepare the ground for the free society." The FAI's founders "mingled idealistic devotion to a cause with a taste for conspiracy, a justification for illegality and tyrannicide—and a leaning toward social experiments of a primitive communist nature."[1]

---

1   Woodcock, op.cit., p. 358.

Gabriel Jackson believed "the FAI combined anarchist idealism with gangsterism, often in the same persons." The FAI is presented as the Mafia and the CNT as a Spanish Teamsters Union. "They collected the dues of the CNT unions, forming prisoner funds, buying arms, 'protecting' the workers from the police." Jackson portrays the "Zaragoza" anarchists as being divided into three types. "There were a handful of self-educated idealists, readers of Bakunin and Tolstoy, sometimes mystical pacifists, sometimes vegetarians or nudists. They lived aesthetically, on the proceeds of their own proud but ill-paid labor, and believed literally that the declaration of *comunismo libertario* throughout the Peninsula would lead immediately to a peaceful, prosperous, egalitarian society. Then there were the mass of unskilled and semi-skilled workers... Before the days of the FAI, these people might easily have been cajoled into settling their strikes... But the class consciousness and the revolutionary mystique which had been inculcated by the FAI, made them determined to show their bosses that society depended upon them, the workers. They enjoyed demonstrating their power by tying up the city and looked upon their general strikes as a rehearsal for the eventual revolutionary achievement of *comunismo libertario*... Finally, there were a small but important group of professional gunmen, by no means all Spaniards."[2]

The "foreign" gunmen, the "stormy petrels" so beloved by conspiracy buffs, were, in Jackson's view, an important element in the FAI. The sources on which this view is based were "businessmen" who had had "repeated dealings" with the CNT and FAI in the 1920s and 1930s:

"When the residents of Zaragoza observed twenty or thirty strangers with foreign accents selling ties on the streets, they knew that another general strike was coming."[3]

Frank Jellinek took a slightly more sophisticated view of FAI members. He described them as "killers," rather than "mere gunmen," who were "entrusted with what may be called without intention of insult, the CNT's dirty work." It recruited "from among the most skilled and intelligent workers at one end and from the Murcians and Almerians who are engaged in the

---

2 Jackson, op.cit., pp. 126–127.
3 Ibid.

great cities at the other. Naturally, lumpenproletariat elements inevitably creep in, but are sooner or later liquidated."[4]

For Gerald Brenan, the advent of the FAI brought with it an increasingly noticeable trend in Spanish Anarchism: "the inclusion within its ranks of professional criminals—thieves and gunmen who certainly would not have been accepted by any other working class party—together with idealists of the purest and most selfless kind."[5]

---

4   Jellinek, op.cit., pp. 92–93.
5   Brenan, op.cit., p. 251.

8

A Parallel CNT?

Trotskyist historian Felix Morrow described the FAI as "a highly centralized party apparatus through which it maintained control of the CNT."[1] This view was shared by American liberal historian Gabriel Jackson who depicted it as "the tightly organized elite, which, since 1927, had dominated the CNT."[2]

This view of the FAI is not shared by contemporary participants. Francisco Carrasquer, a *faista*, noted:

"Each FAI group thought and acted as it deemed fit, without bothering about what the others might be thinking or deciding, for there was no intergroup discipline such as was found between communist cells in respect of territory, etc. Secondly, they had no competence, opportunity, or jurisdiction—though they might have preferred that—to foist a party line upon the grassroots. They were like the rest, no more. Had it been otherwise how come a Francisco Ascaso would have been allowed to his death in the front ranks."[3]

With regard to what many observers have referred to as the "elite" of the anarchist movement, it is important to remember that anarchists do not object to the principle of leadership and that organization does not mean submission to concentrated authority. Anarchists have never denied the legitimate authority of a person to exercise leadership in the area in which he or she is knowledgeable. What they do object to is the view that such authority should be coercive.

---

1 Morrow, op.cit., p. 100.
2 Jackson, op.cit.., p. 126.
3 Carrasquer, op.cit.

The anarchist attitude to such authority was expressed clearly and succinctly by Bakunin sixty years earlier:

"There should be no fixed and constant authority, but mutual and voluntary authority. Society should not indulge or exalt men of genius, nor should it accord them special rights or privileges because: it would often mistake a charlatan for a man of genius; because through such systems of privilege it might even transform a genius into a charlatan; it would establish a master over itself."[4]

The basic units of the FAI were not individuals, but small autonomous affinity groups of anarchist militants. This cohesive quasi-cellular form of association had evolved, gradually, over the period of time it takes for relationships to be established and for mutual trust to grow. The affinity groups consisted, usually, of between three and ten members bound by ties of friendship, and who shared well-defined aims and agreed methods of struggle. Once such a group had come into existence it could, if it so wished, solicit affiliation to the FAI.

The small size of the group implied a minimal structure of decision making, if only on the level of commitment to majority decisions or group consensus. It also permitted the greatest degree of intimacy and trust between those who composed it. The essence of the affinity group, however, is that it is the members who decide who is and who is not a member. The loyalties of group members always lay with each other and the shared ideal, not with the concept of the organization as an organized institution. Also, although small groups can be easily led by force of personality, this drawback was felt to be balanced by the fact that dominant individuals who do emerge are restricted in the area in which they can dominate. The affinity groups were also highly resistant to police infiltration. Even if infiltration did occur, or police agents did manage to set up their own "affinity" groups, it would not have been a particularly efficient means of intelligence gathering; the atomic structure of the FAI meant there was no central body to provide an overview of the movement as a whole.

---

4 Mikhail Bakunin, *God and the State* (*Bakunin on Anarchism*), Montreal, 1980, p. 230.

It should also be stressed that affinity groups are not without their drawbacks either. There are as many inherent dangers within small, self-selecting, and self-perpetuating groups as there are within larger formal organizations. The CNT, for example, took as its basic unit the workplace, by necessity, and this may have had its weaknesses, but it also had the enormous strength that the workers cooperated daily and struggled against a common and real enemy. They were obliged to get on and they had to practice solidarity. It was this daily practice of cooperation and solidarity that provided the basis of revolutionary unionism. Affinity groups, on the other hand, because of their exclusive and cohesive nature, run the risk of being nothing but ideological groupings or terrorist cells, both of which, however necessary at times, are in constant danger of perpetuating the split between class-conscious or revolutionary cadres and the non-militant mass of the workers. No matter how idealistic the members of the group may be, there will undoubtedly come a time when conflict develops between obligations to one's comrades and the society of the outside world. Tension between the ideal and practice becomes inevitable when ideologically committed people form exclusive groupings. An unbridgeable gap is created between them and people outside their immediate circle and ideology; in other words, an "affinity group" can become just as "institutionalized" as a mass organization.

The founders of the FAI were, however, sensitive to the oligarchical dangers inherent in organization and conscious of the perpetual struggle between "freedom" and "authority," with the associated problems of "deference" and "obedience," and made a conscious effort to reduce its negative features to a minimum. In fact the term "organization" hardly fits the FAI: it had no collective identity other than a commitment to libertarian communism as an immediate objective. It did not issue membership cards or collect dues (although voluntary contributions were made), so there was never a roster of members, nor were there any formal procedures for replacing members. Above all, it was not a representative body and involved no delegation of power either within the affinity groups or in the regional or national administrative bodies to empower those bodies to make decisions on behalf of the collectivity. Drawing on many years of revolutionary experience, the FAI was firmly rooted in federal principles and structured in such a way that its coordinating function did not deprive its constituent members of their autonomous power. "The [Peninsular] committee's title was 'Liaison Committee' [*comité de relaciones*] nothing more. It took no initiatives itself of any sort; it merely passed them on to other comrades and the assemblies approved or rejected them."[5] In situations where it was necessary for delegates to take decisions, e.g. at plenary meetings during times of crisis or clandestinity, those decisions were required to be ratified by the whole membership who, in effect, constituted the administration.

Not only was there no program of activity, as Francisco Carrasquer noted, other than the agreed immediate objective of toppling capitalism and the State and the introduction of Libertarian Communism, no common ideologically cohesive line was possible.[6] The views, activities, and priorities of the different groups covered such a broad range of options that any attempt to impose an official program could only have been a source of division and friction. The public views of the FAI were expressed as general statements by the Peninsular Committee, but these in no way bound the sovereign constituent affinity groups who remained free to pursue their preferred activities and propagate their views within their own spheres of influence.

The FAI was, in its initial phase, simply an ad hoc instrument, the cutting edge of the CNT. It was a voluntary and mutualist association of militant anarchist unionists who, in response to a perceived threat at a precise point in time, refused to go along with the reformist leadership of the CNT. These anarchist workers combined their energies under the convenient banner of the FAI to achieve a specific concrete end, the defense of the revolutionary objectives and principles of the Confederation. The intention of the *faistas* was not to exercise dominion, but to carry out the historic role of anarchism, namely to combat authoritarian ideas within the working class movement and keep alive the anarchist spirit in a CNT, which was increasingly under pressure from a class collaborationist leadership. Juan Manuel Molina, secretary of the Peninsular Committee of

5   *El moviemiento libertario Espanol*, op.cit., p.288.
6   Carrasquer, ibid.

the FAI from 1930 to 1932, described it as being, above all, "a symbol," rather than "a rigorously structured organization." He went on to point out that, although the majority of anarchists agreed and sympathized with it "and spoke in its name even, they did not in fact belong to it."[7]

Each individual in the FAI affinity groups, if a wage earner, was expected to join and be active within a CNT-affiliated union. As has already been noted, most of the founding members of the FAI were, first and foremost, CNT militants. As José Llop recalled in conversation with Frank Mintz:

"The groups organized themselves in such a way that union problems were dealt with by amalgamating the different views of the anarchists who were also members of the union organization, or the co-operatives, etc. The union question predominated in the activities of the groups. That is, the group was set up for the sole purpose of being active within the union ranks."[8]

In what I have described as the instrumental or youthful and mature period of the organization, 1927–1933, the FAI's commitment to direct action and class war meant it attracted few intellectuals. During this phase most of its affiliates were young and enthusiastic working class revolutionaries who, based on their own experiences and knowledge, understood that all economic gains were short term and that the only lasting solution to the alienation and misery of the society in which they lived was immediate social revolution. They were the sworn enemies of all attempts to compromise fundamental anarchist principles through pacts with bourgeois democracy. They championed a society that worked from the base upwards, not from a centralized State or administrative apparatus run by an intellectual elite with a theoretical view of social processes.

An important binding factor in the relationship between anarchist organization and the union was its federal structure, which directly paralleled that of the CNT, with local, district, and regional federations. The groups in a city or town constituted a Local Federation, while the rural groups, combined, formed a District Federation. These were administered by a secretariat

7 Molina, ibid., p. 223.
8 Llop, ibid., p. 290.

and a committee composed of one mandated delegate from each affinity group. The Local and District Federations were obliged to convene regular assemblies of all groups in its area. These usually took place on Sundays under the guise of picnics in the countryside. They were small meetings with one or two delegates from each group and "never," according to Fidel Miró, "general assemblies."[9]

Local and District Federations constituted a Regional Federation. These, in turn, were co-ordinated by a Peninsular Liaison Committee. None of these committees, local, district, regional, or national, could be described as having a bureaucratic apparatus. Nor did they wield executive power of any description. Their function was purely administrative.

Regional liaison was always conducted by letter. "It was never an option to allocate a comrade. The national committee was seconded several times, but always within Catalonia. Later, when funds were more plentiful, this became an option. It would have been interesting to second a comrade to Asturias, for there was a federation of anarchist groups up there. But liaison with the national committee was rather hit and miss. A meeting would have been necessary, but many a time we did not have the wherewithal to send letters."[10]

---

9 Fidel Miró, a member of both the FAI and the FIJL, argued that this structure was undemocratic as it permitted the influential groups to dominate and manipulate the meetings to their advantage. The meetings themselves were rarely raided, according to Miró, because of the danger to the police from heavily armed FAI members. *Catalonia...*, op.cit., p. 49. It is equally possible the police depended on these meetings for their intelligence on anarchist plans.
10 Llop, op.cit., p. 290.

9

Unionism versus Anarcho-syndicalism

By the winter of 1927–28 the grip of the dictatorship had begun to loosen. This led to a corresponding upsurge in working-class militancy. The CNT began to re-group its scattered forces. On 16 and 17 January 1928, the official FAI delegate to a CNT National Plenum held in Madrid proposed the *trabazón*, the joint defense and solidarity committees, as the most efficient and suitable way to link both organizations and prepare them for the task of confronting the dictatorship and easing the eventual re-emergence of the confederation from clandestinity.

"It is not proposed," stated the delegate, "to create a new organization, but connect like-minded organizations for the realization of activities and resolving problems common to both, forming committees or general councils that will harmonize and develop their relationship and avoid prejudicial friction."[1]

The proposal for joint FAI-CNT action committees, the forerunners of the Defense Committees, was accepted by the Madrid plenum with little opposition, as was the joint National Prisoners' Aid Committee. Clearly, at that point in time, the leading spokesmen for the legal union position, including Angel Pestaña, then CNT National Secretary, did not see the FAI as an incompatible competitor. Indeed, it was the anarchist groups influenced by the Urales family journal *La Revista*

---

1 "La FAI a la CNT," *Acción Social Obrera*, 6.4.1928.

Blanca who were expressing doubts as to the wisdom of the "understanding" between the two organizations.

Pestaña himself endorsed the *trabazón* when its advisability was questioned by the Valencia Local Federation of Anarchist Groups. His reply, on behalf of the National Committee of the CNT, appeared to say that the FAI was entitled to intervene in "political" matters, i.e. that the CNT was only concerned with economic demands:

"Collaboration between the two national organisms (CNT and FAI) is not a confusion of the respective missions of both organisms...

"There is union question that is the exclusive competence of the CNT, but whenever the situation is such as to allow support from the FAI, and when there is another question which, by virtue of its blatantly revolutionary nature, may be described as political, it is only natural and logical that there should ensure close collaboration of both organisms on a basis of complete equality."[2]

That the FAI should have accepted the idea that the political struggle could be separated out from the economic is curious and difficult to explain; for anarchists there is only one class, one enemy, and one struggle, and the latter can only be waged by one organization, not two!

The endorsement of the *trabazón* by an anti-revolutionary CNT National Committee is equally curious. Perhaps their fears had been allayed by the poor resources and relatively minuscule membership of the FAI. Compared with the CNT leaders' apparently strong position within a mass organization that numbered its strength in hundreds of thousands, the 1,000 or so FAI affiliates could hardly have appeared to present much of a threat.

Perhaps Pestaña hoped that, by formalizing the relationship and mapping out the boundaries between the two organizations, friction could be reduced. There also appears to have been some confusion as to the composition and jurisdiction of these

2   Letter from the National Committee of the CNT to the Valencia Local Federation of Anarchist Groups. Quoted by Alexander Schapiro in his confidential report to the AIT on the CNT: *Rapport sur l'activite de la Confederation National du Travail d'Ëspagne* 16 Decembre 1932–26, Fevrier 1933.

committees. According to Alexander Schapiro, the minutes of the Plenum do not refer to regional or local committees, only to a National Prisoners' Aid Committee.[3]

By the Spring of 1928 the dictatorship had lost the support of the officer and professional classes, and was drawing uneasily to a close. At the same time, anarchist rank and file discontent with the attitude of the CNT leadership over the question of collaboration with political and statist bodies became increasingly acute. Pestaña and his unionist colleagues had almost completed the process of transforming the National Committee of the CNT into a body with a life and purpose of its own, one with views very different from the revolutionary objectives of the Confederation.

It would be wrong to argue that Pestaña acted as he did out of treachery, opportunism, hypocrisy, or that he had in some way lost his moral sense. There can be little doubt he did what he did out of a sense of obligation and duty. Pestaña had come to believe that anarchism was compatible with capitalism and statism.

How did the revolutionary anarchist of the 1910s cross the unbridgeable gulf from class war to class collaboration, and still claim to be an anarchist?

Like anyone else in a similar position, Pestaña, a dedicated union leader, professionally committed to representing what he saw as the best interests of his members, had fallen prey to what Robert Michels has described as "The Iron Law of Oligarchy":

"It is organization that gives birth to the dominion of the elected over the electors, of the mandatories over the mandators, of the delegates over the delegators. Who says organization says oligarchy?"[4]

Bureaucratic conservatism, inherent in all formal representative organizations, reinforced by the distorting effects of the years of clandestinity, had finally taken its toll. Pestaña's moral and logical senses had acquired a radically different focus. He no longer saw himself as an individual, morally accountable either to his own ethical yardstick or to the

---

3   Ibid., p. 30.
4   Robert Michels, *Political Parties*, New York, 1962, p. 365.

"idealistic" demands of the base of a democratic organization whose contradictions were becoming increasingly apparent: demanding, on the one hand, piecemeal improvements and, on the other, immediate social revolution.

The ideals that had originally inspired him had now become an obstacle to the realization of his ends. He now regarded himself as the agent of an organic whole whose survival and growth took precedence over everything else, including his own principles and, if necessary, the wishes of the structure's constituent parts, the autonomous industrial unions.

Mikhail Bakunin, an astute observer of human nature and politics, had warned of the inevitability of this outcome when anarchists were seduced into believing their ideas were compatible with statist and party political activity:

"This explains how and why men who were once the reddest democrats, the most vociferous radicals, once in power become the most moderate conservatives. Such turnabouts are usually, and mistakenly, regarded as a kind of treason. Their principal cause is the inevitable change of position and perspective."

Nourished by the tactical collaboration with political and military groups for the purpose of overthrowing the dictatorship—something which many sections of the CNT had been involved in since 1923, as indeed had the Peninsular Committee of the FAI since 1927—the seeds of reformism began to sprout during 1928. Supported by his power base, the Solidaridad group, which sought precisely those ends he and his colleagues objected to in the FAI—the wish to impose its hegemony over the CNT (it was also to be the seedbed of what later became known as treintismo)—Pestaña stepped up his campaign to bring the CNT "in from the cold," by agreeing to abide by the Corporation Law, the legislative brainchild of the dictatorship.

To unionist colleagues Pestaña argued that it would be a superficial compromise, but one that would permit the Confederation to reorganize and ensure a ready-made conduit for the workers' demands once the state of emergency ended. If they did not re-form, legally, as he argued, they would be left behind once the dictatorship had fallen, a time that could not be far off.

Pestaña and his friends had fallen prey to the imperialist obsession to establish an absolute majority position within the Spanish labor movement. For Pestaña, the struggle had ceased to be a matter of principles, it was not one of competition with Largo Caballero, the Socialist Party leader. What concerned him most was that the CNT would lose its ascendancy over the workers, and leave the UGT with all the advantages. He tried to reassure the rank and file, promising that the organization's anarcho-syndicalistic values and principles (i.e. those of a directly democratic union based on the workplace, aiming at workers control) would be retained and nourished within a parallel, clandestine organization.

Pestaña, however, was saying something quite different to the authorities. In secret discussions with General Mola, the CNT leader clearly led the Director General of Security to understand that, in spite of the rhetoric, the objectives of the CNT were not those expressed by the anarchist rank and file. Pestaña sought to reassure Mola that power did not interest the Confederation and that it would look with greater sympathy on the regime, which most closely approximated its ideal. If legalized, the union would confine its activities to pure social and economic demands such as seeking better pay and improved working conditions. Mola recalled:

"Insofar as their aspirations were concerned, they were simply none other than achieving for the working class those legal rights that were due to them as producers...applying constant pressure to progress, little by little."[5]

It was assurances from union leaders like Pestaña which allowed Mola to state confidently that the trade union bureaucracy could be relied on to keep the rank and file out of militant action, although, it must be added, that he doubted their ability to do so.

The renewed pressure from the national leadership to accept legalization, a move clearly to the detriment of anti-statist and social revolutionary principles, re-awakened the combative spirit of the "conscious minority" who constituted the anarchist heart of the CNT.

---

5   General Emilio Mola, *Obras Completas*, Valladolid, 1940, pp. 351–353.

Although they were a minority in the union, the anarchists exerted a powerful moral influence on the mass of the membership who, as Salvador Caño points out: "Identified with the ideas of the FAI, and the majority of the confederal militancy responded to the anarchist spirit."[6]

The movement was also invigorated by the emergence of more dynamic elements of a younger generation of union militants. These young men had served their revolutionary apprenticeships defending their class interests, not only in the factories, but also on the streets where they stood against the gunmen (*pistoleros*) sent out to shoot them down by intransigent employers' and government agencies.

For them, the emergence of the FAI with its reaffirmation of fundamental anarchist principles reflected the spirit of the age. It also provided a convenient banner around which they could rally the broad mass of confederal unionists to the defense of those principles. Faced with a radical groundswell by the rank and file, and anxious to defend the union organization at any cost from what they saw as the disastrous consequences of upholding revolutionary theory and practice, Pestaña and his colleagues began to pull out all the stops in order to neutralize resurgent anarchist influence within the CNT. Under pressure from the CNT members, rather than by its own initiative, the FAI gradually became the instrument and focus for opposition to the legalitarian union faction that dominated the National Committee.

One solution the Solidaridad group came up with was to set up their own answer to the FAI, the so-called Union of Militants, an organization that would compete with the FAI for influence within the CNT. Joan Peiró, a member of both the FAI and the Solidaridad group, attempted to mediate between the two factions within the CNT, but the ideological gulf that separated them was, by now, unbridgeable and growing wider by the day.

Pestaña had attempted to force this issue to a head in April 1928 with a series of articles in the Vigo CNT paper *Despertad!*, under the heading "Situemenos!" (Where we stand!), in which he had called on the base of the CNT to reconsider its position. The unions, he urged, should be free to adapt themselves "to

---

6   *El Movimiento Libertario,* op.cit., p. 175.

accommodate all manner of principles." They were not tools that, in the hands of the anarchist groups, would permit them to impose their values on the majority.

He also proposed that the workers should be organized by profession, rather than through the federally structured and autonomous industrial unions. This fundamental structural change in the organization, if accepted, would clearly have strengthened the influence of the higher committees at the expense of the membership. In effect, what Pestaña was proposing was, in anarchist terms, nothing short of degenerate. It was a classical piece of political sophistry (which re-emerged during the British miners' strike of 1985 over the question of the balloting of members) that claimed to defend democratic values by "giving the unions back to their members." In other words, they wished to destroy the class content of the unions, which would become little more than coffin clubs.

To Joan Peiró (whose own position, belonging as he did to both organizations, was, to say the least, ambivalent), Pestaña's maneuvering was an outright perversion and betrayal of the principles of the CNT. He vigorously denounced his erstwhile comrade's proposals in *Acción Social Obrera* as "deviationist," class collaborationist, and leading, ultimately, to a legally tamed union:

"In 'Situemenos!' we have examined the hasty assertion that 'the Confederation' is its content, not a 'container' [i.e. that the CNT should be ideologically neutral], which means to say that the CNT is not the expression of enduring principles, but can adapt itself to all manner of precepts however reformist these may be. This, of itself, is tantamount to claiming that 'principles' are made by men (is there anyone who believes them to be God's work?) and that 'men have it in their power to change them,' and so on. No. Let me tell comrade Saltor and all the Pestañas that may have been or are yet to come that, yes, the CNT's principles are susceptible to change and adjustment insofar as they affect the process of economic, political, and social change (to some effect and with ineluctable imperatives), so the CNT has certain basic precepts whose essential and enduring nature cannot be foresworn.

"The confederal congresses can change all of the principles of the CNT should they deem such amendment necessary. What no congress may do, much less any man, no matter how well endowed with a 'grasp of reality' and a 'practical mentality,' is renounce the principles that are the CNT's essential premise, its foundation, and *raison d'être*...its anti-parliamentarianism and direct action.

"What I have been saying amounts to a declaration that, were it possible to speak freely today at a regular congress, then everything amenable would be amended... But the CNT's two basic and intangible principles—direct action and anti-parliamentarianism—would remain. Otherwise the CNT would lose its *raison d'être*. And what I am defending here is nothing more than that which gives the CNT its *raison d'être*."[7]

The FAI enters the debate

In spite of the oft-repeated charges that the FAI provoked the split within the CNT, the truth of the matter is that it did not enter the debate between the unionist and anarchist wings of the CNT until fairly late in the day.

Its first public pronouncement on the subject was a statement issued by the Peninsular Committee in December 1929. It denounced as naive the idea that the labor movement could be ideologically neutral. If the anarchists withdrew their influence from the CNT, other groups such as communists, Catholics, or any other power-seeking group, including pure syndicalists, would quickly attempt to fill the vacuum. The statement also seems to suggest the implicit threat that FAI members would withdraw from the CNT if it refused to recognize the FAI!

"It is sophistry to believe in the neutrality of the labor movement and in the independence of trade unions in terms of their ideological outlook and subversive propaganda, especially by their very nature as libertory movements and their undeniable implications for society, they cannot, in any way, escape the more or less preponderant influences of those ideologies that seek hegemony over society. More especially since their whole moral and sociological consequences are the product of the most powerful minority at work within their ranks. This is why we find as many labor movements on the international scene with corresponding social, political, and religious inclinations.

7   *Acción Social Obrera*, 7.12.1929.

"Every labor movement, whatever its nature, whether it be an imperative of the capitalist, statist system, or has its origins in a condition of political inferiority and economic inequality that afflicts the workers, or whether its short-term activity focuses upon the pursuit of material and moral improvements... cannot, and should not, forget that, in its field, albeit displaying different characteristics and features, there are other social movements that are also struggling towards and desirous of, not merely the economic betterment of the oppressed and humanization of the labor that these perform, but also of the absolute eradication of the prevailing blights and the complete disappearance of all political and economic privileges.

"Hence the need for the CNT (if it truly wishes its activity to be transcendental and demolitionist in the most comprehensive sense of the words) to seek an accommodation with that organism which sees eye to eye with its tactical procedures and agrees with its premise, without thereby—let us say it again— without thereby losing its peculiar independence. On the other hand, should the CNT not accept the proposition formulated by this Secretariat, it is highly likely that it runs the risk of a deviation greatly detrimental to its cause of comprehensive recovery, and of losing that moral and revolutionary value that is its distinguishing feature unless...through the unstinting work of anarchists, it openly describes and declares itself anarchist."[8]

The sharp difference in perception between leadership and base as to realizable objectives increased the friction within the CNT.

Pestaña's proposal that it should "adapt to reality" and form a lawful and compliant union organization, abandoning the undiluted revolutionary principles of the CNT in the process, evoked such intense feeling that Pestaña was obliged to resign as Secretary of the National Committee of the CNT (although he did remain a member of the NC). He publicly denounced the union as being organizationally defunct and devoid of members. Events were soon to prove him wrong.

The Primo de Rivera dictatorship finally collapsed at the end of 1929. Alfonso XIII appointed General Berenguer as premier and promised elections, but the working class and the

8 José Peirats, *La CNT*, op.cit., Vol. I, Ch. 2.

bourgeoisie sensed the weakness of the old regime and began to press in for the final confrontation.

On the economic front, the value of the peseta had dropped to almost unheard of levels. As unrest grew among the professional classes and the commercial and manufacturing bourgeoisie, so too did the number of strikes and disturbances among the workers. The CNT, dismissed the previous year by its own leader Ángel Pestaña as "an empty shell," erupted back on the scene with renewed vigor and vitality. Membership soared to 800,000. Anarchist newspapers once again began to circulate openly on the streets.

From late 1929 it could be argued that the FAI was as much a hybrid creation of the bourgeois press, declassé freelance intellectuals such as Diego Abad de Santillán, and the reformists, as a collection of militants. The capitalist press, reflecting the bourgeoisie's unease at growing working class militancy and their doubts as to the ability of the union leaders to control the rank and file, fell upon the FAI, as Santillán notes, as "the scapegoat for all sorts of accusations and insults."[9]

Nothing could have been further from the truth. Between 1927 and 1930, the FAI had only a nominal existence. Its activities, in the main, had concentrated on anti-clerical and free-thought propaganda, as well as providing a distribution network for the clandestine anarchist press.

Only after Juan Manuel Molina (Juanel) returned from exile in Brussels to take over as Peninsular Secretary of the FAI from José Elizalde did the organization begin to experience growth and live up to its reputation as the voice of revolutionary anarchism. Molina's colleagues on the Peninsular Committee included Merino; an Aragonese militant, Portula; from Barcelona, Luzbel Ruiz; and the Andalucian/Portuguese militant Ricardo Pena.[10]

---

9 Diego Abad de Santillán, *De Alfonso XIII a Franco*, Buenos Aires, 1974, p. 171.

10 Ricardo or Rafael Pena, also known as Carlos Chavez (born Lisbon 1889, died Panama 1975). Pena was a well known militant in the Seville area, as well as in Oporto and Lisbon during the Primo de Rivera dictatorship. He worked closely with the Portuguese anarcho-syndicalist union, the CGT, and the Portuguese Anarchist Union, and was associated with the editors of *La Batalla* and *Comuna*. He returned to Spain in 1927 where he became an active militant in the CNT and played an important part in ousting the Communists who had seized control of the Seville CNT unions in 1930. He represented Seville's textile union at the CNT Congress the following year.

Molina described the state of the FAI when he took over as "unsatisfactory." "When I arrived in Barcelona from exile in the early weeks of 1930, the FAI did not amount to much... When I was appointed Secretary of the Peninsular Committee, it did not even possess a typewriter or anything. The ancient machine of the Federation of Spanish Speaking Groups in France [of which he had previously been secretary], which had virtually been dismantled, plus an up to date duplicator that I bought, were the tools with which we began the march of the FAI."[11]

Active throughout the period of the Republic, he became Secretary General of the Andalucian CNT at the outbreak of the military rising. It was in this capacity that he attended the Andalucian FAI Congress in Almeria. He later commanded a confederal centuria in Malaga. *Cuadernos para una enciclopedia historica del anarquismo español,* No. 28, Vitoria, 1984.

11 Letter from Molina to Juan Gómez Casas, 28.6.1975. (Quoted in *Historia de la FAI,* op.cit.)

10

1930—A Revolutionary Instrument

By the beginning of 1930 the unionist faction held the upper hand, they had their own paper, Acción, and were in full control of the National Committee. Pestaña's meeting with General Mola had secured legal recognition for the union which was now beginning to reorganize nationally. More and more of the leading *cenetistas* openly began to press for closer contacts with republican politicians, not just a tactical alliance but as a strategy to ensure the future growth of the union.

The degree to which tactical collaboration led to reformism and tied in the leadership of the anarcho-syndicalist union with the bourgeois republican politicians became clear with the publication of *Inteligencia Republicana* in March 1930.

This political and statist document had been signed by Joan Peiró and other well-known confederal leaders such as Marti Barrera, Pere Foix, José Viadiu, etc. It gave the seal of approval to the social democratic thesis that parliamentary democracy permitted the labor movement to achieve worthwhile social and political benefits within capitalism. [1]

As José Peirats noted, drily:

"Some *cenetistas* were reticent in breaking relations and persisted in an ambiguous position. This gave rise to suspicions. Their argument was one of expediency. Given the current state of moral disorder and economic disarray caused by the disintegration of the old regime they claimed it was the duty of

---

1 *El movimiento libertario*, op.cit.

all men of goodwill to join together to help restore normality and re-establish legal order under popular sovereignty:

"We state that we stand ready to put in the spade work in order to ensure a new political order which, rooted in the supreme condition of justice, may thwart subversion of authority once and for all and lead the country along the juridicial byways indispensable to the progress of nations.

"This new political order, the Federal Republic, may be broken down roughly into the following basic points:

I   —   Separation of powers.

II   —   Recognition of equal individual and social rights for all citizens.

III   —   Recognition of the full entitlement of groups federated through their express collective will to use their own language and develop their own culture.

IV   —   Freedom of thought and conscience. The separation of Church and State.

V   —   Agrarian reform and the break up of the big latifundist estates.

VI   —   Social reforms on a par with the most advanced capitalist states."[2]

As the swing toward class collaboration gathered momentum, the Peninsular Committee of the FAI warned against the "profoundly reformist deviationism of those militants who, during the dictatorship, had linked themselves, intentionally and premeditatedly, to 'political principles.' The Committee suggested that on return to full normality the union cadres should transform themselves into militant nuclei to prevent the permeation of the CNT by political and authoritarian tendencies."[3] The syndicalists seized upon this statement as a declaration of intent on the part of the FAI to transform the existing union cadres into FAI groups.

Peiró's alliance with republican and separatist politicians was not surprising. The close friendships forged between libertarians, politicians, and disaffected military elements in the joint struggle against the Dictatorship had sucked them, inexorably, into the dubious political maneuvers and secret

2   Peirats, *La CNT*, op.cit., Vol. I, pp. 24–28.
3   Ibid., Vol. I. Ch. 2.

lobbying that led up to the proclamation of the Second Republic.

As José Peirats points out:

"Confederation members and political leftists had linked arms in the common aspiration of bringing down the dictators; no matter that the aspirations of the former with regard to revolutionary aims may have been more ambitious. Jointly they participated in conspiracy and jointly they suffered the punishment of exile. And this circumstantial camaraderie of arms which, in strict doctrinal terms, should not have induced certain CNT members to commit themselves overmuch, flattered the age-old politicians' illusions about bridling the CNT, or at least seeing it become just another faction embroiled in the concerns of parliamentarianism. And, insofar as the CNT had the capacity to reveal its true strength, the deputies and ministers of the future showered their importuning and flattery upon the visible heads of the confederal organization."[4]

Such public support from the confederal leadership for political collaboration with bourgeois politicians threatened to provoke an open split in the union. In the face of massive pressure from union members, Viadiu and Pere Foix recanted and withdrew their signatures, but Peiró insisted on standing by his support for the republican document. He had become enmeshed in the all too human predicament he had created for himself by separating his principles and practice. He now found himself obliged to act against the dictates of his conscience: as an anarchist, in theory at least, he was compelled to believe in certain principles, as a union leader he was obliged to act as though he did not.

Unwilling to weaken or compromise the CNT in any way, Peiró announced his resignation from all positions of responsibility within the organization:

"It is evident that, in signing the manifesto at odds with my beliefs and I accept that my action, mistaken or not, was perpetrated in full awareness of the fact that I was striking a contradictory stance. Let me state formally that it was then and

---

is now a purely personal act of my own. No one can claim that I have tried to influence anyone into following my example…

"Given the reasons which prompted me to endorse it, I find no reason to withdraw my signature; aside from which, the act of cancelling my signature would not—if there was any obscenity in what I did—absolve me of my error. The only course left open to me is to pay the price of my error, if error it be, by prostrating myself.

"This being so, I hereby declare that, in order to avert any sort of threat to things which, for me, must remain sacred, I henceforth stand down from whatever activities I have been engaged in with the organization, in the realm of ideas and in the press and thus come to be only one among the many who follow in silence the vanguards which guide our ranks."[5]

Peiró's isolation was apparent rather than real. Although few would have admitted it publicly, his views were shared by a substantial number, if not all, of the members of the National Committee of the CNT. Since the advent of the Berenguer regime, this body had adopted an openly reformist and collaborationist position that was virtually indistinguishable from *Inteligencia Republicana*. The month after the republican document had appeared, the National Committee, following a plenum of Regionals held on 16 and 17 February 1930, issued a manifesto, approved by a number of individual regional committees, which recognized the need to convene a *Cortes* (parliament) to revise the Constitution and introduce a new legal and political structure for the country "in which we have to live." It also demanded the re-establishing of constitutional guarantees, freedom of union organization, an eight-hour day, and an amnesty for all political prisoners. Ignoring the rhetoric, it was a declaration of intent to collaborate with the political parties in the reconstruction of the State. The National Committee, conscious of the controversial repercussions this would cause within the movement, tried to cover themselves by adding, almost as an afterthought, that the manifesto did not represent the official position of the CNT, simply that of some Regionals, and that "One should not read into this manifesto

---

5   *Un ano de conspiración (antes de la republica)*, Pau y Magrina, Barcelona, 1933, p. 28.

support for political candidates nor, even less, suggestions that
one should vote in the elections."[6]

How reformists and "gradualists" managed to establish
themselves in positions of prominence within an avowedly
revolutionary body such as the CNT is one of the central
questions with regard to the CNT—indeed in any consideration
of any mass revolutionary movement. One reason is that
the leadership of the CNT was never recruited from among
anarchist militants, who shunned all permanent positions of
responsibility within the union. They preferred, instead, to
retain their independence as rank and file activists. This meant
the higher committees were inevitably drawn from among
those who saw the CNT, first and foremost, as a politically
neutral union, not as the instrument for overturning an unjust
society and building a new one in its place. Joan Domenech,
secretary of the Catalan glass workers' union explained:

"When you joined the CNT as a worker, no one asked what
you believed or thought. A carpenter joined the woodworkers'
union, a barber the barbers' union, and that was all there was
to it."[7]

It would be presumptuous to assume CNT members of the
period were somehow more revolutionary than workers in
other unions; it would be equally presumptuous to assume that
anarcho-syndicalism, i.e. democratic revolutionary unionism,
did not satisfy the workers' needs at the time, and reflect their
awareness that they were involved in a bitter class struggle with
a ruthless ruling class. Undoubtedly, the majority of workers
were attracted to the CNT, not just because of its democratic
and revolutionary content, but also because it was the only
union willing to challenge both the State and employers. It was
also a leadership that, because of its anti-political constitution,
was less likely to sell them down the river in negotiations with
employers and deals with political parties maneuvering for
power. In spite of its reformist dynamic, the CNT leadership was,
they undoubtedly felt, sufficiently controlled by an aggressive
and non-deferential "conscious minority," through a directly
democratic structure, who wanted to ensure their interests as

6   *Acción Social Obrera,*. 16.5.1930.
7   Fraser, op.cit., p. 187.

workers (in the semi-feudal and early capitalist society that was Spain in the 1920s and 1930s) would be safeguarded and advanced.

For the leadership, the revolutionary rhetoric, objectives, and zeal of the "conscious militants" were powerful bargaining weapons in negotiations with a violent, reactionary, and totally unbending ruling class. But, at the end of the day, the leadership of the CNT saw their sole function as securing immediate economic gains. This was reformist, not revolutionary, activity. So far as the mass of the members were concerned, as long as no problems occurred and the "influential militants" continued to fulfil their leadership role with relative effectiveness, they were happy to defer to them. Unfortunately, they did so with a trusting pride that wholly undermined traditional anarchist opposition to the leadership principle.

The "conscious minority" of anarchist workers were aware of the anti-democratic and anti-revolutionary degeneration inherent in unionism, but they appear to have believed it was a process that could be controlled (or at least kept in check) through the democratic apparatus of the union and their revolutionary example at rank and file level. They seriously underestimated the tendency of power, even in avowedly anti-authoritarian and democratic organizations, to become concentrated in the higher committees, a tendency that was accelerated by the long periods of enforced clandestinity in which the base of the CNT had little contact with or control over the leadership.

It should also be pointed out that in spite of its revolutionary objectives, the practice of the CNT proved not to be directly democratic. Surprisingly, CNT delegates were non-revocable. If a delegate failed to act on the instructions of his or her branch there was no procedure for recalling them. A further flaw was that the locus of decision-making had gradually shifted from the general assemblies at workplace and local federation level to the five-yearly national congresses.

Effectively, there was no provision for an independently appointed body that could monitor and re-assess CNT policies regularly and frequently, and provide an independent system of checks and balances by which the national and regional committees could be controlled.

With the statutes of the CNT approved by the Civil Governor of Barcelona on 30 April 1930, the CNT finally emerged from clandestinity. This had been the result of much backstage negotiations with the authorities, including a meeting on 4 April between the Director General of Security, General Mola, and Ángel Pestaña. The union leader stressed to Mola that the CNT did not constitute a revolutionary threat and, although unable to co-operate overtly with the State, it would maintain an attitude of benevolent neutrality.

The legally constituted Confederation returned to center stage as the predominant union organization in Spain. In the early months of the Republic, its growth was spectacular, quickly reaching a membership of 500,000. It retained its traditional ascendancy in Catalonia, the Levante, Eastern Andalucia, and Aragón. However, in Seville, an earlier CNT stronghold, the Communists had managed to seize control of most of the unions.

Joan Peiró had been publicly rehabilitated, in the spring of 1930, by the CNT leadership at a public meeting called to explain the National Committee's attitude to the Berenguer government, which had been taken on after the departure of Primo de Rivera. Speaking on the same platform as Pestaña, Peiró received an enthusiastic welcome from a mass audience that spilled out from the Teatro Nuevo into the adjacent Parquelo. Given up for dead by reactionaries such as Martinez Anido and even, as we have seen, some of the union's own leaders, the CNT had sprung fully armed upon an unsuspecting bourgeois society. As if to underline his restoration to grace—if he had ever fallen in the first place—Joan Peiró was appointed the first editor of the newly revived *Solidaridad Obrera.*

In August 1930, representatives of the Socialist, Nationalist, and Republican parties—the parties of the capitalist and professional classes—met in secret in San Sebastian to form a Revolutionary Committee and to plan the strategy for toppling the old regime and seizing political power for themselves. The CNT, as a revolutionary working class body, was not officially invited to these meetings, but "unofficial" representatives were requested to attend as "informal observers." The representatives who attended were Progreso Alfarache, a member of the National Committee of the CNT and a member of the

Peninsular Committee of the FAI, and Rafael Vidiella.[8] As José Peirats points out, "It was an intrigue by which the politicians were trying to embroil the Confederation in a revolutionary revolt without entering into any formal agreement with it."[9]

As the world recession hit Spain and political discontent began to bite deep, the winter of 1930–31 saw a massive wave of strikes sweep the country. For four days, from 15 to 19 November, Barcelona was paralyzed by industrial action. The CNT threw its full weight behind the Republican, Socialist, and young officers' conspiracies aimed at toppling the Berenguer regime.

The year ended with unsuccessful Republican uprisings in the Jaca and Cuatro Vientos garrisons. The refusal of the king to pardon two young officers involved in the risings and their subsequent execution exacerbated hostility towards the monarchy. By February 1931, Berrenguer had no option but to resign. A caretaker government under Admiral Juan Batista Aznar was formed and Municipal elections were announced for 12 April.

On 19 March, during the run-up to the April elections, a National Plenum of the CNT was held in Valencia. The Plenum agreed to advise members, "without political compromise," to vote, tactically, for the leftist candidates. The overwhelming Republican-Socialist victory in the elections, assisted by a "massive turn out of confederal voters at the polls," provoked the final collapse of the monarchy.[10]

---

8 Emilio Mola, op.cit., p. 572.
9 Peirats, op.cit.
10 E. Horacio Prieto, *Marxismo y socialismo libertario*, Paris, 1947, p. 109.

11

The Bourgeois Republic

The Second Spanish Republic was declared on 14 April 1931. It was met with enormous popular enthusiasm by the people of Spain who saw in it the engine of change and the promise of new beginnings. Article No. 1 of the new Constitution read:

"Spain is a democratic republic of workers of every class, organized in a regime of liberty and justice. The powers of all its organs emanate from the people. The Republic represents an integral State, compatible with the autonomy of the municipalities and regions."

The CNT leadership had contributed much to the new Republic. In a truly Pilatesque speech, Joan Peiró confirmed, with obvious satisfaction, that the CNT had acted as midwife to the Republic:

"Our subversive labor from *Solidaridad Obrera* and from the tribunes, contributed directly to the electoral triumph of 12 April 1931… We never said to the workers that they should go to the polls; but neither did we say keep away."[1]

Their enthusiasm for the Republic, however, quickly transcended the boundaries of their functions as mere spokesmen for the anarcho-syndicalist union. Having been so closely involved with other political parties in anti-dictatorship and republican plots over the years, many of the CNT leaders had come to believe in the Republic as an abstract impersonal machine, not something of human origin serving specific ruling

---

1 "El sindicalismo y el problema politico de españa," *El Combate Syndicalista*, Valencia, 6.9.1935.

class interests. Concerned now with the success of the Republic for which they had sacrificed so much and on which so many hopes were pinned, many of the CNT leaders became absorbed and sidetracked by the desire to be "practical." The Republic, they hoped, would provide a framework of stability in which the Confederation could thrive in an atmosphere of class harmony. What they overlooked was that the "success" of the Republic, i.e. the piecemeal resolution of the problems of capitalism and arbitrary authority by compromise, chicanery, dissimulation and self-deception, was the concern of republicans, authoritarian socialists, and enlightened conservatives—but not anarchists! The task of anarchists was to constantly challenge established authority—to a greater or lesser degree according to the nature of the government in power. Anarchists moved as free and independent agents, outside the authority system, sharing the sacrifices and revolts of the people, not their weaknesses, compromises, and surrenders.

For some time, bourgeois politicians, particularly in Catalonia, had been cultivating union leaders such as Pestaña. Their objective was to ensure a healthy and stable investment climate by winning the passive or active collaboration of a CNT that had been neutered and transplanted from its historic roots, and which it hoped to tie in to the apparatus of power. As early as 13 April, Pestaña had been offered a cabinet post in the new Catalan government by Macià, leader of the Esquerra, a Catalan petty-bourgeois nationalist party disguised as Socialists. The reformists grew more assertive by the day. On 14 May, *Solidaridad Obrera*, under Joan Peiró's editorship, announced:

"We have stated that the CNT is not against the Republic. Furthermore, conscious of that which it represents in the soul of the masses, the CNT has agreed to oppose, by all means available to it, any rising which the reaction might attempt. Whether we want to or not, the consequence of the CNT's policy obliges us to defend the Republic."[2]

April 1931 constituted a political revolution for which the old order had been totally unprepared. It had been anesthetized

2 "La CNT ante el momento actual," *Solidaridad Obrera*, Barcelona, 14.5.1931.

and disoriented by the rapidity with which events had developed, but its economic and social power bases remained unchallenged. For the Republicans and authoritarian socialists, their ultimate goal of a liberal democratic Republic had been achieved, they had reached the end of the line. Their revolution was over. For the anarchists, whose goal was a classless society in which the exploitation and oppression of man by man had been eliminated, it was only the first way-station on the road to Libertarian Communism. As far as they were concerned, the only thing the CNT should defend was the working class. If this meant supporting the Republic so be it.

One of the charges levelled against the anarchists by Liberal and Marxist historians is that anarchist intransigence was one of the contributory factors that undermined the Republic and led to economic, social, and political overload on the system. The people were making demands that neither the new born state nor capitalism could hope to meet. The credibility and future prospects for the stability of liberal democracy in Spain were steadily eroded to the point of complete collapse.

How well does this charge stand up to analysis? The widespread discontent with the policies of the Second Republic was not a problem unique to Spain in the 1930s, nor was it attributable to anarchist intransigence. The problems of the Spanish Republic were ones of political alienation, which arose (and have subsequently grown increasingly acute in the Western democracies) from the contradictions and tensions inherent in the unholy alliance between the bourgeois liberal concept of the State, as a mechanism for facilitating control over the system in the interests of the capitalist class, and the working class ideal of democracy as essentially egalitarian and participatory. Popular disenchantment and frustration with the political process was inevitable and had nothing to do with anarchist intransigence. The anarchists were simply the only ones willing to publicize these contradictions. They were not prepared to pander to the illusion that democracy and capitalism were compatible.

With the democratic surge of April 1931, the people's long-standing expectations of social change became a direct challenge to the complex power structure. Agrarian reform and the break up of the large estates, the fundamental problem of the Republic, which cried out for a solution, was one that could never be tackled within the framework of the parliamentary system. Neither did the political parties of the Republic have the capacity, or will even, to attempt to resolve it. The weak and vacillating bourgeois politicians understood only too well that to do so would bring them into direct conflict with the enormously powerful landed interest, which had the ideological support of the Church and the military support of the army. The whole structure would collapse in an orgy of violence.

12

The "Storm Petrels" Return

The declaration of the Republic permitted the return from exile and the regrouping of the dispersed younger anarchist activists who were to challenge the campaign, engineered by Pestaña's Solidaridad group, aimed at weaning the CNT away from its anti-statist and anti-political statutes. As well as confronting what they saw as the institutionalized leadership of the older generation, these young men were to infuse the Spanish anarchist movement with a fresh revolutionary ardor which was to enable it to resist, successfully, a military uprising and lay the foundations of the most profound social revolutions in history. Prominent among these were the members of the old Los Solidarios and Los Treinta group.[1]

A few days after his return from exile, textile worker Buenaventura Durruti, one of the better known members of the old Los Solidarios, clarified the anarchist position toward

---

1 The activists of the Los Solidarios group had been dispersed throughout the dictatorship. Durruti, Ascaso, Vivancos, and Jover formed the Los Treinta group (not to be confused with Pestaña's *treintistas*), which had been active in Europe and Latin America while García Oliver and others had been in prison. There had also been disagreements between Durruti and Oliver that were finally patched up, if not resolved, in the summer of 1931, when all the comrades were reunited. According to Marcos Alcón, when the Republic was proclaimed, Aurelio Fernández returned to Oviedo and had no contact with the others. Sanz, Jover and Vivancos confined their activities to work within their respective CNT unions: "They never attended FAI meetings except on a limited number of occasions. Their meetings were with one another since they all worked in the textile industry." Letter to Juan Gómez Casas, *Historia de la FAI*, op.cit., pp. 141–142. When the group met again at the first meeting of the Anarchist Groups of Catalonia in 1931, they discovered another group had adopted the name during the period of the Dictatorship. To avoid confusion, the comrades decided to change the name to the Nosotros group.

the new bourgeois Republic in a speech in Barcelona on 18 April. They understood only too well that the Republic could not provide a satisfactory solution to the workers' problems; but it had to discredit itself in the eyes of those who hoped for so much from it. The revolutionary anarchists, like every other section of the anarchist movement, including the Urales family, were at least prepared to give the Republic the benefit of the doubt, believing they could steer the institutions of the bourgeois democratic regime into "constructive" work.

Durruti gently reminded those comrades who held out great hopes for the Republic that the traditional role of anarchists in relation to governments, revolutionary or otherwise, was in opposition. He emphasized that the degree of anarchist opposition would be geared to the willingness of the Republic to confront the major problems facing the Spanish workers. In everything constructive it did, the Republic could rely on the enthusiastic support of all honest revolutionaries. But he also warned the bourgeoisie and the reformist unionists that they would not default on their revolutionary commitments as anarchists or act contrary to their anti-statist and anti-capitalist principles:

"If we were Republicans, we would maintain that the provisional government is incapable of making a success of the victory given to it by the people. But we are authentic workers and in their name we say that, following this path, we will not be surprised if the country finds itself on the edge of a civil war tomorrow. The Republic does not interest us, but we accept it as the springboard of a process of social democratization. But only provided, of course, that this Republic goes guarantor for the principles according to which freedom and social justice are not merely empty words. Should the Republic scorn to take into consideration the aspirations of the working class, then the slight interest it has aroused in the workers will be whittled away to nothing because that institution will cease to correspond to the hopes which our class placed in it on 14 April."[2]

---

2   *Solidaridad Obrera*, 21.5.1931.

Later, Durruti added: "As anarchists we declare that our
activities never have been and never will be at the service of any
political party or any state. The anarchists and the syndicalists
of the CNT, united with all the revolutionaries and backed
by pressure from the street, have as their goal to compel the
people in government to carry out their mandate."[3]

Despite its optimistic commitment to social reform the
Republic was incapable of acting as guarantor of either
freedom or social justice. Neither was it possible for the CNT
to expect anything from a government that contained Largo
Caballero, Indalecio Prieto, and Fernando de los Rios—the
three Socialist leaders whose careers had been predicated on
establishing and consolidating the bourgeois Republic and
strengthening the UGT, at the expense of its only rival for
the hearts and minds of the Spanish working class: the CNT.
Bookchin quotes an unnamed socialist leader in 1932, which
shows clearly the distance and antipathy between the two
contending ideologies:

"There is a good deal of confusion in the minds of many
comrades. They consider Anarchist Syndicalism as an ideal
which runs parallel with our own, when it is its absolute
antithesis, and that the Anarchists and Syndicalists are comrades
when they are our greatest enemies."[4]

The bourgeois Republican and Socialist politicians, anxious
to appease the powerful landed interest and their rightist
supporters in the army and church, sought to reassure these
reactionary forces that the new regime did not intend to
upset the delicate balance of social forces in the nation. As if
to underline this, a series of labor and public order laws were
introduced, which clearly targeted the revolutionary threat—
the CNT. The compulsory arbitration of Caballero's agrarian
"mixed juries" (*jurados mixtos*), although intended to relieve
the misery of the Andalucian peasants, effectively banned the
right to strike and undermined the CNT's principles of direct
action and opposition to political collaboration.

Laws that assert the rights of labor can also affirm the rights
of capital and the legitimacy of state power. "Apart from the fact

3   Abel Paz, *Durruti: The People Armed*, Montreal, 1976. p. 104.
4   Murray Bookchin, *The Spanish Anarchists*, New York, 1977, p. 236.

that these laws ran contrary to the Anarcho-syndicalist principles
of negotiating directly with employers and interfered with the
practice of lightning strikes," observed Gerald Brenan:

"It was clear that they represented an immense increase in
the power of the State in industrial matters. A whole army of
Government officials, mostly Socialists, made their appearance
to enforce new laws and saw to it that, whenever possible, they
should be used to extend the influence of the UGT at the
expense of the CNT. This had of course been the intention of
those who drew them up. In fact the UGT was rapidly becoming
an organ of the State itself and was using its new powers to reduce
its rival. The Anarcho-Syndicalists could have no illusions as to
what would happen to them if a purely Socialist Government
should come to power. To that they almost preferred a military
dictatorship, which would force their organization to disband,
but could not destroy them."[5]

To remind the new Provisional Government, with its
hotchpotch of disparate groups, parties, and interests all
contending for power, what the working class expected of
it, the CNT and FAI organized a joint meeting on 1 May in
Barcelona's Palace of Fine Arts. The anarchists' demands
were a direct challenge to the bourgeois Liberal and Socialist
politicians and the old semi-feudal order alike: the dissolution
of the hated Civil Guard, the expropriation of the investments
of the religious orders to fund public works, land to the
peasants, and the factories to the workers.

The meeting ended with a peaceful march through
Barcelona to the Generalitat Palace. Francisco Ascaso disarmed
a Civil Guard officer who refused to let the marchers through
to deliver a petition and who ordered them to disperse at pistol
point. At this crucial moment, Durruti emerged from the crowd
brandishing the red and black anarcho-syndicalist flag shouting
"Make way for the FAI!" The marchers followed. Within
moments they had filled the Plaza de la Constitucion. When the
workers' commission leading the demonstration attempted to
hand in their resolutions, Civil Guard and Carabineros opened
fire on the crowd. Armed workers, supported by a company
of infantry troops stationed nearby, returned fire, forcing

5   Brenan, op.cit., pp.258–259.

the Civil Guard and Carabineers to retreat. The tally was one demonstrator dead and fifteen wounded. Two Civil Guards were killed and an unknown number wounded.[6]

The confrontation between the workers and the forces of order of the new Republic, on 1 May 1931, marked the beginning of the end of the period of grace that the working class anarchist revolutionaries had been prepared to grant the bourgeois-socialist coalition government. The blood spilled in Barcelona's Plaza de la Constitucion gave substance to the anarchists' denunciation of the reactionary nature of the Republic and its incompatibility with revolutionary working class objectives. Tension between the collaborationist leadership and revolutionary base of the CNT had reached breaking point. The FAI, still numerically and organizationally weak, now began to emerge as the instrument through which the anarchists, anarcho-syndicalists, and working class militants— the vast majority of whom were not affiliated to a FAI group— could focus their opposition to the class collaborationist stance adopted by the leadership and reaffirm the anarchist content of the CNT.

The reformist challenge from such an influential sector of the CNT leadership, goaded by the cajolery of Republican politicians seeking a neutered and malleable union movement, left the revolutionary anarchists with no alternative but to respond to the sustained attacks on the anarchist spirit of the union. From a fairly low key and not particularly efficient propagandist and educational body under the dictatorship, the FAI became the voice of the revolutionary cutting edge of the CNT.

The unionists upheld the virtues of moderation and compromise. They believed that the liberties and reforms which the Republic could offer, albeit gradual and piecemeal, would constitute a beneficial opportunity for the unions to fulfil their economic and welfare functions. Mass consciousness would be raised, values would change, human freedom would advance, and the foundations for long-term revolutionary objectives would be laid.

For the anarchists, this argument served only to legitimize the interminable exploitation and injustice of existing

---

6   Paz, op.cit., p. 107.

society. As long as revolutionaries were prepared to make accommodations with capitalism and accept the sovereignty of the State, both these institutions would thrive at the expense of the oppressed. Comfortable in their relationships with the bourgeois politicians, and lacking confidence in the workers' ability to overcome capitalism and build a free society, the union leaders had, by opposing the revolutionary violence of the oppressed, opted for what they presumed to be the "lesser" evil. In so doing, they helped perpetuate the already drawn out misery, oppression, and violence that the workers faced in their everyday lives, and dashed all prospects for qualitative change. As long as capitalism and the State remained, there would continue to exist powerful vested interests who would oppose and resist the working class drive to a less repressive, more just, and freer society.

The break with repressive capitalism and the State had to be complete and, if necessary, violent, if only, as Barrington Moore points out, to ensure subsequent peaceful change and avoid the even more horrendous costs of going without a revolution:

"These are the tragedies of the victims of fascism and its wars of aggression, the consequences of modernization without a real revolution. In the backward countries today, there continues the suffering of those who have not revolted."[7]

The "mass consciousness" and "change in human values" talked about by social democrats and Marxists as a prerequisite for revolutionary change were abstract and theoretical ploys in the arsenal of liberal democracy and authoritarian socialism. The anarchists argued that the "level of mass consciousness" required to change human values and the fundamental nature of capitalist and statist society was a illusory ideal that could never be achieved within a class divided society. Changes in attitude may well be gradual and ongoing, but if there was ever to be a quantitative shift in human values it would only come as a consequence of the revolutionary process.

Around this time the revolutionary anarchists developed the concept of the "revolutionary gymnasium." The idea came

---

7 Barrington Moore Jr., *Social Origins of Dictatorship and Democracy*, London, 1981, p. 506.

from the activists of the CNT Defense Committee, not the FAI (although it came to be associated with that organization simply because the CNT militants, many of whom did not belong to FAI-affiliated groups, spoke in its name in matters of ideas). It postulated that the only viable revolutionary option open to them under the prevailing conditions in Spain was to embark on a succession of direct insurrectionary attacks against the State whenever the time and the opportunity presented itself.

The two irreconcilable tendencies within the CNT prepared for a major confrontation at the forthcoming Extraordinary National Congress of the CNT, set for 1 June at the Conservatorio theater in Madrid. Companys and Macià's Esquerra party, a petty bourgeois Catalan party that tried to pass itself off as Socialist, also supported the Pestañista faction, which they knew would adapt itself to Republican and Catalan legality. The Pestañistas also received the support of the national bourgeois press. On the eve of the National Congress, *El Sol*, the Madrid daily, published a major feature article promoting Ángel Pestaña as a responsible, strong, and masterful leader of a labor union that was attracting Republicans and Socialist alike. In the interview, Pestaña outlined the state of the CNT and described what he saw as its immediate objectives. Asked if he believed in revolution, the syndicalist leader replied: "I believe firmly that a revolution is inevitable, but not as soon as some people believe."[8]

By the time the Third (Conservatorio) Congress of the CNT began in Madrid on 11 June 1931, the battle lines were drawn. Although numerically weak, the position argued by those CNT militants who belonged to the FAI reflected the mood of the 400 or so delegates who represented over half a million workers. The rise to prominence of these militants was not the result of infiltrating committees, a tactic which they left to reformists, or from any numerical predominance or gerrymandering by anarchists, but because the FAI was the only organ that voiced the collective dissatisfaction of the rank and file with the policies of the leadership. In the atmosphere of social conflict that hung over Spain in the summer of 1931—strikes in Andalucia, Asturias, Catalonia, and Aragón—the anarchist position expressed by the FAI reflected

---

8 *El Sol*, 31.5.1931.

the hostility of the base of the CNT to the now embarrassingly conciliatory, deferential, and compromising attitudes of the union leadership to the reactionary and anti-anarchist policies of the new government.

13
1931—
The Conservatorio Congress

The 1931 CNT Congress was opened by Ángel Pestaña on behalf of the solidly Catalan fourteen-man National Committee. These men represented a generation of leaders who had been compromised through their relationship with Catalan politicians and who had opted for pragmatic social reform. Their main criterion was that the Republic had to be supported until the organization could be consolidated and all threats of a rightist military coup overcome. They wished to transform a union committed to revolutionary change into the defender of the status quo.

The hostile undercurrents boiled to the surface early on in proceedings. Congress quickly became a battlefield in the struggle between the two tendencies. Francesc Arín and Joan Peiró spoke on behalf of the National Committee, reviewing the recent activities of the organization and outlining CNT collaboration since 1923, with the political and military groups in the plots against the dictatorship. This admission appeared to come as a revelation to most delegates and sparked heated and angry discussions. Francisco Arín accused the FAI, the focus for the hostility of the National Committee, of hypocrisy. According to Arín it had been the FAI-dominated Catalan Regional Committee and the FAI Peninsular Committee, bodies with overlapping membership, that had originated and sustained the contacts with political and military elements, without consulting the National Committee.

Collaboration with the new Constituent Cortes was another theme that raised fundamental issues at this Extraordinary Congress. Item eight on the Agenda read:

"The position of the CNT with regard to the convening of the Constituent Cortes and the political, legal, and economic resolutions to be presented to it." The inclusion of this provocative political proposition on the Agenda of an anti-political body was justified by the National Committee on the grounds that the Cortes was the "outcome of a revolutionary act in which, directly or indirectly, we had been involved."[1]

For the anarchists, the formulation of a petition for presentation to the Cortes—whether to do with unemployment, schools, teachers, individual rights, freedom of the press, speech, or association—implied recognition of the legitimacy of governmental institutions. This was quite incompatible with the principles of the La Comedia Congress of 1919. The thrust of the collaborationist argument was that although the Republic might conflict with the revolutionary principles and objectives of the CNT, it was an improvement on the dictatorship. Consequently, they argued, a certain measure of trust should be placed in it. As Murray Bookchin notes:

"Apparently, many delegates to the congress saw no contradiction between preparing for a revolution and voting for a minimum program that proclaimed the need for democratic rights, secular schools, and the right to strike."[2]

For union leaders like Joan Peiró, a gradualist who believed in a war of attrition, or standoffs rather than spontaneous and full frontal assaults on the system, the problem was simply that the CNT was unprepared for revolution. It required time to consolidate and build up its base. The Confederation should, conceivably, he felt, overthrow the capitalist State, but it was in no position to reconstruct the free society subsequently.[3]

Congress finally approved the following ambiguous amendment to the motion:

1   Peirats, op.cit., Vol. I, Ch. 2.
2   Bookchin, op.cit., p. 237.
3   Confederación Nacional del Trabajo, *Memoria del Congreso Extraordinario celebrado en Madrid los días 11 al 16 de Junio de 1931*, Barcelona, 1931, p. 208.

"We are opposed to the Constituent Cortes just as we are opposed to any authority which oppresses. We are still at daggers drawn with the State. Our sacred, noble mission is to educate the people to an appreciation of the need to join us in full awareness and to secure their and our total emancipation through social revolution. Aside from this principle, which is an integral part of our very being, we have no hesitation in conceding that it is our ineluctable duty to place before the people a scheme of minimum demands that it must pursue by creating a revolutionary force of its own."[4]

Another hotly debated issue was the proposed adoption of new National Industrial Federations to operate alongside and complement the work of the sovereign geographic federations of the CNT Sindicato Único. The supporters of the resolution envisaged the Federations fulfilling two functions, one permitting the organization to cope more efficiently within the prevailing capitalist economy and the other in the building of the free society to come.

Proposed by Joan Peiró, the motion read:

"The object of the national industrial federations is to bring together all the unions in the industry which it represents and coordinate its industrial action on the technical, economic, and professional level."

These new organisms, it was argued, would function in parallel with the local, district, regional, and national federations of single unions. The working class had to adapt its methods of struggle to the increasingly sophisticated structure of modern monopoly capitalism. Peiró continued:

"The national industrial federations serve to focus the initiative and activities of the proletariat, divided by industry on a nationwide scale, in opposition to capitalism. They also serve to lay the practical foundations for the structuring of the economic apparatus of tomorrow."[5]

The anarchists, defending the autonomy of the basic unit of the CNT, the Sindicato Único, pointed out the centralizing, reformist, and bureaucratic dangers that would result from

---

4   Ibid.
5   Ibid., p. 123.

the adoption of such a structure. Julio Roig, a delegate from the Santander Construction Union, challenged the supposed inevitability of the laws of the capitalist economy on which the resolution was based. He argued that, if accepted, the proposal would lead inevitably to all the industries being represented in one national center, which would be the equivalent of nationalization:

"That would mean a bureaucracy worming its way into our organization... The Confederation would give birth to a bureaucracy such as exists inside the UGT, or is to be found inside the German organizations and in England. Solidarity cannot be contrived. There is something more than professional and trade improvements; something represented in the doctrine that drives this organization of ours, and we have to be consistent and, if we truly identify with our principles, we must stand by them. In return for improvements, we must defend the cause, which is worth more."[6]

José Alberola, a CNT delegate and FAI member, also repudiated the motion:

"There are two very clear-cut schools of thought; one that places the stress on methodology, and the other that places it on the individual. Those who advocate industrial federations do so because they have lost faith in the element of purpose, and trust only in the ticking over of the machinery. And I hold that the machine does not create strength but, rather, consumes it; this being so, let us conjure into existence a mentality hostile to anything which implies the mechanization of the individual. Capitalist society is run through monopolies and huge corporations because it dances to a hierarchical tune—let us create a mentality inimical to that trend."[7]

García Oliver was another CNT delegate who spoke against the motion. He also expressed clear hostility to what he saw as the negative influence of the theories imported from the German-dominated International Workingmen's Association, the AIT:

---

6 Peirats, op.cit., Vol. I, Ch. 3.
7 Ibid.

"The Industrial Federations come from Germany and appear to have come out of a barrel of beer. The AIT are completely ignorant of Spain and know as much about it as do [Spanish intellectuals] Azorin, Unamuno, and Ganiver—nothing."

In spite of the powerful arguments of the anarchists, Peiró's National Industrial Federations offered the majority of delegates a convincing counter and practical alternative to contemporary Spanish capitalism. The motion was adopted by Congress by 302,343 to 90,671 against, with 10,957 abstentions. Had the FAI controlled or dominated the CNT, as alleged, such an overwhelming defeat would not have been possible. It should be added, however, that the plans for the National Industrial Federations were never implemented and were not even mentioned at the Zaragoza Congress of 1936.[8]

In the meantime the FAI, anxious to counter the influence of the collaborationists whom they felt would lead the CNT into an inevitable integration of revolutionary syndicalism into the State structure, had held its own National Congress immediately prior to that of the CNT. Those militants who belonged to the CNT and were delegates had discussed the motions and tactics they intended to pursue at the union congress. This practice of parallel congresses and conferences was to continue until late in the Civil War. The reason was explained by Juan M. Molina:

"The delegates were all union members and, on this occasion, they brought union resolutions... As secretary of the Peninsular Committee, I attended the Conservatorio congress. Although I took no part in it, I was, in that capacity, flanked by other delegates such as José Alberola, Progreso Fernández, and García Oliver, all of whom argued the FAI case—which was shared by the vast majority of the delegations."[9]

At the FAI congress, the outgoing Peninsular Committee was strongly censured for collaborating with politicians and army officers both during the period of the dictatorship and in the run up to the Republic. Three of its members, Elizalde,

---

8 Ibid.
9 Ibid., Vol. I, Ch. 2. Molina did, in fact, attempt to address the Congress as the official FAI representative, but the syndicalist-controlled National Committee refused to let him speak because he was a spokesman for "an external organization."

Sirvent, and Alfarache were expelled for activities incompatible with the aims of the organizations.[10]

The Conservatorio Congress failed to clear the air between the two main factions within the CNT. The atmosphere remained bitter and acrimonious with the National Committee denouncing the *trabazón* as "dictatorial." Ángel María de Lera, Pestaña's biographer, recorded that during the Congress he and some friends came outside for a breath of fresh air to find Pestaña sitting on the pavement, weeping. "I am in despair," he told them, "I have dedicated all my life to the workers' struggle—all my life—and now when I hoped to harvest the fruits you see what has happened. This is not unionism—he pointed to the theater—this is chaos. This way we can go nowhere. These men are either mad or malicious."[11] De Lera believes that although he continued to describe himself as an anarchist, this was the crucial moment when Pestaña turned his back on anarcho-syndicalism and began thinking seriously about an alternative—the Syndicalist Party (Partido Sindicalista).

The radical mood of the Spanish workers, reflected by the growing influence of the uncompromisingly anarchist or insurrectionist tendency, caused considerable worry to the bourgeois politicians. The FAI, the "NCOs," as it were, of the CNT, had not only captured the attention of the media and the imagination of the most radical section of the Spanish anarchist movement, they were more importantly ensuring the struggle was being steered along clear class lines.

The complexities of divisions within the CNT are disguised by the terms *treintista* and *faista* and it would be a misleading oversimplification to reduce them to such. In spite of appearances, the FAI was never a cohesive body competing with the reformist unionists along clearly definable ideological lines. The FAI, or at least what the FAI represented to many anarchists, was simply an ad hoc association encompassing a broad spectrum of anarchist opinion within the CNT, one which was divided geographically, generationally, and ideologically.

Two main tendencies existed within the FAI in the period 1930–1931: anarcho-syndicalist and revolutionary. A third—

10 "Conferencia de la FAI celebrada en Madrid durante los dias 8 y 9 de Junio," *El Luchador*, 19 June, 1931.
11 Ángel María de Lera, op.cit., p. 279.

intellectual—tendency was also emerging at this time, but the full consequences of this were not to become apparent until much later. The first drew its strength mainly from the older generation of anarchist activists and those based in the socialist UGT strongholds of Madrid and Asturias. Although close to Pestaña and friends, they opposed the class collaborationist line. Many of these, like Joan Peiró, who was a member of a group affiliated to the FAI, did not believe the situation was propitious for revolutionary activism. They emphasized the educative role of the union and the need to preserve and protect the organic fabric of the CNT and build up a strong organizational base before embarking in revolutionary confrontations with the State.

Strong regionalist influences and hostilities were at work as well. Referring to the Solidarios/Nosotros group, Miguel Gonzales Inestal, a Madrid-based CNT and FAI member, complained that these activists were Catalan-based and their group had been "formed in the shadow of certain groups which wanted to control the CNT—although this was not part of the FAI's founding principles—and succeeded to a large extent in its aim in Barcelona… Many times one could say it was the Barcelona tendency against the rest of Spain. Madrid remained solidly in the first tendency, although when the split occurred, it opposed the *treintista* movement as reformist."[12]

The Asturian FAI adopted a position close to that of the Madrid groups over the interpretation and implementation of the social struggle. Ramón Alvárez, secretary of the Asturian Regional Committee of the CNT from 1933 until the defeat of the 1934 October insurrection, a FAI affiliate, and a member of Pestaña's Solidaridad group, explained his members' views to a National Plenum of the CNT in Madrid:

"Revolution isn't the same as a general strike that can be called for a certain day of the month. Revolution is a social phenomenon, which ripens in its own time, which man's conscious influences, accelerates, retards, but which does not happen simply because one sets a date… In Asturias, we thought that those who believed Spain was ready for revolution were victims of their own enthusiasm—an enthusiasm we

---

12 Fraser, op.cit., p. 549.

shared up to a point—instead of making a calm, lucid analysis of the situation."[13]

Perhaps the key identifying feature of the "conscious minority" within the CNT was their unshakable faith in the creative capacity of the working class to fulfil their own destiny—without the advice of ideological theorists or political leaders. This caused friction between the third sub-tendency, led by freelance intellectuals such as Diego Abad de Santillán (whose position had shifted from the abstract revolutionism of the early 1920s to an obsession with economic planning, a hallmark of corporate thinking in the 1930s), and the working class revolutionaries whose ideas were rooted in experience and practice. Francisco Ascaso of the Nosotros group described the views of the latter in an article entitled "Nuestro Anarquismo":

"Our movement is often criticized for its lack of ideological content and this objection is perhaps not without foundation. Nevertheless, we are victims of a lack of understanding and misinterpretation.

"If we compare our movement with those in other countries, I sincerely believe that its 'theories' are not brilliant. But if the Spanish proletariat isn't educated at the European level, it has, to even things out, a richness of perception and a far superior social intuition. I have never supposed or accepted that the problem of intellectual improvement can be solved by mentally accumulating a large number of theoretical formulas or philosophical concepts which will never be carried to a practical plane. The most beautiful theories only have value if they are rooted in practical life experiences and if they influence these experiences in an innovative way. This is how we operate, and it is this that allows us to expect a lot from our movement.

"I don't pretend, far from it, that intellectual mediocrity is an advantage. On the contrary, I would like every proletarian, every comrade, to exhaust every source of learning. Since this isn't the case, we must then act, taking into account the real possibilities of each person.

---

13 Ibid.

"Anarchism has gone through various phases during its history. In its embryonic period it was the ideal of an elite, accessible only to a few cultivated souls who used it as a sharp criticism of the regime under which they lived. Our predecessors didn't do so badly since it is because of them that we are today where we are. But comrades, the time for criticism is past. We are in the process of building, and to build, muscular energy is also needed, perhaps more so than the mental agility required for exercising judgement. I agree that one cannot build without knowing ahead of time what one wants to do. But I think that the Spanish proletariat has learned more through the practical experiences that the anarchists have caused them to live through, than through the publications published by the latter, which the former have not read.

"One must try to increase, as much as possible, the theoretical content of all our activities, but without the 'dry and shrivelled doctrinalism' which could destroy, in part, the great constructive action that our comrades are carrying forward in the relentless fight between the haves and the have-nots. Our people stand for action on the march. It is while going forward that they overtake. Don't hold them back, even to teach them 'the most beautiful theories.'"[14]

It is important here to understand the sequence of events of the first eighteen months of the Republic. By comparing it with the various accounts offered by Liberal historians of this crucial period we can understand better how their political prejudices have come to color subsequent generations' attitudes towards the viability of anarchism, by turning the history of the unionist-anarchist dispute within the CNT on its head. Those who opposed the attempts to overturn the anarchist constitution of the CNT are presented as outsiders—FAI members, not CNT militants—and are invariably presented as "bully-boys" and "extremists" who drove the "moderates" out of the union.[15]

These accounts are distorted by their insistence on judging the CNT against their own authoritarian model of the ideal union, one firmly controlled by an elite "moderate" centralized leadership, contending for a bigger slice of the profits. The CNT was, in fact, a federal organization, founded on the libertarian

14 Francisco Ascaso, Peninsular Committee of the FAI, 1937.
15 Raymond Carr, *The Spanish Tragedy*, op.cit., p. 41.

principles of participation and direct action, and committed to overthrowing capitalism and coercive, centralized power. Leadership did not come from the higher committees down, but from the membership and the autonomous industrial unions.

Raymond Carr suggests that the FAI militants, whose "task as a semi-secret pressure group was to permeate the CNT with revolutionary activists," had, by 1932, not merely discredited the Republic; they had brought the CNT itself to a serious crisis. Relying on the autonomy of the individual unions, FAI activists could propose revolutionary strikes against the will of the CNT leadership. When the leaders refused to sanction such activity, they were denounced as traitors. "By these tactics the FAI gained control of the core of Catalan anarchism and its paper *Solidaridad Obrera*; in protest the moderates signed the declaration of the Thirty which denounced the FAI infiltration and its disastrous effects. Expelled from the CNT, they sought to build up their strength by organizing *sindicatos de oposición*. Frank speaking and resistance to mindless revolutionism had cost Pestaña and his friends the leadership of the movement and divided it against itself."[16]

George Woodcock, another Liberal writer, views the FAI in much the same conspiratorial and elitist light. He compounds his ignorance of the anarchist organization with a disregard for the chronology of events: "Partly because of the unity of purpose of the FAI and the almost religious dedication of its members, and partly because of the romantic appeal of the more flamboyant insurrectionary leaders like Durruti and García Oliver, the extremists were able to retain control of the CNT, to such an extent that they ousted the veteran secretary of the organization, Ángel Pestaña, and Joan Peiró, the editor of the Confederation's paper, *Solidaridad Obrera*. Pestaña, Peiró, and a number of other leaders who distrusted the rule of the FAI in union affairs issued a public protest; since it bore thirty signatures, those who supported it became known as the *treintistas*. With an almost totalitarian intolerance, their opponents engineered the expulsion of these dissidents from the CNT; but the reformists were not entirely without support, and a number of local unions in Valencia and the smaller

---

16 Raymond Carr, *Spain 1808–1975*, Oxford, 1982, p. 625.

Catalan towns followed them into minority movement known as the *sindicatos de oposición*.[17]

For Gerald Brenan, the years of repression led to "the triumph of the more violent party" within the CNT. "But the disapproval of the 'tyrannical' leadership of the FAI persisted."[18] Broué and Temime have their own Trotskyist version:

"Not all Syndicalists were prepared to accept FAI domination. In 1931, many of the leaders rose up against the adventurist and 'putschist' policy that is imposed on their union. Well-known leaders such as former general secretary, Ángel Pestaña, chief editor of *Solidaridad Obrera*, Joan Peiró, and Juan López, called for a return to a more genuine Syndicalist action, involving less indifference to immediate claims and more long term prospects of action."[19]

The revived combative and revolutionary spirit of the CNT, which has been identified as the effect of the growth of influence of the FAI within the organizational apparatus of the union—not its cause—did not take long to manifest itself. Within a few weeks of the end of the Conservatorio Congress, provoked by the unmasked hostility of Largo Caballero attacking the CNT from the privileged offices of the Ministry of Labor, 3,700 CNT unionists, of the 4,000-strong Barcelona dockworkers, announced their refusal to work alongside workers who did not have a confederal union card. On 6 July, 6,200 members of the CNT telephone union (out of a total workforce of 7,000) declared a national telephone strike. Caballero immediately broke the strike by creating a new UGT-affiliated telephone union, a move that provoked considerable anger and violence among the striking CNT workers who attempted to occupy the Madrid exchange.

By the late summer of 1931, growing popular impatience with the Republic's failure to effect, or even begin to implement, genuine social and economic reform, led to a dramatic and rapid deterioration in the situation... Strikes, crop burning, land seizures by peasants, police violence, and the arbitrary arrest of militants such as Durruti (June 1931) provoked

17 Woodcock, op.cit., p. 363.
18 Brenan, op.cit., p. 255.
19 Broué and Temime, op.cit., p. 57.

increasingly violent confrontations with the forces of law and order of the new Republic.

The mask of enlightened bourgeois Republican-Socialism slipped badly during a general strike in Seville when Interior Minister Miguel Maura declared martial law and ordered in the military. In an attack on the CNT-run Casa del Cornelio in La Macarena, heavy artillery was used and the Civil Guard killed thirty-nine workers in Seville alone, and an unknown number elsewhere throughout the province. In his memoirs, Pedro Vallina, the Seville CNT leader, claims to have received information that the general strike was being deliberately provoked by Maura in order to break the CNT. Vallina and his comrades were arrested before they could call a halt to the strike and prevent the massacres that followed.[20]

In his statement to the Cortes, one that was approved by the Socialist Party (PSOE), Maura publicly declared the government's intention to break the CNT and FAI:

"My duty is to say to the CNT and FAI, seeing that they don't accept the laws which govern work, that they ignore the round table committees (*comités paritarios*), the mixed juries (*jurados mixtos*), and especially the law of the government that for them there will be no law of association of meeting, nor guarantee that will protect them. Let them submit to the social legislation and respect the law that regulates relations between workers, employers, and the government, and they will have the right to live normally in relation to the government."[21]

The CNT responded tersely:

"This is a decisive movement. Either we allow ourselves to be murdered, vilely, cowardly, in the streets, allow them to destroy our CNT, through the maneuvers of Maura, Galarza, and Largo Caballero, or we launch ourselves into the streets, declare the general revolutionary strike throughout Spain, and give final battle to these miserable characters who wield power and who machine gun the people in the name of republican

20 Quoted in Santillán, *Contribucion a la historia del movimiento obrero español*, *op.cit.*, p. 106.
21 Miguel Maura, *Asi cayo Alfonso XIII*, Barcelona, 1966, p. 289.

liberties... and do away once and for all with these murderers, imitators and heirs of Martinez Anido and Arlegui."[22]

As class tension increased that summer, divisions within the CNT polarized along clearly-defined revolutionary and reformist lines. Radical arguments were replaced by muted and ambiguous statements from the leadership who identified the union's interests with those of the bourgeois Republic. They stressed the need for internal unity to prevent a military coup, and the disastrous consequences for the organization of divided opinion and premature action. Their main concern was to avoid anything that threatened or compromised the efficient working of the union apparatus.

Early in August 1931 the National Committee of the CNT issued a statement attacking its own militants for provoking "excessive conflicts," which, lacking moral and material support, it argued, could not be won. It proposed that in future all member unions should obtain the agreement of the local, district, or regional federation before going on strike. To continue to "abuse" the autonomous rights of the unions was to place them in jeopardy and weaken the strike weapon.[23]

Augustin Gibanel argued the anarcho-syndicalist position, stressing the overriding need for organization and preparation. "Each day it is becoming more and more evident that the social revolution is a problem of economic and social organization. Without it, nothing would prevail in the present, nor could freedom be guaranteed after the revolution."[24]

Alejandro Gilabert defended the spontaneist anarchist position of the FAI:

"Is the revolution a problem of organization? Is it not, on the contrary, a question of audacity that, in a given moment, sets in motion the impetuous force rooted in the hearts of the masses—which can be mobilized by frequent events that occur in the life of the people? It is the economy that determines events, or the will of men?"[25]

22 De Lera, op.cit., p. 282.
23 "Confederación Nacional del Trabajo a todos los trabajadores," *Solidaridad Obrera*, 16.8.1931.
24 "La mision social del sindicalismo," *Solidaridad Obrera*, 23.6.1931.
25 Alejandro Gilabert, *La CNT, la FAI, y la revolución española*, Barcelona 1932, p. 14.

14

"The Manifesto of the Thirty"

The bitter conflicts between unionists and revolutionaries finally exploded in late August 1931, with the publication of what was to become known as the "Treintista Manifesto." While unionist influence had been steadily eroded over the previous year by the polarized political situation and the failure of the reformist leadership to defend working class interests, an increasingly radicalized rank and file had adopted the FAI as its voice. The violence of the strikes that summer and the increasingly revolutionary atmosphere appeared to presage disaster for the union leaders. Thirty CNT members, from the editorial group of *Solidaridad Obrera* and the National and Regional Committees of the CNT, many of them members of the Solidaridad group, met during August to draw up a manifesto; it was a final gamble to force the issue to a head and isolate the revolutionaries.[1] "With it," said José Peirats, "they nailed their colors to the

1 In 1928, members of the Pestañist Solidaridad group included the Portuguese Germinal de Sousa, a member of the 1936 FAI Peninsular Committee, which approved the CNT joining the Caballero government; Progreso Alfarache, a member of the CNT National Committee until 1936; Patricio Navarro, the member of the Catalan CNT Regional Committee who ordered confederal militants to return to work during the October 1934 uprising; Antonio García Birlán, later the FAI representative on the Generalidat's Economic Council and Councillor of Health in the 1936 Catalan government. Juan López Sánchez, one of the four CNT ministers in Caballero's 1936 government was also a member of this group. *Cuadernos para una enciclopedia del anarquismo español*, No 25, 1984, Vitoria. According to Ramón Alvárez (*El movimiento libertario*, op.cit., p. 159), Regional Secretary of the Asturian CNT, other members included José María Martínez; Segundo Blanco, the CNT minister in Dr Juan Negrín's Cabinet; and Avelino G. Mallada.

mast, and awaited the hostilities they provoked."[2] At stake was their faction's credibility and continued control of the positions of responsibility within the union.

"To the comrades, to the unions, to everybody:—A superficial analysis of the situation in which our country finds itself will lead us to pronounce that Spain finds herself in circumstances of intense revolutionary propensities from which deep-seated collective excitement is going to derive. There is no denying the magnitude of the moment, nor the dangers implicit in this revolutionary period, because, whether we like it or not, the force of circumstance alone must ensure that we all suffer the consequences of the upheaval. The advent of the Republic has opened a parenthesis in the normal history of our country. With the monarchy toppled, the king driven off his throne, the Republic proclaimed by the tacit concerted efforts of groups, parties, organizations, and individuals who had suffered the attacks of the dictatorship and of the period of repression under Martínez Anido and Arlegui, it will be readily appreciated that this whole succession of events had to bring us to a new situation, to a state of affairs different from what the nation's life had hitherto been over the past 50 years, from the Restoration onwards. But if the aforementioned facts were the mobilizing factor that induced us to destroy one political situation and to try to usher in a period different from the past, what has come to pass since has borne out our assertion that Spain is living in truly revolutionary times. With the way made easy for the flight of the king and with the expatriation of the whole gilded and 'blue-blooded' rabble, capital has been exported on a huge scale and the country has been impoverished even beyond what it was. The flight of the plutocrats, bankers, financiers and the gentleman stock and bondholders of the State has been followed by shameful and brazen speculation which has given rise to formidable depreciation in the value of the peseta and a 50 per cent devaluation in the nation's assets.

"This assault upon economic interests, calculated to produce hunger and misery for the majority of Spaniards, has been followed up by the covert hypocritical conspiracy of all the cowl and soutane wearers, of all whom, in order to ensure their

---

2   *El movimiento libertario español*, op.cit., p. 231.

victory, do not shrink from lighting one candle to God and another to the devil. The power to dominate, subjugate and live upon the exploitation of an entire people which is reduced to its knees is being given primacy over everything. The upshot of this conspiracy of criminal procedures is a deep-seated and intense blockage of public credits, and consequent collapse of all industries, leading to a fearful crisis such as our country has, perhaps, never before known. Workshops are shutting down; factories are laying off their workers; projects are coming to a standstill or no longer being launched; in commerce, there has been a fall in orders, and no outlet for natural produce; workers go week after week without finding work; countless industries have to cut back to two or three (and a very few to four) days working. Those workers who manage to find a whole week's work and who can show up at the factory or the workshop six days, account for no more than 30 per cent of the workforce. The pauperization of the country is already an accepted *fait accompli*. Alongside all of these misadventures that have befallen the people, one notes the lethargy and exceedingly legalistic approach of the government. Though every one of the ministers owes his position to revolution, they have reneged upon it by clinging to legality the way a mollusc clings to a rock, and they show no signs of energy except when it comes to turning the machine guns on the people. According to them, it is in the name of the Republic and in order to defend that republic that the entire repressive apparatus of the State is deployed and the workers' blood spilled daily. Now it is no longer a case of this or that village, but in every village that the dry bark of the Mausers has cut short lusty young lives. Meanwhile, the government has done nothing in the economic sphere, nor is it going to do anything. It has not expropriated the great landowners, the true bogeys of the Spanish peasant; it has not reduced, by as much as one single centimo, the profits of those who speculate upon the public interest; no monopoly has been done away with; nothing has been done to limit the abuses of those who exploit and grow fat on the hunger, pain, and misery of the people; it has struck a contemplative pose when what was needed was the crushing of privilege, the destruction of injustice, and the prevention of thefts as infamous as they are vile. How should we wonder, then, at what has happened?

On the one hand, superciliousness, speculation, tinkering with public affairs and with collective values, with that which belongs to the common man, with society's values. On the other hand, leniency, tolerance shown to oppressors and exploiters who victimize the people, whereas the people are imprisoned and harassed, threatened, and exterminated.

"And, down below, as a worthy counterpart to this, the people...suffering, languishing, undergoing hunger and misery, and watching as they trifle with the revolution that the people have made. Still ensconced in public office, on the judicial bench... from where they may betray the revolution... are the ones who achieved those positions through the official bounty of the king or the influence of his ministers. This situation, after having brought destruction to one regime, demonstrates that the revolution left unmade is becoming inevitable and a necessity. We all acknowledge that...the ministers by recognizing the collapse of the economic system... the press, by recording the disaffection of the people, and the people by revolting against the offenses perpetrated against them. So everything appears to confirm the imminence of decisions which the country will have to make in order to save itself by saving the revolution.

One Interpretation

"The position being one of thoroughgoing collective tragedy, the people's wish being to shrug off the grief which torments and kills them, there being but one option, revolution... How are we to go about it? History tells us that revolutions have always been the work of daring minorities that have exhorted the people against the constituted authorities. Is it enough that these minorities should so desire and so scheme, that, in a similar context, the destruction of the prevailing regime and of the defensive forces that uphold it should become a fact? Let us see. One fine day, perhaps availing of the element of surprise, these minorities, complete with some aggressive elements, confront the security forces, stand up to them and spark the violent clash that may lead us to revolution. A little rudimentary training and a few shock elements are more than enough to begin with. They entrust the success of the revolution to the valor if a handful of individuals and to the problematical intervention of the multitudes who would rush to their aid once they were on the streets.

"No need to make provision for anything, no need to make calculations, no need to think about anything other than taking to the streets to rout the mastodon: the State. Thoughts about its having formidable means of defense at its disposal, or about its being hard to destroy as long as its resources of power, its moral sway over the people, its economy, its courts, its moral and economic credit have not been smashed by its thievery and vileness, by the immorality and incompetence of its leaders, and by the undermining of its institutions: it is a waste of time to think that unless this comes to pass the state cannot be destroyed. This is to turn a blind eye to history and to display ignorance of human psychology itself. And that blind eye may be turned at the present time. And so that this blind eye may be turned, a blind eye is turned also even to revolutionary morality itself. Everything is trusted to the serendipity factor, everything is expected of the unforeseen: there is belief in the miraculous feats of the blessed revolution, as if the revolution were a cure-all and not a painful, cruel event that has to forge men with bodily suffering and mental distress. This concept of revolution, the spawn of the sheerest demagogy peddled over decades by all men of the political parties that have tried, very often unsuccessfully, to storm into power—paradoxically though it may seem—has advocates in our own ranks, and it has reasserted itself in certain groups of militants. Without their realizing that they are falling into all the vices of political demagogy—vices that would induce us to hand over the revolution, were it to be made successful in those circumstances, to the first political party to come along, or even to become the government ourselves, to take power so as to govern as if we were just another political party. May we, must we…may the National Confederation of Labor (CNT), must the National Confederation of Labor (CNT)…rally to this disastrous concept of revolution, of the revolutionary act, the revolutionary feat?

Our Interpretation

"Opposed to this simplistic, classical, and somewhat cinematic concept of the revolution, which at the moment would lead us to a republican fascism disguised under the Cap of Liberty, but nonetheless for all that, stands another concept, the true, the only practical and universal concept that may bring us, that will ineluctably bring us, to the attainment of our ultimate objective.

"The latter concept means that it is not merely the aggressive, fighting personnel that have to be trained, but these plus moral factors, which today are the sturdiest, the most destructive, the hardest to overcome. It does not trust the revolution solely to the daring of the more or less daring minorities, but wants there to be an ongoing movement of the people en masse, of the working class en route towards its ultimate liberation, with the unions and Confederation determining the date, technique, and precise timing of the revolution. It does not hold that revolution is only order, only method: this is a large factor in the training and in the revolution itself, but sufficient scope must also be left for individual initiative. Against the chaotic, incoherent concept of revolution entertained by the first group, stands the ordered, prescient, coherent concept of the second. The former is tantamount to playing at riot, ambush, revolution; it amounts in fact to delaying the real revolution.

"So the difference is very considerable. A moment's deliberation will show us the advantage of one approach or the other. Let each person decide which of the two interpretations to make his own.

Last Words

"It will be readily understood by anyone who reads this that we have not written and put our signature to the foregoing for pleasure's sake, nor out of any whimsical desire to have our names featured at the bottom of a text that is of a public nature and that concerns doctrine. Our attitude is unwavering: we have espoused a course that we deem necessary in the interests of the confederation, which is reflected in the second of the interpretations of revolution set out earlier.

"Yes, we are revolutionaries; but no, we do not cultivate the myth of revolution. We seek an end to capitalism and to the state, be it red, white, or black; but not so that we may erect another in its place, but so that, once the economic revolution has been made by the working class, that revolution may thwart the reintroduction of all power of whatever persuasion. We seek a revolution sprung from the innermost feelings of the people... A revolution along the lines of the one being forged today...and not a revolution that is offered to us, or that a few individuals seek to deliver to us...individuals who, were they to succeed in this, would turn into dictators on the morrow of that success, regardless of how they call themselves. But we seek and desire that success. Is this what the bulk of the organization's membership also desires? This is something worth exploring, something that needs clarification as soon as possible. The Confederation is a revolutionary organization, not one that has a hankering for ambush or riot, nor one that makes a cult of violence for its own sake, or of revolution for revolution's sake. This being the case, we address ourselves to all members, to remind them that these are grave times and we remind each of them of the responsibility he assumes by virtue of his action or inaction. If today, tomorrow, the day after, or whenever... they are urged to participate in a revolutionary revolt, let them not forget that they have obligations towards the National Confederation of Labor (CNT), an organization that has a right to be its own master, to monitor its own movements, act upon its own initiative and determine its own fate. And let them not forget that the Confederation itself must be the one to determine, in accordance with its own reckonings, how, when, and in what circumstances it should act; that it is possessed of an identity of its own and the wherewithal to do what must be done.

"Let all be alive to the responsibilities imposed by the extraordinary times in which we live. Let them not forget that, though the act of revolution may bring success, one should go under with dignity in the event of failure to succeed, and that any reckless attempt at revolution may lead to reaction and to the triumph of the demagogues. Let each of them now adopt whatever stance he deems most suitable. Ours you already know. Steadfast in our purpose, we shall always and everywhere stand by our choice, even though others not of the same mind may overwhelm us.

Barcelona, August 1931

(Signed)

Juan López, Agustín Gibanel, Ricardo Fornells, José Girona, Daniel Navarro, Jesús Rodríguez, Antonio Villabriga, Ángel

Pestaña, Miguel Portolés, Joaquim Roura, Joaquim Lorente, Progreso Alfarache, Antonio Peñarroya, Camilo Piñón, Joaquín Cortes, Isidoro Gabín, Pedro Massoni, Francesc Arín, José Cristià, Juan Dinarés, Roldán Cortada, Sebastià Clara, Joan Peiró, Ramon Viñas, Federico Uleda, Pedro Cané, Mariano Peat, Espartaco Puig, Narciso Marcó, Jenaro Minguet"

Juan López of the Solidaridad group has left an account of the events immediately leading up to the Treintista Manifesto:

"Shortly after the Conservatorio Congress, a Regional Plenum of Syndicates of Catalonia was held in the Calle Cabana in Barcelona. At the time the Catalan Regional had 500,000 affiliates:

"I took part as a delegate for my union. García Oliver and Durruti were delegates for the Fabric and Textile Union. At one of the sessions, the Fabric and Textile delegation proposed a session in camera. During this session Oliver and Durruti proposed that the Plenum agree to send a revolutionary plan to the Defense Committee—constituted by the FAI groups, without any connection with the superior organs of the CNT...the campaign for revolution [rejected by the Plenum] gathered momentum among the local groups... In response to this growing threat from the rank and file, the group around Solidaridad and the pro-unionists, who held positions of responsibility, took the initiative at a meeting held in the Transport Union local in Barcelona."[3]

The manifesto itself had been proposed by Francisco Arín of the Solidaridad group. Ángel Pestaña was delegated to write it. According to López and de Lera, his first draft provoked a long and heated discussion. It was virulently anti-revolutionary and obsessively anti-FAI. Pestaña justified his somewhat hysterical tone by claiming to have access to secret information about the real plans behind the FAI's revolutionary proposals, plans that coincided with rightist and anti-republican conspiracies. Unhappy with Pestaña's first effort, a second draft was drawn up, one that stressed the positive aspects of the *treintista* line, but even this failed to satisfy the anti-revolutionary unionists. After a third unsatisfactory meeting, it was decided to nominate

3 De Lera, op.cit., p. 282.

a three-man commission who, working on Pestaña's last draft, would decide on the final text. These were Agustín Gibanel, Progreso Alfarache, and Ricardo Fornells.

The final draft was, then, neither a hasty nor an improvised document. It had gone through at least three detailed readings and much heated discussion among those involved before publication.[4] It outlined what the signatories saw as a synthesis of confederal thought, upheld the "independence" of the Confederation, and denounced as naive the idea that the revolution could be achieved by the actions of an audacious minority—this could only be done through the constructive and co-ordinated labor of the masses.

The attacks on "adventurous excesses" and "unrealizable objectives" redounded against the *treintistas*. In the heated political atmosphere of the time, the mood of the rank and file was hostile to the Republic. The attack on the FAI was seen for what it was—an attack on the union's own militants, a political maneuver to re-assert the waning authority of the union leadership. If successful, the *treintistas* would subvert the CNT's independence by suborning it to an irresolute middle class government. García Oliver later pointed out:

"In reality it reflected nothing more than the disgust of a group of militants who could not come to terms with the fact that they had lost, in less than a year, prestige and leadership within the CNT. It is very easy to explain the war of *faismo* and *treintismo* and the complete collapse of the latter. When the Republic was introduced in Spain, some old confederal militants felt socially and politically satisfied with the mediocre bourgeois content of the new Republic and advocated the renunciation of the traditional social revolutionary spirit of

---

4 Marcos Alcón, Secretary of the CNT's Glass Workers' Union and a FAI affiliate, visited Joan Peiró to ask him to explain why he had signed the manifesto. "When the manifesto came out, I took the day off work and set off for Mataro to get Peiró to give me an explanation... For the glass workers of Spain Peiró was a symbol. He and I had an especially high regard for one another... Upon reaching the plant where he worked I said to him: "What's the meaning of this here signature?" His reply was categorical. "That son of a bitch"—a reference to Pestaña—"stitched me up!" Peiró was a man easily caught off guard. He was too trusting. After the trickster had decamped, he realized that he had been duped and let loose a broadside." Letter from Alcón to Juan Gómez Casas, *La FAI*, op.cit., p. 147.

the CNT and of adapting our organization to the republican situation."[5]

The manifesto's presentation of anarcho-syndicalist ideas contained nothing that directly conflicted with the traditional approach of the CNT. Where sharply conflicting differences did arise was with regard to the question of revolution. This was the key issue that provided the "Thirty," or class collaborationist faction, with the justification it felt it required to launch its overt declaration of war against anarchist influence within the CNT. Although the FAI was nowhere referred to by name in the document, it was implicitly accused of developing a "simplistic, classical, and somewhat cinematic concept of the revolution" and attacked for attempting to impose its "negative," "adventurist," and "putschist" policies on the union by potential dictators with a predilection for "ambush" and "riot" and "violence for its own sake." In fact, as we have seen, the proposed plans for an insurrection, which Juan López claims led to the belligerent attack on the FAI, did not come from that body, or even FAI affiliates as it later emerges, but from the properly delegated representatives of the Fabric and Textile Workers union of the CNT. Durruti and Oliver, who proposed the plan, had been speaking as union, not FAI, delegates.

The manifesto provided useful grist for the mills of the political groups who wished either to control the Confederation or neutralize it. The heated public debate was seized on by the bourgeois press who orchestrated a massively hyped blitzkrieg against the class war anarchist position. The State was being given carte blanche to repress and eliminate what were described as the "uncontrollable" (*incontrolados*) elements within the CNT, presumably a reference to the Los Solidarios/ Nosotros group. The bourgeois press, particularly in Catalonia, gave the manifesto maximum publicity, publishing the text in full, with accompanying editorial articles emphasizing its constructive nature and the positive influence of the moderate leadership. Catalan politicians seized the opportunity to fan the smouldering embers of schism. Macià and Companys, in anticipation of the statute of autonomy, which was to establish

5   Letter from García Oliver to John Brademas dated 9.3.1953. (Quoted in *Anarcosindicalismo y revolucion en España (1930–1937)*, John Brademas, Barcelona, 1994, p. 81.)

the independent Catalan Generalitat government, sensitive to the need for a responsive labor movement, encouraged what they described as "the level-headed portion of the Confederation."[6]

For the anarchists, the *treintista* document was not just an attempt to adapt the CNT unions to the circumstances of the moment; it signified not only the complete abandonment of the fundamental anarchist principles of social revolution as the only acceptable goal for libertarians, but a challenge to the wishes of the base of the union. It displayed an arrogant disregard for the creative capacity of the working class. Buenaventura Durruti launched the counter-offensive with a public defense of the position that the FAI represented to the broad mass of the movement:

"In an energetic, but high-minded way, we anarchists shall reply to the attack on us by some Confederal leaders. I hope that note will have been taken of the fact that the attacks were aimed directly at García Olivares [sic] and myself. This is only to be expected, for as soon as I arrived in Barcelona I clashed with the Confederation's leaders and, following a discussion that lasted for several hours, we clearly arrived at the two stances that have increasingly come to prominence.

"We men of the FAI are not, by a long chalk, what many folk think we are. Around us, there has grown up a sort of unwarranted aura that we must dispel as quickly as we can. Anarchism is not what many timid would suppose it to be. In point of fact, our idea is much more comprehensive than the privileged classes think, and constitutes a serious threat to capital as well as to those phoney defenders of the proletariat who occupy the highest offices. Of course, the manifesto recently published by Pestaña, Peiró, Arín, Clara, Alfarache, and others was a source of much satisfaction to the bourgeois in government and to the Catalan unionists, but no way does the FAI associate itself with the *mea culpa* of the aforementioned gentlemen, and it will press on along the road upon which it has set out, believing it to be the best one. How can they want us to see eye to eye with the present government, which four days ago allowed the murder of four workers in the streets of Seville, lapsing back into the infamous system devised

6   Peirats, *La CNT*, op.cit.

by Martínez Anido and now put into effect by the Interior Minister, Señor Maura? How do they expect us to see eye to eye with a government that fights shy of imposing sanctions on the stalwarts of the late dictatorship and leaves them completely free to go on with their plotting in Lasarte? How do they expect us to see eye to eye with a government partly made up of those who collaborated with the dictatorship?

"We are absolutely apolitical because we are convinced that politics is an artificial system of government that flies in the face of nature, where many men back down in order to hold on to their positions, making a sacrifice of whatever they need to, especially the humble classes.

"What is presently happening is only what necessarily had to come to pass by virtue of the fact that the revolution was not carried through on 14 April. We should have gone a lot further than we did, and now we workers are paying the price. We anarchists are the only ones who defend the principles of the confederation, libertarian principles that others apparently have forgotten. Proof of this claim is the fact that they quit the struggle precisely when they should have begun to escalate it. It is all too obvious that Pestaña and Peiró have assumed moral commitments that hinder their libertarian conduct.

"The Spanish Republic, as presently constituted, is a great threat to libertarian ideas, and of necessity, unless anarchists act vigorously, we will inevitably lapse into social democracy. The revolution has to be made; and made as soon as possible, since this Republic has offered the people no guarantees, economic or political. No way can we wait until the Republic finishes consolidating itself in its present make up. Even now, General Sanjurjo is asking for a further 8,000 Civil Guards. Naturally the Republicans have had the example of Russia in mind. They have seen that of necessity the same thing must happen as during the Kerensky government, which was merely an incubation period for the making of the real revolution, and this is what they seek to avert.

"The Republic has not been able to resolve the question of the Church, for example. The bourgeois have not dared do battle with the workers, but they have taken up their positions. There are two courses to choose from: either social democracy, as in Germany and Belgium, or expropriation by the organized masses of labor. Of course they have opted for the former.

"Macià, a man all goodness, a pure man of integrity, is one of those to be blamed for the dire straits in which the workers find themselves today. If, instead of stationing himself, as he has done, between capital and labor, he had inclined once and for all to the side of labor, the libertarian movement of Catalonia would have spread throughout Spain and throughout the whole of Europe and even Latin America would have had its adepts. Macià has chosen to build a little Catalonia were we would have turned Barcelona into the spiritual capital of the world. All of Europe's workers monitored the libertarian movement of Catalonia, awaiting the opportune moment when they too might achieve their claims. Now, after the false situation conjured up by Macià, he fears us and does not know what to do next.

"Spanish industry cannot compete with foreign capitalism and on the other hand the worker is a lot more advanced. Industry being constituted as it is in Spain, if it were brought up to date and able to compete with industry abroad, the workers would have to take a step backwards and this we are not disposed to do.

"It is necessary, vital, that a solution be found to the problem of unemployed workers whose numbers are growing daily and it is we workers who have come up with the solution. How? By means, necessarily, of the social revolution. The way must be made clear for the workers. Though it may seem a paradox, Spain's wealth has to be defended by the workers and the workers only.

"Turning to that manifesto again, I have to repeat that at one of our meetings I suggested to Pestaña and Peiró that they were the theorists, and we youngsters the dynamic portion of the organization. That is to say they follow in our wake, reconstructing. We of the FAI have only 2,000 members enrolled in the Confederation; but in all we can call upon 400,000 men in that, at the last meeting held, when it came to a vote, we took 63 votes as against 22. The issue was whether or not to reply with revolution to the first provocation offered by the present government.

"On Sunday, the first meeting will take place of the local federation and at it we shall register our protest against the document made public. We anarchists are the ones who have in our hands the true leadership of the labor organization of Catalonia and of many another region in Spain. This has been acknowledged by the Catalanist deputies who publicly expressed their fears with regard to the FAI's organization. We know that our organization strikes a lot of fear into the bourgeois and petty bourgeois of Catalonia; but we shall not take one step backwards where the claims of labor are concerned.

"I do not believe that this unity, which has seemingly come about in the Confederation because of the failures of recent times, can be a lasting one. Similar responses have been forthcoming in other times in the bosom of the Confederation, but have still, in the face of the opinion of the bulk of the unions, had to follow the route mapped out by the confederated workers."[7]

On 3 September, the Barcelona CNT paper *Solidaridad Obrera*, flying in the face of the membership, published an editorial supporting the *treintista* line and denouncing aggressive and insurgent tactics. It proved to be ill-timed and ill-advised. The rank and file of the CNT, subjected to a sustained campaign of terror and intimidation by the employers and the state were angry to find their leaders seeking an accommodation with their tormentors. Pestaña's response had been to write what was seen as a servile letter to President Azaña asking him to intervene against the employers. Azaña, viewing the problems as a crisis of public order, rather than reflecting genuine social grievances, ignored the union leader leaving what little credibility he had left in ruins.

Unfortunately for the *treintistas*, the day the *Soli* editorial appeared, the workers of Barcelona had taken to the streets in protest against the ill-treatment of political prisoners. The Republican authorities met them with force. Barricades quickly appeared in the workers' quarters: shops and bars were closed. The police attacked the Construction Union local with what was seen as unnecessary brutality. Three CNT members were murdered in cold blood under the infamous fugitives' law during this attack.

---

7   *La Tierra*, 2.9.1931.

Again the Republic had been unable to distinguish itself as an improvement on any other Spanish regime. *Solidaridad Obrera* referred to the disturbances dismissively as "an explosion of sentimentalism," but did not go as far as to condemn them outright. The position of the editorial board of *Solidaridad Obrera* in the face of the bloody repression was now clearly untenable. On 22 September, its editorial staff, under pressure from the union membership, resigned.[8] They were replaced by a new team with a *faista* majority, which included Eusebio C. Carbó, T. Cano Ruiz, Liberto Callejas, E. Labrador, and J. Robuste. Felipe Alaiz, a member of the old editorial staff and a FAI member, was appointed editor to replace Joan Peiró. The CNT daily was once again solidly under anarchist control.

A widely-read and influential article by anarchist writer and teacher Federica Montseny (at the time unaffiliated to either the CNT or the FAI) helped put the dispute in perspective for the broad mass of militants. The article, entitled "The Internal and External Crisis of the Confederation"—which denounced the anti-anarchist repression of the Madrid and Catalan governments and the secret intrigues aimed at splitting the movement, as subsequent events proved—reflected the opinion of the rank and file.

"Of late, the agreements with Macià, entered into by union leaders, with an eye to securing approval of the famous statute [of autonomy], indicate what lie in store for us. Once Catalonia has her statute she will pursue a policy of tolerance with regard to the 'good little boys' of the CNT, but 'the screws' will be put on the FAI types (the phrase is Companys') and the celebrated 'extremists.' 'Extremist' will be the term for all those who refuse to see the CNT become in Barcelona what the UGT is in Madrid, vis à vis the Generalitat and Republican governments respectively. A Catalanized CNT, with its National Committee based here for life, will ignore the rest of Spain, just as it has already ignored the strikes in Seville and Zaragoza, which were

---

8   Brenan wrote: "All that summer their influence [the FAI's] in the CNT was increasing, and in October they were able to force the resignation of the editor Juan Peiró, and of the whole staff of the famous anarcho-syndicalist paper, because they refused to support the FAI policy of revolutionary action by small groups." Brenan, op.cit., p. 255.

lost and won with more honour and more intelligence than the strike here in Barcelona was pursued and lost."[9]

Growing unemployment and general dissatisfaction led to a further wave of social unrest. The repression entered a new, sharper phase. On 21 July, Prime Minister Azaña introduced the "Law of the Defense of the Republic" (*Ley de defensa de la República*). Equally harsh was the "Criminal Vagrancy Law" (*Ley de vagos y maleantes*). The forces of public order were also empowered to fire on suspects without prior warning. For the new anarchist editorial board of *Solidaridad Obrera* there was little doubt who these laws were aimed at: "The Law of the Defense of the Republic is the pretext to intensify the persecution of the CNT and make the regular functioning of the unions impossible." In addition to repressive legislation, the bourgeois politicians turned to more subtle and sophisticated ways of manipulating opinion against the anarchist activists. The FAI, as the rallying point of uncompromising class war anarchism within the largest labor union, became the focus of a massive disinformation and hate campaign at the hands of the bourgeois media and officialdom.

The view of the FAI as a conspiratorial, elitist, manipulative body was not shared by all its unionist opponents. José Borras Cascarosa, a member of the Federación Ibérica de Juventudes Libertarias (FIJL) and the CNT from 1932, disliked the FAI, describing it as "the worst plague" suffered by the union, but added:

"One has to recognize that the FAI did not intervene in the CNT from above or in an authoritarian manner as did the other political parties in the unions. It did so from the base through militants who were prime examples of abnegation and heroism. But the decisions that determined the course taken by the CNT were taken under constant pressure from these militants and launched the union into premature defeats for which the rank and file were not prepared and had little enthusiasm."[10]

José Campos, another CNT militant who was not a member of the FAI, points out the often overlooked fact that relatively

---

9 Peirats, op.cit., Vol. I. Ch. 3.
10 *El movimiento libertario español*, op.cit., p. 163.

few anarchists in the CNT were affiliated to the FAI; they saw it essentially as a symbol.

"I did not belong to the FAI, as did many others who considered themselves anarchists. The CNT was constitutionally anarchist because anarchists had created it... We can say that the FAI and *faismo* always existed in the CNT, even before its birth in 1927. It was the spirit of the FAI that sustained the confederal cadres during the terror in Barcelona in the period 1919–1923, and that expelled the Bolsheviks from the National Committee of the CNT, and that kept the union outside Moscow's orbit."

Campos added that the myth of the conspiratorial FAI arose with the *treintistas*.

"Among the promoters of the FAI myth can be found the reformists who, born in the CNT, have little in common with it today." Asked how FAI militants operated within the unions he said that they "tended to reject control of confederal committees and only accepted them on specific occasions... I was in Graficos and if someone proposed a motion in an assembly, the other FAI members would support it, usually successfully. It was the individual standing of the *faista* in open assembly... The attack on the FAI was, in essence, a conscious attack on the basic principles of the CNT, in its anti-governmentalism and anarchism. The attack began with Pestaña and others. The first imagined an aseptic CNT and, later, a unitary union in which the workers would leave behind their political opinions. This was postulated by the Charter of Amiens."[11]

This view is supported by José Peirats, secretary of the Barcelona Anarchist Groups in 1933.

"The FAI was a popular wave that adopted the name FAI because it needed a flag, and there was a mythical concept of the FAI. Some personalities who spoke in the name of the FAI wielded greater influence than ourselves, who represented it officially. These men had their own FAI in the Los Solidarios group, which was only loosely controlled by the Local Federation, at least during my period as secretary. There were

---

11 Ibid., p. 169.

other well-known personalities who had considerable weight in the battle: Felipe Alaiz, Eusebio Carbó, Dionysios, and the very influential *Revista Blanca*. Properly speaking, the FAI exercised enormous influence through its publications and its journal *Tierra y Libertad.*"[12]

Well-known anarchist personalities, speaking in defense of the anarchist objectives of the union, were presumed to be doing so, ex cathedra, in the name of the FAI. Many of these were never members of FAI-affiliated groups or controlled in any way by the FAI. A good example of this is the case of García Oliver, who subsequently claimed never to have been a member of the FAI. Interviewed by anarchist journalist Eduardo de Guzman in October 1931, Oliver, described as "one of the most outstanding representatives of the FAI," explained the concept of "revolutionary gymnastics," the crisis within the CNT, and the reasons behind the media hostility towards the FAI.[13]

"The reason behind the attacks on the FAI escapes those who do not live in our circles. The reason for the indignation which the signatories of the manifesto feel with regard to us is that the anarchist groups have shrugged off the tutelage that they managed to saddle them with at a certain time. In point of fact, the struggle is not of recent vintage. It began in 1923 when anarchists saw that Pestaña and Peiró and the bulk of the manifesto's signatories alike did not have the necessary capacity to face up to the difficult times Spain was passing through, an atmosphere in which the possibility of a military dictatorship was in the air. At one congress we went as far as to point out that an absolutist-style coup d'état would be mounted before three months were up and indeed, regrettably, the dictatorship was set up, confirming our fears.

---

12 Ibid., p. 237.
13 In a letter to Juan Gómez Casas, García Oliver (27.6.1974) claimed he had never belonged to the FAI: "I was never a militant, nor a member of its committees. While I was imprisoned, they tricked Ascaso and Durruti into affiliating our group, which at the time did not exist, to the FAI. The Nosotros group was formed to provide some bureaucratic satisfaction." However, Juan Manuel Molina, who was Peninsular Secretary of the FAI until 1935 (with the exception of 1932, when he was in jail), claims that he was succeeded by García Oliver. The confused relationship of the Nosotros group to the FAI is borne out elsewhere by José Peirats.

"This, the mishandling of the transport strike and the manifest inability to discover a solution to the terrorism problem induced anarchists to launch a movement that, while not designed to split the CNT, sought to extract from that body a revolutionary solution to the problems with which Spain was confronted.

"Anarchists then distanced themselves, not from the Confederation—for they have always been the most active elements of that—but from the men like Pestaña, Peiró, etc., who were influencing the organization along unrealistic lines.

"The same thing is happening now as happened then. Some months ago Pestaña and Peiró were interpreting the reality of Republican Spain in terms of giving credence to the effectiveness of Parliament in respect of social legislation; we anarchists on the other hand, convinced that the dictatorship had been toppled, not by pressure from the political parties, but because the Spanish economy was stretched to breaking point, disagreed with them, affirming that social problems could only be solved through a revolutionary upheaval that would transform the economy, as well as destroying bourgeois institutions.

"Without specifying a date, Oliver continues, we advocate the act of revolution, not trifling about whether we were or not prepared to mount the revolution and introduce Libertarian Communism, in that we take the line that the revolution is not a question of preparation but of will, a question of wanting it made, when circumstances of social decomposition such as Spain is going through pave the way for any attempt at revolution.

"Without in any way belittling revolutionary preparation, we relegate it to a secondary position because, following the Mussolini phenomenon in Italy and the fascist (Hitler) experience in Germany, it has been shown that any ostensible preparation and propaganda for the act of revolution leads to a parallel fascist preparation and act.

"Formerly, all revolutionaries accepted that the revolution, when it knocks upon the doors of a people, inevitable triumphs, whether those elements hostile to the prevailing system like it or not. This could be believed up until the fascist victory on Italy, for up to that point the bourgeoisie believed that the democratic state was its last line of defense. But after Mussolini's coup d'état, capitalism is convinced that when the democratic state fails it can discover in its organization the forces to topple liberalism and crush the revolutionary movement.

"The FAI has been labelled by the signatories of the manifesto as aspiring to carry out a Marxist-type revolution, in a deplorable confusion of revolutionary techniques (the same for everyone who intends to mount a revolt) with the basic principles (so very different) of anarchism and Marxism. The FAI, in these times in Spain, represents the revolutionary ferment, the factor of social decomposition needed by our country if she is to arrive at the revolution.

"In ideological terms, the FAI, which is the enshrinement of anarchism, aspires to make a reality of Libertarian Communism. So much so that if, once the revolution has been made in Spain, there should be installed a regime along the lines of the Russian one or the dictatorial syndicalism advocated by Peiró, Arín, and Piñón, the FAI would instantly enter the lists against those sorts of society, not so as to overthrow them in favor of reaction, but in order to make the necessary progress beyond them to install Libertarian Communism.

"The signatories of the manifesto have never believed in the possibility of the Spanish revolution. In far-off days they made revolutionary propaganda but today, now that the time has come, the fiction that they peddled has fallen apart in their hearts. Nevertheless, the manifesto's signatories, realizing that they had been overtaken by events, are now making revolutionary assertions, fending off the realization of the act to utterly absurd dates two years and more hence as if this was an option given the general crisis in which the bourgeois economy finds itself. Also, within two years, the revolution would not be needed by the workers because between Maura and Galarza, not to mention the fact that by that time, should any workers survive, they would be ground down by a military dictatorship (Monarchist or Republican) that will necessarily come about due to the failure of the Spanish parliament."

Asked about the line the Confederation should take, Oliver continued:

"The CNT need not waste time of preparing the act of revolution in both its facets of, first, organizing destruction and, then, organizing construction. In the collective life of Spain the CNT is the only solid presence, for in a country where everything is pulverized, it represents a national reality that all political elements together would not be capable of overtaking. When it comes to revolutionary construction, the CNT should not on any pretext postpone the social revolution for anything that can be prepared, in fact already is. Nobody will suppose that after the revolution the factories have to operate in reverse, nor will it be argued that the *campesinos* will have to operate the plough by using their feet.

"After the revolutionary act, all workers have to do the same as they did the day before the upheaval. Essentially, a revolution boils down to a new concept of law and the law being effective as such. After the revolution, the workers should be entitled to live according to their needs, and society entitled to meet their needs as far as this is economically feasible.

"None of this requires any preparation. All that is required is that today's revolutionaries be sincere defenders of the toiling class and do not seek to set themselves up as petty tyrants under cover of a more of less proletarian dictatorship."[14]

As the economic and political situation deteriorated, during the period between September and December 1931, Spain was swamped by a wave of general solidarity strikes. Barcelona was particularly badly affected. Governor General Anguero de Sojo suspended a number of meetings and closed the offices of the Transport Union. In Zaragoza, an anarcho-syndicalist solidarity strike led to a confrontation with the police, which left one anarchist dead, a number wounded, and many imprisoned. Important strikes also took place in Bilbao, Huelva, Cádiz, and a number of other cities. In December, Security Guards in Barcelona opened fire on a group of *cenetistas* on their way to a meeting to commemorate the Jaca uprising of the previous year. The labor policies pursued by Largo Caballero were seen by the CNT as benefiting the socialist UGT at the expense of the Confederation. "From now on we know that the Constituent Cortes are against the people," commented the Catalan CNT paper *Solidaridad Obrera*. "Henceforth there can be no peace,

14 *La Tierra*, 3.10.1931.

nor one minute of truce between the Constituent Cortes and the CNT."

The FAI paper, *El Luchador*, published horrifying photographs of the victims of the Republican security forces and took the national committee of the CNT to task for not offering more support to the strikers—particularly in Aragón, Asturias, and Seville. The pestañistas, now on the defensive, spent the final months of 1931 attacking *Solidaridad Obrera* and justifying the *treintista* position. At the beginning of December, during the Lérida Regional Plenum, the *treintistas* announced the publication of their own paper, *Cultura Libertaria*.

15

1932, Insurrection—
The Revolutionary Gymnasia

For anarchists, social revolution is the ultimate collective instrument of the oppressed against the hierarchical and exploitative social and economical structure under which they are forced to live. It is the only means by which the old order can be displaced. Compromise with capitalism, and collaboration with the State through the parliamentary process, serves only to institutionalize misery, injustice, and violence in its broadest sense.

With the coming to power of the Alcalá Zamora presidency in January 1932, working class discontent with the frustrated and impotent bourgeois Republic boiled over into violent confrontation. The first incidents of the new year took place in Arnedo, in Logroño, on 5 January, when a number of people were killed in clashes between the Civil Guard and strikers. The wave of revolutionary militancy steadily gathered momentum. On 18 January, the anarchist miners of Alto Llobregat near Figols and Cardoner in the neighboring valley, triggered what they hoped would be the first hammer blow on the locked doors of the future.

It has been widely assumed that the cycle of insurrections that began in Figols in January 1932 were organized and instigated by the FAI. "The first days of 1932," wrote Gerald Brenan, "saw a rising organized by the FAI in Catalonia."[1] Hugh Thomas also

---

1 Brenan, op.cit., p. 254.

confirms that these were "inspired by the FAI,"[2] as do Broué and Temime[3] and a number of other commentators.[4]

In fact, the rising had nothing whatsoever to do with the FAI. It began as an entirely spontaneous local affair directed against a local employer, but quickly mushroomed into a popular movement that threatened to engulf the whole of Catalonia and the rest of Spain. In spite of the assurances of the First Article of the Constitution that Spain was now a Workers' Republic, the wages and working conditions of the Catalan miners and textile workers had changed little with the Republic. In January, Juan Selvas, the deputy for Manresa, informed the Cortes that with two exceptions, the weaving and textile employers of his region had refused to comply with the nationally recommended minimum wage agreements, and workers in his constituency continued to be paid starvation wages.

The owner of the mines of Alto Llobregat was the powerful and autocratic Conde de Olano, a landlord who steadfastly refused his workers the right to organize public meetings or organize a union. Not only did the Count own the coal and potash mines, he ruled over them as a feudal lord and master. He set the minimal wages the workers received for working in virtually inhuman conditions, the prices they paid for their food in the company store, and the rent for the company houses. He wielded almost absolute power throughout the two valleys, including control of the Civil Guard.

Tension had been rising in the valleys for months. It finally came to a head in the early hours of 18 January in the remote mining camp of San Cornelio at the head of the Llobregat valley. That same morning the textile workers in nearby Berga had gone on strike over the refusal of the employers to comply with the Republic's labor legislation and the government had proved itself incapable of enforcing its own laws. Anarchist miners, acting on behalf of a local revolutionary committee, spread the news to the morning shift that the inhumane

---

2   Thomas, op.cit., p. 103.
3   Broue and Temime, op.cit., p. 56.
4   Miguel Iniguez claims that the Figols uprising was "the exclusive handiwork of the FAI." Juan Manuel Molina and Diego Abad de Santillán both argue in their memoirs that it would be more accurate to say it was organized by the Los Solidarios/Nosotros group "who were often indistinguishable from the FAI."

conditions, in which they had been forced to live and work for generations, had ended and Libertarian Communism had been proclaimed. Money, property, and the exploitation of man by man had been abolished. Armed workers quickly took over the key points of the town of Figols and seized the company store. The Civil Guard and the Somatent, the armed civilian corps, were disarmed without bloodshed, and informed that they had been relieved of responsibility for order in the area. The red and black flag of the CNT was run up on the church steeple and at the town hall. Not a shot had been fired, nor a blow exchanged. Neither the bourgeoisie nor their agents had been strung up, no priests had been hacked to death, no nuns raped, churches burned, or bars looted.

Within two days, the revolt had spread down the valley from Figols to the textile and weaving towns of Berga, Balsareny, and Salent into the neighboring Cardoner valley to Cardona, Suria, and Manresa. The Revolutionary Committee of Figols, having seized the opportunity and proclaimed Libertarian Communism, then turned to the National and Regional Committees of the CNT to support their example. These higher committees of the CNT, totally confounded by the revolutionary initiative of the Llobregat and Cardoner workers, were uncertain how to respond to what the miners had done. Confederal militants Vicente Pérez Combina, Arturo Parera, and Buenaventura Durruti were sent to Figols on a fact-finding mission and to speak to the workers. (Arturo Parera later confirmed that the FAI had not participated in the aborted movement "as an organization."[5]) In spite of their report and pressure from the local and district Federations, it took the National Committee six days before they finally decided to call a general solidarity strike, but by that time it was too late—the rising had been savagely crushed.[6]

These miners of Llobregat and Cardoner were not millenarians, madmen, or dreamers who heard "voices in the air" or "(distilled) their frenzy from some academic scribbler."[7] They were practical, hard-working men, who had come to

---

5   *El Luchador*, 10.6.1931.
6   Cristina Borderias, *La insurrección del Alto Llobregat Enero 1932. Un estudio de historia oral*, Masters' thesis, University of Barcelona, September 1977. Pedro Flores, "Ramón Vila Capdevila," *Ruta*, No 40, Caracas, 1980.
7   J. M. Keynes, *General Theory*, London, p. 383.

realize that if any qualitative change was too come about in their lives, it would only come about through a complete break with the past. To instinctive and natural revolutionaries such as these, ideas were irrelevant unless transformed into action. The abstract, theoretical, and subjective anarchism of people such as Pestaña and Peiró was of no consequence when their diffidence perpetuated the tyranny and violence of their miserable everyday lives under the intransigent Conde de Olano and his fellow mine owners and industrialists. They were fully aware that Libertarian Communism was not something that could be achieved overnight, or even planned. It was an aspiration, an ideal, which would require tremendous ongoing commitment, but they knew that if they managed to throw off the shackles of capitalism and the State now, progress towards that ideal could at least begin with some degree of assurance that the main obstacles to the free society—exploitation and coercive authority—would not hinder that progress. By their example, they hoped to provide the spark required to ignite similar hopes and aspirations among the rest of the Spanish working class.

The psychological mood of the Llobregat and Cardoner miners was not shared, however, by workers elsewhere in Spain. The moment of revolution had not yet come and the miners' unsupported challenge to the bourgeois and oligarchic order was brutally crushed after five days, by troops sent from Zaragoza, Lérida, Gerona, and Barbastro. CNT members were denounced by Catalan and Madrid politicians and journalists as "card-carrying bandits." The hysteria provoked by the bourgeois press did, however, provide the extremists of the center, the republican and socialist parties, with an opportunity to promote the reformists at the expense of the so-called "uncontrollables" within the Confederation. There were no trials for the arrested militants, all so-called *faistas* (no *treintistas* had been arrested). The Workers' Republic sought to avoid embarrassing public scrutiny of the intolerable conditions that had provoked the rising in the first place, and the excessive and selective repression with which it had been put down and the CNT activists criminalized. The authorities had used the opportunity to isolate the "conscious minority" from the mass of what they took to be the neutral, a-political mass of the CNT. Apart from the hundreds thrown into the prisons of Manresa and Barcelona, 110 confederal militants from Catalonia, Levante, and Andalucia, most of whom had not participated in the rising, were deported to the Spanish West African colonies. Among the deported were rank and file "uncontrollables" (*incontrolados*) such as Durruti, the Ascaso brothers, and Francisco Jover of the Los Solidarios/Nosotros group, and Ramón Vila Capdevila, the last of the rural guerrillas to be ambushed and killed in the Pyrenees in 1961.

Although the revolt failed to trigger a nationwide insurrection, the spontaneous action of the workers of Llobregat and Cardoner proved a heartening inspiration to many activists within the anarchist movement. It had proved, they felt, more effective, in emotional and practical terms, than all the written propaganda and revolutionary rhetoric of the previous sixty years. Alto Llobregat appears to have been read by the defense committees and activist core of the CNT as their cue from the workers that revolution was now a feasible option.

The belief that revolution was now finally "on the agenda" in the heady atmosphere that followed the January 1932 rising, provoked renewed interest in ideas as to how the free society might be organized. There was a spate of articles and pamphlets exploring the theory and formulating a program of Libertarian Communism. One of the most influential of these studies to appear that year, perhaps because it avoided detailed theorizing on economic and social planning, was "Apuntes sobre el comunismo libertario" by the Basque doctor and writer on preventive health care, naturalistic medicine, and sex education, Isaac Puente Amestoy. The FAI Peninsular Committee were so impressed with this title they commissioned Puente to draft a more detailed pamphlet on the concept of Libertarian Communism. This work, the influential *El Comunismo Libertario*, was published in Valencia in 1933 and republished in Barcelona in 1935 under the title *Finalidad de la CNT: el comunismo libertario*. It was to be Puente's ideas, rather than the more economic ideas of Diego Abad de Santillán, which provided the basis for the resolution on Libertarian Communism adopted by the CNT at the Zaragoza Congress in May 1936.

The *treintistas*, led by Pestaña, roundly condemned the Llobregat and Cardoner uprisings. This was read as an attempt to make political capital from the disaster at the expense of those who had died, been imprisoned, tortured and sent into exile. A split was now inevitable. In her famous article "¡Yo Acuso!," Federica Montseny publicly accused Emilio Mira, the Catalan Regional Secretary, of preventing the spread of a solidarity strike in support of the Llobregat workers in Barcelona to the rest of Catalonia. García Oliver accused Pestaña of circulating a letter to the regions informing each of them that the others supported a propaganda campaign against the deportations and not a social general strike as had been agreed by the National Committee.

Pestaña replied that the strike option was only to be used in an attempt to impose a dictatorship. The National Secretary's failure to endorse a solidarity strike in support of the imprisoned and deported comrades finally opened the floodgates that were to sweep him away. Demands for his resignation poured in from the rank and file led by the 200 CNT prisoners in Barcelona's Modelo Prison whose solidarity and trust, the cornerstones of the Confederation, he had betrayed.

Pestaña, his credibility and power base gone, was obliged to resign as National Secretary in March 1932. His place was taken by Manuel Rivas, a revolutionary anarchist and a member of the FAI.

The February deportations had exacerbated an atmosphere already stretched to breaking point by vicious repression. Pio Baroja, one of the best known novelists of the Generación del '98, said on 5 February in Villena:

"As far as repression and violence go, the months we have had of the Republic have produced more dead on the streets of our cities than forty years of the monarchy."[8]

The wave of revolutionary fever continued to gather momentum; general solidarity strikes were declared in Grenada and Valencia, while partial stoppages were organized in many other towns. Violent confrontations, including prison demonstrations, erupted all over the country. On 14 February, the anarchist groups of Tarrasa, an industrial town

---

8   Santillán, op.cit., p. 125.

near Barcelona, followed the example of Alto Llobregat and declared Libertarian Communism, occupying the town hall and laying siege to the police station and Civil Guard barracks. Similar actions took place in Andalucia, Zaragoza, and the Levante. In mid-March, peasants in Zaragoza, Puente Genil, and Ciudad 'Real began to seize the estates of the large landowners. The Republic had lost its legitimacy and was becoming ungovernable.

At the end of April, in the midst of a massive wave of strikes, inspired mostly by CNT unions, an important Regional Confederal Plenum was held in Sabadell, a small industrial town near Barcelona. Present were more than 300 delegates representing 250,000 workers. The tide of rank and file opinion was by now obviously running against the *treintistas* with their commitment to a totally discredited Republic. The throwing out of Pestaña and Arín, both signatories of the manifesto, from the National Committee the previous month had signalled the beginning of the end for the reformists within the CNT. With the election of Alejandro Gilabert, a member of the FAI, as Regional Secretary of the CNT in place of the *treintista* Mira, by the April Plenum, the last reformist stronghold in Catalonia collapsed.

The CNT unions in Sabadell were heavily influenced by the Pestañista faction. They had been used by them for some time in their political maneuvers to neutralize the anarchists within the unions. In a confidential report on the internal problems of the Spanish libertarian movement at this time, Alexander Schapiro, a member of the AIT Secretariat, noted:

"They wish to use the Sabadell Local Federation as a lever with which some day to topple the Regional Committee—and, if at all possible, the National Committee too, and to recapture the leadership of the CNT. Maybe the Sabadell comrades were unconscious of this ploy, but in effect, they became, albeit unwillingly, the instruments of revenge in the hands of the *treinta* movement."[9]

Matters finally came to a head in September when the Sabadell Local Federation, in a gambit aimed at pressuring the Catalan Regional Committee to summon a national conference

---

9 Schapiro, op.cit., pp. 33–38.

to condemn the revolutionary anarchist influence of the *faistas*, withheld payment of confederal subscriptions. The Regional Committee responded by declaring that, by refusing to pay their union dues, they were placing themselves outside the CNT. The entire Sabadell Local Federation was expelled on 24 September 1932 for defaulting on its basic obligation. A similar split occurred in Valencia where the local unions were opposed to join CNT-FAI involvement in the Prisoners' Aid Committee. They too withheld the confederal dues and were expelled by the Levante Regional Federation.

The breakaway unions, representing around 60,000 workers, formed what came to be known as the *sindicatos de oposición*, the "Opposition Unions," with their own Regional Committee, but they did hope and plan for eventual reconciliation with the Confederation. They initially enjoyed some strength in Catalonia, Levante, and Huelva, but this position weakened considerably when Pestaña left to form his Syndicalist Party at the end of 1933.

Another important development in mid-1932 had been the founding congress in Madrid of the Federación Ibérica de Juventudes Libertarias (FIJL). The FIJL had been set up with the specific intention of countering the influence of the PSOE's youth group Juventudes Socialistas Unificadas (JSU). Although many of its members belonged to the CNT and the FAI, it was an independent youth organization. It soon came to be regarded as the third force of the libertarian movement. In Catalonia, a traditionally independent area, there was opposition to the motion of a national youth group. They preferred instead to form an independent organization of individual groups and local federations, collectively known as the Juventudes Libertarias (JJ.LL.).

The position of the FIJL with regard to the *treintistas* was outlined in a statement published in the national CNT daily:

"It is no longer a question of tendencies—reformist or extremist—that separates us. Neither is it a form of procedure that varies within the confederal norms. What separates us irreconcilably is, more than our anarchist view of the union movement, a question of dignity and revolutionary sentiment. These ex-comrades have initiated a scissionist movement within the CNT, with the objective of creating a union movement for the support of the Esquerra de Catalunya and its counterparts in other regions."[10]

The final ignominy for Pestaña came with his expulsion from his own union, the metalworkers syndicate, by a majority of twelve branches to one against. Even his own section, the machinists, voted against him. In little more than a year the witch-hunt unleashed by the *treintistas* in August 1931 had ended by consuming its principal authors.[11]

Pestaña still refused to acknowledge the failure of the gradualist position within the CNT. In January 1933, he and his friends set up an organization inside the CNT called the Federación Sindicalista Libertaria (FSL) an organization recruited from among the CNT union members hostile to the revolutionary anarchist line represented by the FAI. It was immediately tied in with the Opposition Unions among whom, for a short time, it played the same role as they alleged the FAI did within the CNT. The First Secretary of the FSL was Ángel Pestaña. This was to be his last stop within the libertarian movement (until shortly before his death when he rejoined the CNT). Pestaña's place was taken by Juan López who, together with Joan Peiró, became the main theoreticians of the reformist body whose principal objective, following Pestaña's U-turn, became reunification with the CNT.

The collapse of the reformist offensive within the CNT by late 1932 signalled that the FAI had served the main purpose that had brought it to prominence. The CNT militants who had spoken in its name and adopted its slogans quickly merged back into the Confederal Defense Committees and everyday union activity. The active phase of the FAI as the defensive instrument of the CNT rank and file had come to an end. Instead of disbanding, however, or reverting to what it had been during the dictatorship—a loose-knit corresponding society of local anarchist groups—new people began to emerge who saw in the FAI a useful vehicle for addressing and influencing the mass audience provided by the CNT. The

---

10 *CNT*, Madrid, 2.6.1933.
11 Pestaña, a watchmaker by trade, had been a full-time paid official of the CNT for five years, during which time he had not worked at his trade. Perhaps this accounts for the oligarchical attitudes he had developed by the time of the Republic. See "La expulsion de Angel Pestaña," *Boletin de la CNT*, March 1933.

vacuum left by the anarchist rank and file began to be filled by maverick theoreticians and planners who believed inordinately in their own mechanical and abstract view of social processes. By early 1933, these people had begun to transform what had been a working class instrument concerned with practical considerations into an organic entity, with a life and will of its own, which indulged in abstract problems of a doctrinal or administrative nature. "There began to emerge," recalled Progreso Fernández, "a form that failed to convince many of us anarchists: a Peninsular Committee was set up which, contrary to our ideas, arrogated certain powers to itself."[12]

---

12 Bicicleta, op.cit.

16

Legitimacy Crisis

By 1932 it was clear to all sections of the population that liberal democracy was clearly not working the way it was supposed to. Dissatisfaction with government affected everyone, cutting across class and regional lines. The politicizing effect of the democratic surge that accompanied the Republic had led the people to make political demands on the State that could not be met. Disappointment was inevitable, and confidence in the Republic began to wither.

The year 1932 was dominated by uninterrupted agrarian and industrial unrest. Strikes and violent confrontations were a daily occurrence. The specter of revolution haunted the agrarian, industrial, and commercial bourgeoisie and the semi-feudal landed elite of Spain alike. On 29 May, a National Plenum of CNT Regionals had organized a successful nationwide day of protest against governmental repression and anti-CNT legislation such as the *jurados mixtos*. "The Law of Professional Associations," passed on 8 April, was seen as a further deliberately provocative attack by the government toward the CNT.

Although the press, including the Socialist press, referred constantly to anarchist unrest, the activism credited to FAI manipulation was, in fact, a reflection of the degree of working class militancy and the strength of popular feeling. In the rural areas, for example, it was not unknown for the landless workers to constitute themselves into a *Casa del Pueblo*, a cross between a Trades Council and a community center, and affiliate to every revolutionary organization they could think of—anarchist, socialist, and Communist. As Paul Preston notes:

"The essential harshness of conditions created a solidarity that rose above the rivalries of the various political factions."[1]

The semi-feudal and fundamentalist right, meanwhile, had recovered from the shock of the Republican victory the previous April. Fearing the bourgeois center would be unable to hold out much longer against an increasingly ungovernable working class in a revolutionary frame of mind, they began to plan the restoration of their political power. In August, General Sanjurjo, ex-director of the Civil Guard and commander of the *carabineros*—also an aristocrat—launched a military coup. The rebels were defeated in Madrid when they attempted to seize the Ministries of War and Communications. In Seville, Sanjurjo had greater success. In the face of widespread apathy and, in some cases, collusion on the part of the local authorities, the CNT called a general strike. Anarchist defense groups attacked and burned the meeting places of the big landowners, employers and rightists. Their quick response mobilized the population to defeat the rebellion and, paradoxically, to save the Republic.

As 1932 drew to a close, the social revolutionary objectives and anti-parliamentary principles of the biggest labor union in Spain appeared to express the mood of the Spanish working class. Durruti, recently released from prison for his part in the Figols uprising, addressed a mass audience at a meeting to launch a FAI propaganda campaign at the Palace of Fine Arts in Barcelona on 1 December 1932:

"Your presence at this meeting and my presence on this platform show the bourgeoisie and government clearly that the CNT and FAI are forces that increase with repression and grow in adversity... The Republican Socialist government thought that, by deporting a hundred or more workers, the CNT would knuckle under. Acting as it did, it showed, once again, its ignorance of social reality and the reason for the existence of anarchism. The bourgeois press has applauded the government's move, the deportations, thinking that once the leaders were exiled, the sheep would go back to the sheep fold. In other words, 'the dog killed, the rabies would

1   Paul Preston, *The Coming of the Spanish Civil War*, London, 1978, p. 61.
Grandizo Munis, *Jalones de Derrota: promesa de victoria*, Mexico, 1948, p. 74.

disappear.' The bourgeois scribblers were mistaken, just like the government itself... the Spanish working class is not a herd of sheep offering their necks so that a yoke can be placed upon them.

"Such dreadful things have been said about me, as well as about my comrades in deportation, believing that I would be discredited, but the effect was entirely the opposite... To fight us they have used the worst weapons. The theory of the 'leaders' of the CNT is identical to the 'scoundrels' of the FAI...

"Those whom the bourgeoisie call 'leaders' are workers whom all the world knows, and their way of life is identical with that of every unfortunate worker. The way they differ is that they have the courage to choose the worst position in the struggle, to be in the front line to stop a bullet or fill the prisons. The real bandits, the real scoundrels, are the politicians who need to fool the workers and put them to sleep, while promising them a month of Sundays so as to wrest their votes from them, which will bring them to the Cortes and will permit them to live like parasites on the sweat of the workers...

"For the government, it was a political error to exile us, for they paid for our trip to the Canaries so that we could make anarchist propaganda...

"Another argument used against us is that we are in the pay of the monarchists, that we play the game of reaction by fighting the Republic. The attitude of the CNT in Seville shows that this argument is also lame. It is the second time that the CNT has saved the life of the Republic. But the Republicans should not fool themselves. Sanjurjo said that 'the anarchists will not succeed,' and the anarchists did succeed, and Sanjurjo had to 'bite the dust.' Let the Republicans take notice: the CNT said no to Sanjurjo, but it says no also to the Republic.[2]

"The Republican Socialists should know that they must either resolve the social problem or else it will be the people who will do it. We think that the Republic cannot resolve it. Also, we say clearly to the working class, that there is now only one dilemma: whether to die like modern-day slaves, or to live like admirable men, on the straight path of social revolution.

---

2 The CNT and FAI defense groups in Seville had played a prominent part in defeating the Sanjurjo rising on 12 August 1932. The Defense Committee had formed a Revolutionary Committee, which called the people out on to the streets and routed the insurgents.

"You then, workers who are listening to me, know what to expect. The change in the course of your lives depends on you."[3]

Durruti's impassioned speech was well received. The Republic, lacking any real power base in the country, faced an impossible task; it had failed completely to live up to the expectations of the Spanish working classes. It was clearly unable, or unwilling, in the face of resolute opposition from the still unchallenged and powerful landed interest, to implement the long hoped-for agrarian reforms that would bring Spain into the modern age.

By October 1932, CNT membership had jumped, in one year, from 800,000 to over a million. Many of these had been recruited from among the increasingly disillusioned members of the UGT rank and file. Draconian repression and the anti anarcho-syndicalist legislation of the Socialists and Republicans, coupled with the hostility and constant harassment and intimidation of the newly created Generalitat government of Catalonia, left the CNT with few options. Two solutions presented themselves—the anarcho-syndicalist one, with its emphasis on building up the organization in the hope that working class pressure would end the persecution and open the doors to an increasingly more rational and just society, or the "cavalry charge" option with its strategy of constant direct frontal attacks aimed at weakening the system, educating the people, and building a revolutionary self-confidence, which would one day allow them to throw off the shackles of state and property and begin to build a more just society.

Spurred on by the explosive atmosphere and the heady revolutionary consciousness, which had built up steadily since the Alto Llobregat rising at the beginning of the year, the joint CNT-FAI Defense Cadres (*Cuadros de Defensa*), under the national and local defense committees, prepared to launch a coordinated national revolutionary insurrection. It was the only viable option in the face of the continuing provocations of the Madrid and Catalan governments. Both governments had adopted the elitist, *Pestañista*, line that the CNT was simply a pawn in the hands of the FAI, and had, since early in the year, systematically attempted to break anarchist influence in the

3 *Solidaridad Obrera*, 3.12.1939.

CNT. Confederal newspapers had been suspended, preventive detention introduced while CNT militants were being beaten up and tortured in the secret detention centers operated by the Esquerra.

The rising was scheduled to take place on 8 January 1933, almost exactly a year after the first rising in Alto Llobregat.[4] A nationwide general strike of railway workers was to provide the backdrop for the planned insurrection. Paralysis of the rail network would, it was hoped, cause maximum economic disruption and limit the government's ability to move troops to cope with the concerted risings in widely dispersed urban and rural areas.

But, when members of the Catalan Regional Defense Committee of the CNT met to finalize the arrangements for the rising with the CNT's National Committee, they were surprised to find that this body, at the last moment, wanted the insurrection called off. The Catalans refused to call it off and insisted on going ahead as planned.

One of the keys to the confusion, and disaster that followed, was the overlapping memberships of the main protagonists in the relevant committees. Manuel Rivas, both National Secretary of the CNT and Secretary of the National Defense Committee, disagreed with the Catalan Regional Defense Committee's optimistic assessment of the situation. But his revolutionary and personal loyalties outweighed his critical judgement and he agreed to cooperate—in the belief the Catalan Defense Committee was acting in the name of the Regional Committee of the CNT.

The Catalan Regional Defense Committee, however, was acting on its own initiative. Rivas' role was to advise all the regional organizations, in accordance with a CNT National Committee circular of 29 December, that Barcelona had risen in revolt and they were to follow suit.[5]

The Catalan Regional Defense Committee consisted, primarily, of members of the Nosotros group, Durruti, Oliver

4 Peirats says there existed a "sort of super FAI, which spoke in the name of the peninsular organization, but neither belonged to it nor was answerable to it. When I say that there was another FAI above those of us who were its official representatives I am referring to Ascaso and Durruti, and in particular to García Oliver, the real Robespierre of the revolution." Letter to Juan Gómez Casas. *La FAI*, op.cit. See also letter to Frank Mintz, op.cit.
5 Schapiro, op.cit., p.8.

and Ascaso. Durruti, representing the CNT's National Defense Committee, had travelled to Andalucia at the beginning of the year to take part in a CNT conference and to coordinate plans for the revolt. Everything hinged on Barcelona. If the movement failed there, the whole thing was to be aborted.

The premature explosion of two bombs close to the central police headquarters in Barcelona forced the insurgents' hand. Joint CNT and FAI Defense Cadres attacked a number of barracks in the Catalan capital, but the authorities had been fully informed of the insurrectionary plans and were waiting for them to make their move. What had been intended as a surprise operation turned into a well-prepared trap. On the morning of 8 January, Premier Azaña noted in his diary:

"At 11 AM this morning, Casares [Quiroga, Minister of the Interior] telephoned me that according to all indications, the anarchist movement that we were waiting for would be launched today, late in the afternoon. Their plans are to assault the military barracks at Barcelona, Zaragoza, Seville, Bilbao, and other points. Something is also expected in Madrid, but of less importance. I am sending instructions to divisional generals."[6]

The railway workers, most of whom belonged to the UGT, failed to come out on strike. Their national union leaders had sided with the UGT executive. The Catalan leaders of the rebellion, including García Oliver and Gregorio Jover, were arrested in the opening stages. By noon, the insurrection in Barcelona had been crushed. Neither the soldiers in the barracks, nor the populace at large, responded to the call to revolution.

In the meantime, however, Manuel Rivas, in his capacity as Secretary of the National Defense Committee, had telegraphed the other Regional Committees informing them that Catalonia had risen. Although he signed the telegram in his name only—not as National Secretary of the CNT—it was assumed that the information came in the name of the National Committee, not the National Defense Committee. On receipt of this telegram, the Levante and Andalucia Regional Committees instructed

6 "Papeles ineditos de Azaña," 8.1.1933. Quoted by Joaquín Arraras, *Historia de la Segunda Republica Española*, Madrid, 1964, Vol. II, p. 79. See also Peirats' *Anarchists in the Spanish Revolution*, Toronto, 1977, p. 98.

their affiliates to follow suit. The anarchist-oriented paper, *La Tierra*, also carried premature reports that day that the insurrection was spreading quickly throughout the peninsula, and that a general strike was in progress. Before the mistake could be rectified, the local defense groups in a number of districts had begun to move into action to declare Libertarian Communism.

In the Catalan town of Ripollet, the anarchists seized the town hall; unfurled the red and black flag of the CNT; proclaimed universal fraternity; the abolition of money, private property, and the exploitation of man by man. They then proceeded to burn all the legal archives, especially property deeds, in the main square. Libertarian Communism was also declared in Valencia and Lérida, as well as the villages of Ribarroja, Betera, Pendralba, and Bugarra. These isolated local movements were soon quashed by the prompt arrival of reinforcements from surrounding areas. In Andalucia, events led to what was to become an infamous incident in the impoverished township of Casas Viejas.

On the morning of 11 January, unaware that the rising had been crushed elsewhere throughout the peninsula, representatives of the local FAI group, Libertarian Youth organization, and CNT *sindicato* called on the mayor of the small town of Casas Viejas to inform him that Libertarian Communism had been declared and that his services as a functionary of the State were no longer required.[7] Given the distorted interpretations of the Casas Viejas rising, it is important to stress that it should be seen in the context of an organized nationwide uprising and not the spontaneous action of a small isolated group of local enthusiasts staging a declaration of "village independence characteristic of the millenarian tradition of rural anarchism."[8] The full tragedy of

---

7   According to the FAI paper *Tierra y Libertad*, the influence of the FAI in Medina Sidonia was "decisive;" with fourteen groups in the area, it rivalled the CNT. *Tierra y Libertad*, 11.3.1932.
8   Carr, *Spain*, op.cit., p. 625. Eric Hobsbawm, in support of his thesis that Spanish anarchism was "millenarian" and lacked "organization, strategy, tactics, and patience" implies that the Casas Viejas rising, the example from which his "millenarian" conclusions are drawn, was called on the orders of *Seisdedos*, who exercised "ascendancy over the masses." *Primitive Rebels*, Manchester, 1978, p. 79–92.

what followed was recorded by Eduardo de Guzmán, anarchist editor of *La Tierra*:

"For a number of hours, the workers were masters of the village and Libertarian Communism was declared. From 7AM until 4PM, they had reason to believe that the revolution throughout Spain had been successful. The red and black flag fluttered in the breeze; armed peasants were in control of the situation. During those fleeting hours of victory it never occurred to the workers to wreak vengeance on anyone, destroy anything or molest anyone who may, possibly, have been their enemies. There were several *caciques* (political bosses) in the village, along with their families. No one was molested nor were any demands made of any of them; all were treated with respect. The same applied to the few shops, as well as the church and its priest. Libertarian Communism began, as in every other village in which it had been proclaimed to date, without violence of any sort, without any murder, robbery, or rape, everyone being left completely at liberty. The sole intention of the people was to disarm those who might have been obstacles to the consolidation of a successful revolution. Thus did the peasants of Casas Viejas behave. Despite their lack of learning and the hunger gnawing in their bellies... (Not that this was to prevent some dolt of a señorito in Medina some days later to speak of some fantastic sharing out of the women which the revolutionaries apparently intended.)"[9]

Eduardo de Guzmán's account of the subsequent cold-blooded slaughter of the peasants of Casas Viejas caused a sensation that cracked the foundations of the Azaña government. At dawn, when Seisdedos' shack had been razed to the ground and the bodies of the old man, his six children, and grandson consumed by fire, Republican troops swept through the town arresting everyone they could lay their hands on. The prisoners were then marched to the smouldering embers where the Seisdedos family had died, where the officer in charge, Captain Rojas, ordered them shot in cold blood. The final death toll was twenty-two prisoners dead, three guards killed, and perhaps four wounded. President Azaña, the alleged author of the order, "No wounded, no prisoners; shoot

---

9   Peirats, *La CNT*, op.cit., Vol. I. Ch. 3.

them in the guts," dismissed the allegations of cold-blooded murder by the Republican troops as a "fairy tale."[10]

In an article in *La Voz Confederal*, an underground CNT paper, Durruti gave his assessment of the reasons for the failure of the January insurrection:

"Certainly conditions were not ripe. If they had been we would not be in prison! But it is equally certain that we are living in a pre-revolutionary period and that we cannot permit the bourgeoisie to dominate it by strengthening the power of the state. In the same manner, we must prevent the state from strengthening itself by tacking over the unions, which is the political ambition of the Socialists and of some of our former comrades.

"It is with this perspective that we must interpret the revolutionary attempt of 8 January. We never believed that the revolution consisted of the seizure of power by a minority who would impose a dictatorship on the people. Our revolutionary conscience is opposed to this tactic. We want a revolution by and for the people. Without this idea no revolution is possible. It would be a *coup d'état*, nothing more. And we, from the factories, the mines, and the country, are seeking to develop an effective social revolution. There is nothing in this of Blanquism or Trotskyism, but the clear and precise idea that the revolution is something that we must work for every day. With this unknown quantity one can never be certain when it will break out."[11]

Faced with the absolute disaster, the National and Regional Committees of the CNT refused to accept official responsibility for the ill-fated January rising.[12] While comrades were still

---

10 Manuel Azaña, *Obras Completas*, Mexico, 1966, Vol. II, pp. 540–541. (Cortes, session of 2 February, 1933).
11 Paz, op.cit., p. 137.
12 The FAI delegate at the May 1936 Zaragoza Congress of the CNT set the official record straight as to the role of the anarchist organization during the events of January 1933: "We fell in for a revolt prepared by the CNT. And we had to look on even as the Confederation's mouthpiece disowned us... Not that we are complaining. We know that the labor organizations, whenever they get involved in the process of revolution, necessarily fall into contradictions. And contradiction is not the same as betrayal... To backpedal was impossible. There was ongoing pressure from every quarter in our movement. Anything which did not suit the current whipped up by

fighting in the streets and villages of Levante and Andalucia the Madrid paper, *CNT* was busy denying all responsibility for the events then taking place. Its headline of 9 January affirmed "This is not our revolution. Is it a trap being prepared for us?"

The following day, *Solidaridad Obrera* stated its somewhat equivocal position:

"We cannot condemn the movement of Sunday. On the other hand, we cannot accept it as an act of the Confederación Nacional del Trabajo, because the organization was not aware of events."

In spite of the fact that the rising had been planned and coordinated throughout by the National Defense Committee of the CNT and triggered by the Catalan Defense Committee, with the FAI playing no organizational role whatsoever, the Peninsular Committee of the FAI suddenly stepped in to claim full responsibility. It was undoubtedly a propagandist gesture aimed at deflecting the inevitable government repression from the open union organization. It was, however, no more than a gesture; as an unregistered, therefore illegal, ad hoc association with no hierarchical chain of command or responsibility before the law, there was little likelihood or possibility even of the authorities acting on this statement.

In a statement of 11 February 1933, entitled *La FAI al Pueblo*, the Peninsular Committee of the FAI declared:

"We say loud and clear, we affirm it absolutely, that we take full responsibility for all that occurred on the eighth and on the following as a violent protest against arbitrary acts. We are sick and tired of so much governmental crime. It is natural

---

revolutionary zeal became suspect. One has to know what it means to order a retreat, as was the intention upon learning that the railmen would not be striking." The FAI delegate's statement concluded: "So the CNT does not acknowledge January? And the FAI does? The revolt was the CNT's. The defense cadres are the CNT's. And the order was handed down to them by the Confederation." (Minutes of the Zaragoza Congress.) According to Juan Gómez Casas, the FAI had apparently been approached beforehand, but had insisted on two preconditions before committing itself to supporting the revolt. First, that five or six guerilla fronts be opened up on a national basis to support the diversionary revolts in the villages. Second, to increase confederal dues to finance the purchase of the material wherewithal for the revolt.

that we should appeal to methods that will make us heard, and reasonable that we should not cease until the insults, the sarcasm, the jeers, and the violent acts against anguished and hungry people are ended.

"We want all the responsibility for ourselves, since we have not asked for the collaboration of anyone or the support of the working people, or even the CNT; and we did not advise our best friends of what we intended to carry out; and we will continue this course in the future, in order to be the only ones with the responsibility that derives from an attitude of straightforward rebellion and protest.

"We know the tactics of the enemy from experience, and, for that reason, we have preferred not to call on the organized workers to second and maintain the protest. We are ourselves strong enough to act on our own, assuming all responsibility.

"The social revolution will take place soon. We have the sympathy of the revolutionary people and the indestructible weapon of reason. Let government oppressors and their accomplices tremble. Forward comrades! Everyone at his post, and wait for the moment. On the red and black banner we have written the words 'Love and Justice.' We are invincible. Long live the free workers of the town and country. Long live Libertarian Communism! Long live the Federación Anarquista Ibérica!"[13]

José Peirats' view of the revolutionary movements of 1932 and 1933 was more critical:

"From a strategic point of view they were catastrophic. There was no plan, or it was deficient. We lacked the means for serious fighting and we limited ourselves to attacking in the populated areas. When we lost these, there were not plans for a rural guerilla campaign. With the exception of Andalucia, we lacked a true peasant organization. We had made enemies of the petite bourgeoisie whom we had terrified with the lack of psychology in our propaganda. Furthermore, many of those who fought for Libertarian Communism did not believe it could be implemented by a simple audacious coup in cold

---

13 *CNT*, 11.2.1933.

blood and at a given time. Many of us took to the streets out of self love, not from conviction."[14]

As to FAI involvement in the risings, José Peirats, Secretary of the Barcelona Local Federation of Anarchist Groups at the time, recalls that, following the January 1933 rising, his Federation asked the Nosotros group to attend a clandestine meeting on Mount Horta to explain their conduct. "García Oliver, Aurelio Fernández, and I can't remember who else attended the meeting. They claimed that, although they did not belong to the organization, they had decided to come along out of deference, nothing else." He added: "In my capacity as Secretary General of the Barcelona groups until the middle of 1934, I am in a position to assure you that neither Durruti nor García Oliver belonged to the specific organization."[15]

The gratuitous violence of the repression that followed the January 1933 rising, fuelled a massive anti-governmental propaganda campaign, which politicians of both left and right exploited to the full. With the government forced into assuming increasingly defensive postures against the combined pressure of the agrarian and industrial power elites, the credibility of the Socialist Party as a party of government and the parliamentary representative of the organized working class slipped even further.

---

14 El movimiento libertario, op.cit.
15 Letter from Peirats to Frank Mintz, 7.6.1985.

17

The Road to 1936

As the world crisis bit deeper into the economy, with unemployment affecting almost every working class family, Spanish workers became increasingly more radicalized. Industrial Barcelona was particularly badly affected. The number of armed robberies and petty theft in the city escalated. In response to this crime wave, which was laid at the door of the anarchists by the bourgeois press, the FAI launched a counter-propaganda campaign to convince the workers that individual solutions were not the answer to their problems. Collective action and the revolutionary general strike were emphasized as the only enduring solutions to exploitation and injustice. Coming from such legendary "expropriators" as Durruti, Ascaso, Oliver, etc.—all of whom had abandoned their underground lives and were now respected and dedicated union and community activists—there could be no confusion in the thinking public's mind that "banditry" had anything to do with the revolutionary practices of anarchism.

Within the Cortes, the political climate was equally tense. The heart of the problem lay in the inherent contradictions and irreconcilable differences between the two contending power blocs. The extremists of the right, the old agrarian based elites, were represented by the Partido Agrario, the party of the Castilian landowners, led by the pro-monarchist Martínez de Velasco, and the Confederación Española de Derechas Autonomas (CEDA), the Catholic party led by Salamanca lawyer José María Gil Robles. These two parties, between them, represented the landed oligarchs and theocrats, who had controlled Spain for centuries and who continued to maintain a tight grip on the economic and social life of the country under the Republic.

Opposing them were the extremists of the center, the agrarian, commercial, and industrial bourgeoisie, who gravitated towards Alejandro Lerroux's Partido Republicano Radical. Both sides saw the struggle for political power in zero-sum terms. The legislative gains of one side meant possibly irreversible material damage to the class interests of the other. The right, for example, saw liberal agrarian reform, the eight-hour day, and curbs on the power of the Church as much as a threat to the foundations of their society—property, privilege, religion, and tradition—as social revolution. They responded to it with all the powerful resources at their disposal as a crusade to reassert the "traditional" values of pre-Republican Spain. The forces of the *ancien régime* aimed to maneuver the socialists and the ascending bourgeois liberal democrats out of government, and to clear the few tentative reforms that they had been able to introduce from the statute book, particularly the irksome law on municipal boundaries.

Durruti and Ascaso, "the terrible *faistas*," who had been in hiding since the January uprising, were finally arrested in April 1933. That same month, Ángel Pestaña formally announced the formation of his Syndicalist Party. Dr José Dencàs, the Councillor for Public Order in the Catalan government, the Generalitat, and his police chief, Miguel Badia, issued a joint statement announcing that the FAI was now "completely in shambles."

From the early summer of 1933, the political pendulum in Spain began to swing to the right. Fascist and rightist provocations increased in direct proportion to the threat to the property, position, and privileges of the landed oligarchy. An assault by young fascist Jonsistas (Juntas de Ofensiva Nacional Sindicalista) on the offices of the Friends of the Soviet Union was blamed on the anarchists. The government seized on this as a convenient pretext to round up a number of anarchists.

A governmental crisis in September 1933 had brought Alejandro Lerroux to power. His cabinet consisted of Radicals, Left Republicans, and Radical Socialists, but no members of the PSOE. Not only had the Socialists been squeezed out of government, the UGT were losing an increasing number of members to the CNT. Largo Caballero's Socialist Party response to the wave of organized working militancy was to adopt, not only the rhetoric, but the apparent tactics of revolution.

The Socialists, too, had come to realize that there was nothing more to be gained by collaborating with a hesitant and weak Republican bourgeoisie who, afraid of the masses, were too frightened to challenge the economic power base of the still-powerful landed elite. Early in October, Socialist leader Indalecio Prieto declared to the Cortes that the Socialists renounced all further compromise with the Republicans, and affirmed there was to be no further collaboration between them and future Republican governments of any persuasion.

Lerroux's premiership was short-lived. Diego Martínez Barrio, the interim premier, dissolved the Cortes. New elections were announced for November.

By the end of 1933, the Republic had lost all legitimacy in the eyes of both the workers and the agrarian, commercial, clerical, and military elite. Historian, Victor Alba wrote:

"The 18 months of the Republican administration, the provocations of the right and the dithering of the left led to the deaths of 400 persons, of whom 20 belonged to the forces of law and order—3,000 persons were recorded as wounded, 9,000 arrests were made, 160 persons were deported; there were 30 general strikes and 3,600 partial stoppages; 161 newspapers were suspended, of which four belonged to the right."[1]

It was in this charged atmosphere that the FAI met in a National Plenum in Madrid in October 1933. Present were 21 delegates representing 569 groups and 4,839 members. In its report to the National Plenum, the Peninsular Committee admitted that the FAI had borne the responsibility for the uprising the previous January simply to spare the CNT the brunt of the repression.

In spite of the fact that an estimated 9,000 anarchist and CNT activists were in prison at this time, the FAI had registered a growth in membership. However, even at this, its pre-1937

---

1   Victor Alba, *Histoire des republiques espagnoles*, Vincennes, 1948, p. 257.

peak, with an estimated 5,500 affiliates, the FAI still represented a relatively small section of the Spanish anarchist movement.[2]

The Plenum agreed that the CNT should continue to be influenced along anarchist lines and retain the *trabazón*. It also agreed to step up the pressure on the deteriorating capitalist economy, and to recommend abstention in the forthcoming elections. Other resolutions included greater anti-militarist activity, building up the anarchist press, and moving the Peninsular Committee to Zaragoza.

Perhaps the most important resolution agreed at the FAI plenum was the decision to oppose further support for the brutal bourgeois Republic through the ballot box, and, instead, issue a call for social revolution. Item No. 5 on the Agenda read:

"[Thus] this working party's understanding is that we must direct our action to undermining the foundations of the capitalist economy by hindering its development in all its manifestations and by precipitating its ruination…

"The anarchist groups of the FAI will devote their best efforts to contriving the decomposition of capitalism and thus to an ongoing revolutionary backlash against any fascist venture by the political parties, without distinction. The groups shall be on a war footing for the struggle against native and international fascism, hatched by the mad determination of the parties to match the ultimate requirements of capitalism. Any possible unleashing of the reaction must be met with by our people's committing themselves to the social revolution."

Catalonia added to the resolution that:

---

2 If the written support of Levante and Asturias is included, there were 632 groups representing 5,334 individuals (8.43 members per group). Neither the North, nor the Canaries were represented. In an article appealing for more members, José Benet wrote: "At the moment, there are many anarchists who do not work within the FAI, directly or indirectly. We remind all of these of the need to form groups and affiliate to the FAI." "Una llamada urgente," *Tierra y Libertad*, 8.8.1933. Figures for the FAI have been grossly exaggerated. David Miller, a writer on anarchism, puts the membership from 1930 onwards at about "10,000 militant anarchists," who exercised "hegemony over the union" (*Anarchism*, London, 1984, p. 137). Brenan also puts the figure at "around 10,000" (op.cit., p.184, N.2), while Woodcock claims a 1936 membership of 30,000 jumping to 150,000 in 1937 (op.cit., p. 363). Hugh Thomas gives a 1936 figure of 160,000, "much the same" as the Socialist Party (op.cit., p. 523).

"We cannot remain silent in the face of the present threat. As an ideological principle we should recommend abstention. In the event of a possible reactionary victory, we should hurl ourselves into revolution without delay."[3]

The Local CNT Federation of Barcelona supported the *faista* position wholeheartedly. The following statement appeared in *Solidaridad Obrera* at the end of October:

"If, as a result of our anti-electoral campaign…the reaction attempts to establish itself in power in Spain, the revolutionary workers of the CNT will have sufficient grace, courage, and honour to place themselves in the forefront of the struggle and destroy the reaction, employing all the violent means and arms necessary."[4]

The previous day, at a National Plenum of CNT Regional in Madrid, it was unanimously agreed that the organization would be put on a war footing in the event of a rightist victory in the elections.

In keeping with the anti-electoral decisions of the FAI National Plenum and the CNT Plenum of Regionals', decisions clearly influenced by the relentless and vicious anti-anarchist mentality and policies of the party political left, the anarchists embarked on a massive anti-voting campaign in the run up to the elections of 19 November 1933.

"Don't Vote!" urged the slogans and posters that covered the walls of all major cities, "because that banal act spells the ritualization of your slavery."

Similar slogans were repeated at public meetings and in the pages of the anarchist press up and down the country.

The decision not to vote was not merely a declaration of war on the leadership of a hidebound Socialist Party and the bourgeois republicans who, during thirty months in power, had relentlessly attempted to limit and roll back the hopes and aspirations of the dispossessed people of Spain.

The anarchists saw their duties as revolutionaries as being to analyze and advise the workers as to the possible consequences of their voting. Tied to a strategy of social revolution the anti-voting campaign was not just a self-indulgent exercise in

3   *Memoria del pleno nacional de regionales de la FAI*, Barcelona, 1933, p. 12.
4   *Solidaridad Obrera*, 31.10.1933.

abstract principles—it became a constructive act of affirmation in the future, and a revolutionary statement of intent.

The campaign culminated on 16 November with a mass meeting at the Palace of Fine Arts in Barcelona. A packed auditorium was addressed by speakers from both the FAI and CNT, including Domingo Germinal, Valerio Oroban Fernández, Secretary of the Asociación Internacional de Trabajadores (AIT) and one of the few CNT leaders who did not belong to the FAI, and Buenaventura Durruti. The slogan was "Social revolution rather than the ballot box."

Durruti wound up the meeting by saying:

"Workers, the storms are approaching. To prepare for all emergencies, the FAI advises the workers of the CNT, since it is they who control the factories and the production sites, not to abandon them. They should stay close to the machines. Let us start to set up workers' councils and use the techniques which should be basic to the new social and libertarian economy.

"The anarchists, as always, will do their duty by being the first to throw themselves into the struggle. The occupation of the factories in Italy should be a lesson to us. They should spread constantly outwards, for, like all insurrections, they must be on the offensive. To be on the defensive always means death to any uprising, so the seizure of the factories without cooperation from outside means death through isolation. The workers have nothing more to lose than their chains. Long live the social revolution."[5]

---

5   *Solidaridad Obrera*, 17.11.1933.

18

December 1933—
Millenarians or "Conscious
Militants?"

Inevitably, the right won the elections. With an abstention rate of 32 per cent in Spain as a whole, and 40 per cent in Catalonia, the authoritarian left, with an estimated loss of 1.5 million votes, was roundly defeated.[1] The Socialists took just 60 seats against 116 in 1931. With the right victorious, it was now the turn of the Socialists to be on the receiving end of some of the repression they had been party to, as members of the previous administration. On 3 December, the Minister of the Interior declared a state of emergency. For the anarchists, the *bienio negro*— the "Black Biennium," as the repressive period that was to follow was dubbed—was merely a continuation of the repression that began in the summer of 1931.

The "victorious" abstentionism of the CNT in the November 1933 elections should not be viewed as a mere passive and empty gesture. For the anarchists, it was a necessary precondition for the insurrection that was to follow. Having committed themselves to social revolution as the only means of cutting the Gordian knot of liberal democracy, the activists of the CNT and FAI had no intention of reneging on that promise. Within days of the rightist parliamentary victory, the National Defense Committee appointed a revolutionary committee to plan and coordinate the uprising. Its members were Joaquín Ascaso, Durruti (according to Oliver, he joined the committee against the views of the rest of the Nosotros group), Cipriano Mera,

---

1 Paz, op.cit., p. 147.

García Chacon, Casado Ojeda, Moises and Jesús Alcrudo, Antonio Ejarque, Felipe Orquin, Ramón Andres, and Dr Isaac Puente, the author of *Libertarian Communism*. Zaragoza was chosen as the base of the National Defense Committee because of its proximity to the CNT National Committee. The date of the rising was fixed for 8 December 1933, the day scheduled for the official opening of the rightist-dominated Cortes.

The uprising was presaged by a spectacular mass escape of fifty-eight CNT prisoners from Barcelona's Modelo prison. General strikes were declared in Zaragoza, Barcelona, Huesca, Valencia, Seville, Córdoba, Granada, Badajoz, Gijón, and Logroño. Libertarian Communism was declared in a number of towns and villages, particularly among the vine-growing villages that dotted the banks of the river Ebro in Aragón and Rioja. Interestingly enough, the majority of the anarchist militants who took part in the rising in the Ebro villages were smallholders, ploughmen, share-croppers, and small tenant farmers, fact which lends weight to the theory that these men and women were moved by revolutionary, rather than purely economic, motives.[2] Significantly, the uprising drew little support in Catalonia, Levante, and Andalucia, regions that had borne the brunt of the repression following the earlier January rising, and whose most reliable and committed militants were in jail.

In the Socialist dominated areas, such as the Asturias and Bilbao, the strikes were partial and sporadic. The failure of the Socialists to respond favorably, the apathy of the broad mass of people, and the demoralizing intervention by the conscript army, meant the rising was doomed from the start. In Barcelona, where most of the leaders had been arrested even before the rising had been launched, fighting was limited to a short exchange of gunfire in a few working class areas. It was, as indicated above, mainly in Rioja, Aragón, and Navarre that the rising proved successful. In Zaragoza, for example, the revolutionaries managed to hold out for seven days before the police and the army were able to recapture the city. When the struggle finally collapsed on 15 December, the final toll was estimated by José Peirats at 87 dead, countless wounded, and 700 who received long prison sentences.

2   *Cuadernos para una enciclopedia*, No. 36, September 1935.

Writing from his prison cell, the Basque Doctor, Isaac Puente, one of the organizers of the rising, reflected on the various factors that contributed to the failure of the insurrection:

"The episode took place during a freeze, against a background of inclement weather, which marshalled all the rigors of cold, rain, and snow against the undertaking. The Confederation's entire anarchist leaven, its vital and active element, deployed to unleash this revolutionary act, in order to galvanize into action the timorous, passive element of the CNT, which mobilized only in some villages. The people, broken by an inheritance of fear and conformist education, did not let themselves be caught up in the revolutionary zeal that moved the "heralds," whose impatience and faith speak of society's urge for renewal. Due to a variety of adverse circumstances, backing which had been counted on failed to materialize and, as a logical consequence of this, the revolt was unable to spread beyond the scale it had attained on day one."

The secretariat of the international anarcho-syndicalist organization, the IWMA (AIT), delivered their judgement in true *esprit de l'escalier.*

"Passive abstentionism in countries where such abstentions may completely invalidate the elections, is a futile gesture unless it carries within it 'dynamic seeds.' The 'victorious' CNT abstentionism of November 1933 was really a 'defeat' for the CNT, because of its failed insurrection of December that same year. If that insurrection missed its mark in certain respects, it was because the CNT, during its phase of abstentionism which was, on the surface, successful...and probably before then, too...failed to concern itself with the immediate follow-up to that victory. Thus the futility of passive abstentionism was merely exacerbated by the pointless victory, for lack of preparation of events which ought to have invested it with a certain actuality. In France, where the aware abstentionism of the revolutionary masses can have no influence beyond propagation of our ideas, and no impact upon the outcome of the general elections, "passive" abstentionism today is inconsequential. It serves only as a declaration of principles that, sooner of later, will have to be implemented on bases researched and prepared in advance.

"In Spain, that groundwork ought to have been in place. Every suitable opportunity ought to be seized for the purpose of steering our struggles along the lines of 'revolutionary direct action.' In the struggle against fascism and the State, a general expropriatory strike can and should be the overture to such action. A successful abstentionism, which leaves the State and its apparatus in a delicate position—and such was the case in November 1933—can and should also be the overture to such action, unless one wishes to squander the dynamic effect of a passive success as borne within that fact."[3]

---

3   Ibid., Vol. I. Ch. 6.

19

The "Planners" Move In

By early 1934, with most of the revolutionary anarchists in jail or in hiding, the changes which had begun to take place in the FAI since the previous year became more noticeable, both structurally and in membership. From being the "cutting edge" of the CNT rank and file, it became the seedbed for a new breed of bohemian intellectuals, administrators, and publicists. There was a clear shift towards centralization and greater emphasis on turning the FAI into an organizational "center of excellence," which would "sharpen the weapons of revolution."[1] De Santillán, one of those maverick intellectuals who had joined the FAI in mid-1933 on his return from Argentina, was the principal architect of this shift away from what he described as "resistance to capitalism" to "revolutionary preparation." "The emphasis now should be on attack, rather than defense, and that attack implies a better disposition of our forces. For, in the economic sphere, output and consumption cannot be interrupted, lest the revolution itself makes itself odious and be forced to reply solely upon new dictatorships. The more thoroughly it has been prepared, and the greater the measure of planning for the seizure and running of the means of production, distribution, and consumption by the producers themselves, the more libertarian and the less bloody will the revolution be."[2]

---

1 Diego Abad de Santillán, *La FORA: Ideologia y trayectoria*, Buenos Aires, 1933, p. 292.
2 Ibid., p. 288.

De Santillán was a man convinced of his own rightness, as were the people he attracted around him in the Nervio group. From an earlier career as a globetrotting journalist and union administrator, he had developed an obsession with the need for economic planning and formulating a "scientific" approach to anarchism. In the early-twentieth century there were two main schools of thought within anarchism: the scientific-rational approach to the search for objective truths, the view upheld by intellectuals such as de Santillán, and the scientific-naturalist method preferred by anarchists such as Isaac Puente, Ascaso, and Durruti.

Conscious that absolute truth did not exist, the members of this latter group were cautious of all pre-determined systems and of imposing solutions of a pre-established nature which might carry within them the seeds of a new dictatorship. Anarchist writer Ricardo Mella had highlighted the dangers of such systems in an essay written at the turn of the century:

"It is science's business to systemize; and by systemizing we wall ourselves up in science, become dogmatic. Behold, the cause behind every fenced enclosure; and see, the reason behind the failure of beliefs...

"Instead, whenever a new structure is being raised and new channels opened and new walls being built, work with your picks and leave not a stone upon a stone. Thought needs unlimited space, endless time and freedom without restriction. There can be no rounded theories, no completed systems, no single philosophies because there is no absolute immutable truth: there are truths and yet more truths, truths undiscovered and truths yet unlearned."[3]

De Santillán, however, was not content to lay down axioms and general principles as Isaac Puente had done. Obsessed with efficiency, he sought to draw up a system which was complete in all its parts and required only to be set in motion. "There is an urgent need for workers to work together in harmony with the greatest possible number of scientists and technicians: for only through science, expertise and hard work will we be able to realize on earth the paradise of which

3   Ricardo Mella, "La bancarrota de las creencias," *Questiones Sociales*, Valencia, 1910.

religions of the old school dream beyond the tomb... Whereas, for resistance to capitalism, the waged worker was the basic and sole factor, when it comes to the reconstruction of society and of the economy, then given the development achieved by the means of production and by culture, all progressive forces are required, especially the aforementioned trilogy of labor, science and technology."[4]

Through the work of these anarchist intellectuals, "the brightest and the best," Abad de Santillán saw the FAI providing Spanish anarchism with the organizational and ideological discipline he felt it lacked to fulfil its historic role of transforming society. He described the work of the new Peninsular Committee with self-effacing modesty:

"We did not take our lead from the higher committees, but rather from below, through educational activity and constructive propaganda. I was on good terms with the hitherto crucial group which consisted of Ascaso, Durruti, García Oliver, and Companys. These were splendid comrades, selfless, schooled in conspiratorial struggle and in the action that was then necessary. Little by little we began to focus attention upon more substantial activities, and the FAI rallied the best equipped, most learned, most responsible militants. The dissidents took a back seat: we published magazines, books and pamphlets and held local, regional and national meetings with a certain quality of agenda. There was a lot of personal dialogue and it was precisely in the men of Los Solidarios that I found my best support. The FAI did not embody systematic subversion: it was a movement loyal to doctrine: in those days the aficionados of heroic, epic action took refuge in the defense committees. And we cannot deny that defense was needed.

"Today, as yesterday, we have had hotheads, revolutionaries in a hurry. But the FAI ceased to be an exponent of such hotheadedness at least from early 1934 on... Not all good comrades were in the FAI, many were outside it, but morally they were a part of it and the proof is that *Tierra y Libertad* had a larger print run than most of the political weeklies put together."[5]

---

4   Ibid., p. 289.
5   Letter from Diego Abad de Santillán, quoted by Fidel Miró, op.cit., pp. 65–68.

It was not long before this new mandarin breed in the administrative organs of the FAI felt strong enough to move against the "disproportionate" influence of the spontaneist and "uncontrollable" elements within the movement, particularly the Los Solidarios/Nosotros and other revolutionary working class groups. The offensive against the activists within the Barcelona Local Federation of the FAI was led by the A group, who argued the need for greater democratic "control" within the organization. Precisely who was to administer this "control" remained unclear. The question of the right of minorities not only to dissent, but to propose organizational changes was also raised. Moves were made to expel the Nosotros group, but nothing came of it and they continued to exert a powerful influence within the FAI and CNT until the outbreak of the Civil War.[6]

Progreso Fernández was one of those sensitive to the shift in direction that had resulted from the influx of newcomers. For him the FAI now ceased to be the anarchist association he had joined in 1927:

"I dropped out of the FAI in 1934 when I returned from exile; its authoritarian tendencies were already evident. Lots of people dropped away then—but we remained anarchists, because anarchism is an attitude to life."[7]

José Peirats, at the time a member of the Afinidad group and Secretary of the Barcelona Local Federation of the FAI, later recalled:[8]

"You mention the proposal to expel Los Solidarios and you speak of my advocacy of the minorities' rights issue. I cannot recall this business of expelling Los Solidarios, but I very well recall the exact reason why I quit the FAI, whose local secretary I had been, in the summer of 1934 (it might have been in July).

6 Miró, op.cit., p. 54. Miró (p. 61) states that the proposal to expel the Nosotros group took place at the end of 1934. The proposal, which originated from the A group, whose members included Jacinto Torhyo, Abelardo Iglesias, Ricardo Mestre, and other well-known anarchists, was based on the charge that the tactics of struggle advocated by the Nosotros group did not coincide with anarchist ideals and were more compatible with the Communist tactic of creating the social revolution through a coup d'état.
7 *Bicicleta*, op.cit.
8 Miró, op.cit., p. 61.

My two colleagues on the secretariat were Magrina (Eusebio) and Cabrerizo. The latter perished in the Plaza de Catalunya during the siege laid to the rebel troops dug in at the Hotel Colón and in the Telefónica building. The exact reason was that some groups advocated the introduction into the FAI of what they termed discipline: voting and observance of the law of majorities. We took the line that in the FAI, an anarchist affinity organization, the implementation of such procedures was a negation of the precept of liberty and thus of anarchism's purest essences. We lost the battle and we withdrew. I handed the seal over to Idelfonso Gonzales of the Nervio group who became the new secretary.

"So that you may understand this matter properly, let me add that the FAI was then (in 1934) little short of deserted. No more than six groups of us would come together in Las Planas or in the hills of Horta. During my term as Local Secretary—a period of exactly one year—we did not lay eyes on Los Solidarios (in the flesh) more than once. We summoned them, García Oliver and others, because they had travelled to Madrid for talks with Lerroux. Their answer was that they had acceded to the summons out of courtesy, but did not feel under any obligation to give us an account of their activities. This would have been well into the spring of 1933.

"What I am trying to get over is that the members of that group, whom we never saw at our meetings, were active more in the defense groups than in the FAI, although on the dais and in the press they always specifically professed to be of the FAI. To support this argument let me tell you that, in the immediate wake of the events of 8 January 1933, we of the Afinidad group called upon Durruti to give an account of himself before the Local Federation of (FAI) Groups. To our astonishment, we were told in reply that none of the leaders of that uprising belonged to the FAI.

"It was in the summer of 1934 that the FAI saw a greater influx of people. There is an explanation for this. I don't know whether you will recall that around that time there was an appeal for every leading CNT militant to join the FAI. Then there was a massive influx, but also lots of arguments, for the motley crew of newcomers were very full of themselves. It was then that I saw Muñoz, Marianet, de Santillán, Toryho, and possibly also your Z group in the Local.[9] It is possible that the fact that there was allegedly another Los Solidarios group in the Barcelona Local Federation was due to the fact that the authentic owners of the title were not, as I say, under its control. The changing of their name to Nosotros may possibly have been as a result of their re-entry at the time of the 1934 influx and their inability to force the others to change theirs."

During the summer of 1934, Largo Caballero, through intermediaries, made overtures to the CNT of Catalonia concerning a possible revolutionary alliance with the UGT. Significantly, the approach was made not to the National Committee of the CNT in Zaragoza, but to the Regional Committee of Catalonia. A meeting was arranged between Rafael Vidiella and Vila Cuenca, chairmen of the UGT and PSOE in Catalonia restively, apparently on behalf of the national leadership, and Francisco Ascaso, the then Secretary of the CNT Regional Committee of Catalonia. Ascaso was accompanied at the initial meeting by Buenaventura Durruti and García Oliver—all members of the Confederal Defense Committee for Catalonia.

According to García Oliver, Vidiella and Cuenca proposed to the Catalan anarchists—effectively the Nosotros group—a joint UGT-CNT-Esquerra rising, which would be "federalist and socialist" in inspiration.[10] The objective was to bring down the right wing government. Ascaso explained that any agreement would have to be formalized at a joint meeting with Largo Caballero. A meeting was arranged for the next time the Socialist leader was in Barcelona. The meeting never took place. Companys refused point blank to have anything to do with "those CNT-FAI types." To do so, he claimed, would be seen by the world as unmistakable evidence of the weakness of the "Popular Front." Companys assured Caballero that, with the support of the *escamots*, his private army of young nationalists, his reputation alone was sufficient to rally the whole population of Catalonia behind them.

---

9   The Z group was an offshoot from the Nervio group, which had joined the FAI towards the end of 1935. It had almost absolute control of the Juventudes Libertarias of Catalonia until 1937. The group contained a considerable number of leading militants of the JJ.LL, and helped keep the anarchist youth organization in Catalonia under FAI influence.
10 Juan García Oliver, *El Eco de los Pasos*, Barcelona, 1979, p. 156.

On 4 October 1934, Alejandro Lerroux patched together a new, predominantly right wing, government. It was made up of Radicals, agrarians, liberal democrats, and three ministers from the CEDA, the party of the Catholic fundamentalists which had still to declare its support for the Republic. The news of this ministry, with the participation of Gil Robles, a man likened to Austrian fascist leader Dolfuss, was the signal for the UGT-PSOE to embark on its gambit for power—revolt.

In the Asturias, the Regional Committee of the CNT, a minority union with a membership of only 22,000, had signed a local agreement with the dominant UGT—the Alianza Obrera (Workers' Alliance). The Alianza was the creation of Marxist Joaquín Maurín, one of the pro-Bolsheviks who had unsuccessfully attempted to infiltrate and take over the CNT in the 1920s. It was an amalgam of the Opposition unions set up following the *treintista* split, the Socialists and Communists. The Asturias was the only CNT region to sign the Alianza.

In spite of the fact that they had committed themselves to the rising and were provided with weapons, something that did not happen elsewhere, the CNT were not invited to participate in the Revolutionary Committee. Neither was the CNT National Committee ever approached by the Socialist leaders of the rising. Miguel Yoldi, the CNT National Secretary, had attempted, on his own initiative, to make contact with Largo Caballero and the Oviedo-based, UGT-PSOE dominated revolutionary committee to coordinate the actions of the two unions, but he had been rebuffed at every turn.

The revolt, organized by the Socialists, with the CNT and the Communist minority in an auxiliary role, began in the Asturian mining region at dawn on 5 October. The UGT declared a general strike without seeking the support of the CNT, but in spite of this deliberate affront, confederal militants throughout Spain supported the stoppage out of moral solidarity. After initial successes by the Asturian workers, government troops surrounded the region and quickly closed in on the revolutionaries. The revolt had failed to extend itself beyond Asturias, parts of Leon, and Catalonia. Confronted with disaster, the PSOE-UGT-controlled Revolutionary Committee finally ordered an ignominious retreat on 11 October.

In Catalonia, it was the Estat Català and the Esquerra, the governing parties, who had been the prime movers in what they hoped would be a palace coup. In a radio broadcast from the Generalitat palace, Companys proclaimed an autonomous Catalan state within a federal Spanish Republic. He also offered the provisional federal government a base in Catalonia, but neither the "Popular Front," the Alianza Obrera nor the Rabassaires responded to his appeals for support. The failure of the Generalitat to issue arms to the Alianza Obrera, and the unprovoked attacks on and arrests of CNT and FAI militants by Badia's police contributed heavily to the workers' suspicions of the bourgeois Catalan nationalists. Immediately prior to the rising, Generalitat police raided the homes of all known anarchist militants. Durruti, for example, was arrested in his bed on 4 October and held in detention for almost a year.

The anti-anarchist campaign waged by the Socialists and the political left since the birth of the Republic had, however, materially weakened the CNT. Until April 1933 it was estimated that upwards of 15,000 CNT members were in jail.[11] The Generalitat's policy of repressing the CNT, which for the previous year had been obliged to lead a clandestine existence, was intensified. *Solidaridad Obrera*, the Catalan CNT daily, had been shut down and all CNT Locals, *ateneos*, and cultural centers had been sealed by the Generalitat police throughout 1934. According to Abad de Santillán, a sympathetic Communist member of the Workers' Alliance had informed them that Dencàs had issued orders to his men to fire on all CNT members spotted on the streets. When the Confederal militants attempted to re-open their closed-down union premises on the morning of the rising, they were fired on by Badia's police. It is ironic that the first shots to ring out in Barcelona were aimed against the CNT, by those in revolt against the central government.

The editorial offices of *Solidaridad Obrera* were also attacked. However, in spite of this hostility, which verged on a state of war, the CNT declared a general strike in support of the rising.

Within a few hours of Companys' declaration, General Batet Mestres, the Captain General of Catalonia, proclaimed martial law. With 500 or so soldiers, he had cleared the Generalitat and

---

11 "Spanish Anarchists and the October Uprising," Diego Abad de Santillán, *Tiempos Nuevos*, II, No. 1, 10.1.1935, p. 5.

Catalanists forces from the streets. When Batet's artillery fired unprimed cannon shells at the Generalitat building, which they had made their headquarters, the leaders surrendered. The weapons, including 300 Winchesters, dropped into the sewers by the fleeing Catalan nationalists, were quickly collected by Ricardo Sanz and CNT members of the council refuse department. These were to re-emerge two years later on 19 July 1936. In Badalona and Granollers, the abandoned weapons had permitted the CNT to gain control of the streets. The Catalan Regional Committee of the CNT, unaware of events then taking place in the Asturias, ordered a return to work after two days general strike.

In the Asturias, the rising was put down with medieval brutality by the director of operations, General López Ochoa, a Republican and Freemason, and the new rising star in the military firmament, General Francisco Franco Bahamonde. The ambiguity with which the UGT-PSOE responded to what was their own rising, with the notable exception of the Asturias and, to a lesser extent, Catalonia, suggests the real intention of the leadership may have been—by unleashing a limited conflict—to force the resignation of the right wing CEDA government—or at least to allow them to negotiate their way back into the government.

20

Interregnum: 1934–35

In the recriminations that followed October, the CNT's alleged lack of solidarity was singled out by the Marxist press as a prime contributory factor to the ignominious collapse of the rising. From exile in Paris, Socialist Party leader Indalecio Prieto claimed, in a statement to the United Press agency, that one of the reasons for the failure of the rising—which they, the Socialist leaders had not wanted, as they regarded it as premature and inadequately prepared, was the abstention of the CNT. This opinion was not shared by Rafael Vidiella, the Catalan PSOE leader, who wrote in *Leviatan*:[1]

"So what happened that, on the morning of 7 October, the Generalitat was to surrender without offering any resistance and without being defended—after a few brief hours…? Quite simply, what happened is that today's revolutions cannot be made by halves. There are two forces present in the world: capitalism and the proletariat, and half-measures cannot satisfy either, because they make both discontented.

"The Esquerra Republicana de Catalunya was a party without tradition in Catalan political life. In Catalonia there were only two real, homogenous factors; the Lliga and the CNT, which is to say, the capitalist factor and the proletarian one. But the latter was and is the irreconcilable enemy of political contest, of the capture of corporations and Parliament. In 1931 the Spanish revolution had a safety valve in the form of the municipal elections. If it had been the CNT that ran candidates in Catalonia, they would have won. For one very simple and

---

1 *Leviatan*, No. 7, November, 1934, pp. 11–15.

yet very potent reason: because no Catalan sector had been so sorely oppressed by the monarchy and the Lliga, and no one had fought so bitterly and so strenuously against these since 1911 as had the CNT. In 1929, I had occasion to anticipate this possible triumph of the CNT, if the Spanish revolution culminated in a political contest: but the Confederation, by its inhibitions, ensured that in Catalonia and in some Spanish provinces the victory went to many lawyers and friends of these who defended the unionists whenever they were persecuted by the monarchy.

"The proletariat were unarmed. Estat Català was afraid that it might be swept aside by the proletariat. On the other hand, and not unreasonably, the working class suspected that it would be gunned down by Estat Català, which possessed over ten tons of arms. In addition, a deep chasm had opened up between the proletariat proper and the Generalitat. The arms in the hands of the Estat Català were useless. A well-known FAI militant, García Oliver, forecast this some months previously... and he was not mistaken."

On 19 October, the government announced that the Asturian uprising had been completely crushed. According to official figures issued in January 1935 by the Dirección General de Seguridad, 1,051 civilian and 284 military and security personnel had died in the rising. Whatever the reasons for the failure of the October rising, an important consequence was the realization, within both legal and fascist rightist circles, that, in the event of future failure at the polls, the military option was the only one that remained open to them. Clearly, the only way their policies could effectively be implemented and their long-term interests defended was by transforming the Republic into a corporate state along the lines of Mussolini's Italy. Plans for a corporatist right wing coup had, in fact, been initiated as early as March 1934 at a meeting in Rome between Mussolini and Air Marshal Italo Balbo, and representatives of the Carlists and Calvo Sotelo's monarchist Renovación Española. Mussolini promised to provide the plotters with a substantial first installment of weapons, ammunition, and money, which would be followed by further, larger contributions when required.

In late 1935, the Peninsular Committee of the FAI was controlled by de Santillan's Nervio group of Barcelona. The

Committee's emphasis was now determinedly intellectual rather than activist: Pedro Herrera, Idelfonso González, Germinal de Sousa, and Fidel Miró. De Santillán was appointed Secretary of the Peninsular Committee. One of the first tasks of the new Peninsular Committee was to revamp *Tierra y Libertad* and turn it into a theoretical and doctrinal journal. Jacinto Toryho, a journalist whose ideas and personality generated mixed feelings within the movement, was among those closely involved in running the FAI paper, as was the outgoing Peninsular secretary, "Juanel." In keeping with the theoretical and intellectual priorities of the new Committee, a publishing house specializing in anarchist economic and social theory was soon established.

Another objective of the new Peninsular Committee was to initiate new organizational changes. These changes were not welcomed by many of the groups, highlighting as it did the accelerating drift toward centralization and the weakening of the autonomy of the affinity groups. With the exception of Catalonia, the new-look Peninsular Committee had a delegate in each of the local federation of groups and another in the regional committees, giving it considerable oversight of the overall organizational position, and, consequently, greater influence and control.

21

Plots, Plans, and the Popular Front

A series of economic and social crises and major scandals in late 1935, involving the bribery and corruption of government ministers, finally brought down the right-wing government of Alejandro Lerroux. The *estraperlo* scandal, one which attracted the most publicity, involved the presentation of gold watches to members of the government and Radical Party in return for the licensing of "fixed" electrical roulette wheels in casinos. New elections were arranged for February 1936. The electoral campaign of the right, centered around Gil Robles, whom President Alcalá Zamora disliked and had been avoiding appointing as Prime Minister, was aimed at establishing a totalitarian regime.

The left, on the other hand, unwilling to go into the elections disunited, formed a "Popular Front" coalition consisting of Socialists, Republicans, Communists, and other Marxist groupings, as well as the Catalan and other bourgeois nationalist groups. Its program, the work of Azaña and Prieto, was a moderate one, promising full restoration of the Constitution, reform of taxation, police, etc., but it repudiated the Socialist program for the nationalization of the land, the banks, and industry. It also offered an amnesty for all political crimes committed after November 1933. This was to be the carrot for the CNT.

Companys, in the meantime, had smuggled a letter from prison to his deputy, José Antonio Trabal Sanz, suggesting an approach be made to the Catalan CNT to ask them to halt their anti-election propaganda in the run-up to the forthcoming elections.

García Vivancos, a Freemason and a trusted associate of the Nosotros group, was approached by two men: Farreras, Grand Master of the Grand Lodge of Catalonia and the Balearics, and Salvat on behalf of the Esquerra. A meeting was arranged with Ascaso, Durruti, and Oliver to discuss Companys' proposals that the CNT refrain from an active anti-election campaign.

Before informing the Regional Committee of the CNT about this approach, García Oliver convened a meeting of the like-minded comrades in Nosotros group and the Confederal Defense Committee of Catalonia (the two overlapped to be almost indistinguishable) to discuss the Esquerra proposals. In Oliver's view, if they ducked out of the meeting with Companys' envoys they would seek a similar accommodation with other CNT militants, either in Catalonia or Madrid. A decision had to be made quickly.

The crucial meeting was held in Oliver's apartment, opposite the Jupiter football ground in Barcelona's Pueblo Nuevo district. All the Nosotros group attended—Jover, Aurelio Fernández, Ricardo Sanz, Durruti, including new members Antonio Ortíz and Antonio Martínez. Also present was García Vivancos. Apart from the one or two militants who held positions of influence in the union—Jover was a member of the CNT Regional Committee, and Aurelio Fernández belonged to the Local Committee of Barcelona CNT Unions—the anarchists assembled that day also constituted the powerful Confederal Defense Committee of Catalonia, the joint CNT-FAI body entrusted with coordinating the defense and revolutionary strategy of the organization.

When Vivancos had outlined the proposals put to him by the Esquerra and Grand Lodge, García Oliver gave his view of the situation. If the CNT helped put the "Popular Front" in, it would provide them with the means to attack them. If, on the other hand, the CNT abstained, the reactionaries would get in and attack both them and the reformists together, morally the same as voting them in—something that no anarchist could ever do—even though the reformists would probably try to sell them out to the reactionaries as a bargaining lever. The only viable option left to the anarchists was to support a tactical vote for the "Popular Front," as a means of keeping the fascists out long enough to allow them to prepare for what they foresaw as an inevitable violent confrontation with the military. Oliver proposed that, in return for supporting the "Popular Front" at the polls, the CNT should be provided with sufficient weapons to resist the military uprising.

Nothing, however, was to be agreed until they had secured the promise of weapons in advance of, or immediately after, the electoral victory of the left.

The Catalan anarchists agreed that when the issue of the anti-election campaign came up for discussion in the run-up to the elections, their duty as revolutionaries was to spell out what they saw as the likely consequences of voting or abstentionism:

"If the working class abstains from voting this time, election victory will go to the fascist right. Should they succeed, we would have to take to the streets to fight them with all available weaponry.

"Should the working class vote this time—and vote for the left—the right, backed by the military, will revolt before six months are up, and we would have to take to the streets to fight them with weapons.

"So we do not say to you that you should NOT vote. But nor do we tell you that you should vote. Let each individual act as his conscience dictates. But you should all be ready for fighting in the streets, no matter whether it is the right who win, or the left."[1]

Two days later García Vivancos set up the meeting between Companys' envoys Trabal, Farreras, and Salvat, and the anarchists Ascaso, Durruti, and Oliver. A letter from Companys was read out in which the Catalan nationalist declared his admiration for the men of the CNT and his apologies for what had happened in October 1934. The problems that united them now, he pointed out, included the thousands of political prisoners throughout Spain. If the right, under Gil Robles and his CEDA associates, won the elections, the political prisoners would remain in jail for many years. If, on the other hand, the CNT was prepared to suspend its anti-election propaganda

---

1   Oliver, op.cit., pp. 163–164.

and encourage the Spanish and Catalan workers to vote for the "Popular Front," the left would win and secure the release of those prisoners. Ascaso, Durruti, and Oliver were, therefore urged to use their influence with their comrades to shift their anti-electoral position.

Oliver gave the Defense Committee case, pointing out that the union, although it had lots of men at its disposal, lacked the weapons necessary for the inevitable confrontation with the army if the left won the elections. The CNT could only face that risk if sufficient weapons were deposited in the anarchist strongholds of Aragón, Andalucia, and the Levante, the "anarchist triangle," either immediately or, at the latest, within two months of a leftist electoral victory.

Companys' reply came a fortnight later. He argued that as a military rising was improbable and, therefore, the Defense Committee demands were excessive and unreasonable. The resources of a legitimate state would be sufficient to deter the right. The prospective Catalan premier did, however, promise to provide the anarchist revolutionaries with arms once victory at the polls had been assured. Having no option but to make do with this somewhat ambivalent assurance, Durruti, Ascaso, and Oliver agreed to use what influence they had to prevent the Confederation and the FAI from embarking on an anti-voting campaign in the run-up to the February 1936 elections.

Largo Caballero, the PSOE-UGT leader, like Lluis Companys and the Esquerra politicians, was equally sensitive to the electoral importance of the 1,600,000 CNT members. The successful anti-election campaign run by the anarchists in 1933 had had a disastrous effect on his own quest for power. Swallowing his hostility, he appealed to the CNT publicly to support the "Popular Front" in the forthcoming elections.

The CNT's Regional Committee in Catalonia responded quickly. It convened a Regional Conference on 26–29 January 1936 to discuss the issue of supporting the "Popular Front" candidates in the forthcoming elections. Another important item on the agenda was the question of a formal revolutionary alliance with the UGT. The discussion revealed a high degree of confusion and ideological uncertainty as to whether the anti-election stance was a tactical issue or a matter of fundamental principle. The fact that activists of such standing as Durruti,

Ascaso, and Oliver, as well as the Peninsular Committee of the
FAI, were lobbying extensively within the movement in support
of tactical voting lent considerable weight to that position.[2]

The secretariat of the anarcho-syndicalist international, the
AIT, sent a letter to the Regional Conference warning against
the dangers of even tactical participation in the capitalist and
statist electoral process:

"The forthcoming elections scheduled for February have
produced the collective hallucination of an age of possible
social achievement being ushered in thanks to a victory by the
left. From moderate Republicans through to the Communists,
the so-called Anti-Fascist Front promises to struggle against all
the forces of reaction.

"In various confederal bodies in Spain the issue is mooted—
'Is it proper to vote? Should we vote or not? Ought the
casting of our votes be deemed a function of our immutable
principles, or should it be construed instead as a mere tactic
which may alter as the needs of the moment alter? Is there a
danger in abstaining in that it represents a boost to the right?'
All these questions are not hotly debated in the bosom of our
Spanish affiliate. Such indecisions, 'correcting of sights,' must
be attributed entirely to this collective psychosis, which has its
origins in the pending danger.

"There are but two alternatives: either many Spanish
comrades, persuaded that this time their abstentionist
propaganda would not be as effective as it was back in 1933,
choose to keep to it because it retains all its values as a
declaration of principles; or that propaganda will once again
lead to a parliamentary and governmental impasse in the
country, in which case the CNT must now take the necessary

2 *Presencia*, Paris, 1967, p. 46. According to Peirats, García Oliver attended
a "restricted" meeting of "notables" immediately prior to the January CNT
Regional Conference. This meeting, which apparently "took place behind the
back of the organization," was to forestall an active and dynamic anti-election
campaign such as that which had cost the Left the elections in November
1933. "Out of it," notes Peirats, "undoubtedly came the summoning of the
conference, which did indeed recommend a low-key campaign against the
elections." The members of the Peninsular Committee of the FAI were also
committed to supporting the Left in the elections. "The initiative in the
campaign," wrote de Santillán, "originated with the Peninsular Committee
of the FAI." De Santillán, *Contribucion a la historia del movimiento obrero espanol,*
Vol. III, p. 267.

steps to exploit the situation...by means of social revolution. For it is an open secret that there is only one way out of the struggle against fascism—that is, Revolution ..."

Although the conference officially re-affirmed the anti-parliamentarian position of the CNT, the anti-voting campaign it organized in the run-up to the elections was half-hearted to say the least. CNT historian José Peirats described it as "so perfunctory as to be scarcely perceptible." A minority of anarchists did abstain, but the vast bulk of the CNT members (of whom perhaps, at most, half a million might have described themselves as anarchists)—particularly in Aragón, where voting had been recommended, and in Catalonia—ignored the pastoral letter of the AIT and voted for progressive candidates. Thus did the CNT militants play as decisive a part in bringing the "Popular Front" of 1936 to power, as they had in the birth of the Republic in 1931 and the rightist victory of 1933.[3] Whether they voted to hasten the revolution, were playing for time, or were swayed by the "Popular Front" bait of total amnesty for the 15,000 or so political and social prisoners (many of whom were anarchists and *cenetistas* imprisoned for their part in the insurrections of December 1933 and October 1934) is impossible to ascertain; what is certain is the confederal workers did not vote for the "Popular Front" as a solution to their problems.

Immediately after the CNT conference, an FAI Peninsular Plenum was held in Madrid between 31 January and 1 February. The reports from the various Regional Federations and Committees were discouraging. The number of groups affiliated to the FAI had dropped from the all-time high in 1933 to 469. This drop could be attributed partly to the repression of the previous two years, but also reflects the growing unease

---

3   In 1931, the provinces with more than 35 per cent abstentions were: 35%–40% Oviedo, Barcelona, Seville, Granada, Almeria, Murcia; 40%–50% Cádiz, Málaga, La Coruna; 45%+ Pontevedra. There was a solid CNT presence in all these provinces. In the 1933 elections, the provinces with over 35 per cent abstentions were: 35%–40% Leon, Almeria, Teruel, Lérida, Gerona, Barcelona; 40%–45% La Coruna, Pontevedra, Zaragoza, Tarragona; 45%+ Huesca, Seville, Cádiz, Málaga. In the 1936 elections, the results of abstention are: 35%–45% La Coruna, Lugo, Zamora, Cádiz, Almeria, Murcia; 40%–45% Burgos, Guadalajara, Málaga; 45%+ Teruel. (Source: Jean Becarud, *La IIe republique espagnole*, doctoral thesis, Fondation National des Sciences Politiques, Paris, 1962.)

felt among anarchists with the centralizing direction taken by the FAI Peninsular Committee under the influence of de Santillán's Nervio group.[4]

Worried by the drop in number of affiliated groups, the FAI Plenum decided to mount a recruitment drive in an attempt to double the organization's numbers. In two years, the FAI had lost 2,000 individuals—from around 5,500 in 1933 to an estimated 3,500 in 1936. An appeal was issued for all anarchists to joint the organization. It also agreed to counter the "Popular Front" alliances between the bourgeoisie and workers, to confront the rising fascist danger, and to increase the work of the anti-militarist groups in the barracks.[5]

One of the most important resolutions put forward was that of the Barcelona Local Federation on "Revolutionary Preparedness" and the coordination of the revolutionary defense forces. It showed a clear awareness of the inevitability of the military coup and the prospects this opportunity held out for "engaging in ultimate battle with the aged edifice of capitalist morality, economics, and politics." These "Local Revolutionary Preparedness Committees" were to be appointed by the local committees and consist of four members (two from the Confederation and two from the FAI), each with specific tasks: Transport and Communications; Technical Preparation

---

4 Abad de Santillán throws some light on how this shift came about: "Little by little we began to focus attention upon more substantial activities (i.e. conspiratorial struggle) and the FAI rallied the best equipped, most learned, most responsible militants. The dissidents took a back seat: we published magazines, books and pamphlets and held local, regional and national meetings with a certain calibre of agenda... Today as yesterday we have had hotheads, revolutionaries in a hurry. But the FAI ceased to be an exponent of such hotheadedness from at least 1934." (Letter to Fidel Miró, *Catalunya los trabajadores*, op.cit., pp. 65–68). Progreso Fernández was one of those who "took a back seat" by retiring from the FAI (*Bicicleta*, op.cit.). Peirats was another of the militants worried by this shift in direction. While agreeing in principle with tactical voting, "I quit the editorial board of *Solidaridad Obrera* in a gesture of protest. I was convinced that this change of pace spoke of the secret desire to see the Left win the elections. I had no shortage of evidence and grounds for believing this. Politicians call this disparity of conduct 'the politics of anti-politics.' Indeed, unless it has a fixed position, valid for any eventuality, apoliticism loses its status as principle to become mere opportunism." (Peirats, *Examen crítico-constructivo del movimiento libertario español*, Mexico, 1967, p. 27.)
5 *Memoria del Pleno Peninsular celebrado el dia 30 de enero y 1o de Febrero de 1936*, El Comité Peninsular, Barcelona, 1936.

for Combat; Industrial Organization; and the Organizational Deployment of the Insurrectionary Forces.

Their function was to act as an anarchist general staff, a forward planning committee that would prepare the local defense committees for the realities of modern combat, to "examine the means and methods of struggle, the tactics to be deployed and the organization of insurrectionary organizational forces."[6] Both the unions and the anarchist groups were to finance the work of the Local Preparedness Committees.

The Aragón, Rioja, and Navarre delegates opposed the proposed Revolutionary Preparedness Committees on the grounds that this was a task best left to the Defense Committees. In their view, the FAI should concentrate wholly on ideological propaganda.[7]

Other plans to cope with war or a military rising included a national sabotage plan; the re-launching of the anarchist paper for soldiers, *Soldado del Peublo*; and the setting up of intelligence-gathering and revolutionary cadres inside the barracks.

On the question of the forthcoming elections, most FAI delegates reaffirmed their classical anti-parliamentary stance, but added that, although the 1933 anti-election campaign was justified at the time, it was not appropriate to repeat the exercise. The resolution, which was finally approved, was noticeably silent on the question of an anti-election campaign: "We reaffirm our anti-parliamentary and our anti-electoral position. World events, bearing out our predictions, have eloquently demonstrated that all democratic experiences have foundered and that only direct intervention by the workers in the problems with which the capitalist system confronts them, has any offensive or defensive value against the reaction. The FAI, therefore, has nothing to amend in its complete abstention from all direct and indirect collaboration with any State politicking."

Interestingly, towards the end of the Plenum, the delegate from the Levante referred to an article in *Tierra y Libertad*, which suggested that going to the polls was a tactical issue and not a

6   Gómez Casas states that the "revolutionary preparedness studies" had been drawn up by de Santillan's Nervio group. (*La FAI*, op.cit., p. 210.)
7   *Memoria del Pleno Peninsular*, El Comité Peninsular, Barcelona, February, 1936, p. 11.

matter of principle. The editorial board of the anarchist paper explained that it was trying to clarify what should be regarded as principle and what should be understood as tactical: "The revolution itself is a question of tactics, method, procedures. Principles, on the other hand, are the fundamental aims for which it strives: how these are to be achieved and encompassed is a matter of tactics."[8]

The left were the undisputed victors in the elections. A "Popular Front" government of 263 leftist deputies led by Manuel Azaña took office. The Center, with 52 deputies, and the Right, with 129 deputies, were powerless against such an overwhelming majority. The train of events, which was to lead inexorably to a military uprising, had been set in motion.

Two days before the election, the National Committee of the CNT issued a statement to its members as to what it saw as the inevitable consequences of a leftist victory in the elections. It was a clear declaration of intent to the Republican bourgeoisie, as well as to the military plotters and the landed oligarchs whose interests they served, that the most powerful labor union in Spain would respond to a military revolt with the ultimate expression of working class power—social revolution:

"On a war footing, proletariat against the monarchist and fascist conspiracy! Day by day the suspicion is growing that rightist elements are ready to provoke intervention by the military... Insurrection has been deferred, pending the outcome of the elections. They are to implement their theoretical scheme of prevention should victory at the polls go to the left. Furthermore, we have no hesitation in recommending that, wheresoever the legionnaires of tyranny may launch armed insurrection, an understanding be unhesitatingly reached with anti-fascist groups, vigorous precautions being taken to ensure that the defensive contribution of the masses may lead to real social revolution under the auspices of Libertarian Communism. Should the conspirators open fire, the act of opposition must be pursued to its utmost consequences without the liberal bourgeoisie and its Marxist allies being countenanced in their desire to apply the brakes, in the event of the fascist rebellion's being defeated in its first stages...in the course of the people's victory its democratic illusions would be dispelled; should it

---

8   Ibid. pp. 31–32.

go otherwise, the nightmare of dictatorship will annihilate us. No matter who opens the hostilities seriously, democracy will perish between two fires because it is irrelevant and has no place on the field of battle. Either fascism or social revolution... Beginning right now and for the period remaining until the re-opening of Parliament—if the sources of danger noted by us should persist—militants ought to contrive frequent comings together in each locality by means of the usual organs of liaison, and keep in touch with the confederal committees so that the latter may keep them *au fait* with the course of events and undertake coordinated activity. Albeit in an irregular fashion, a will to fight must be displayed. Anything is better than our remaining on the fence and being exterminated by the dark hordes through our incredulity, while the others are loaded with chains ..."[9]

The backs of the defeated right were now against the wall. Like their Socialist predecessors in 1934, they, too, had refused to accept the decisions of the electorate. President Zamora was approached to hand over power to General Franco. Clearly, the socially conservative, corporate state would not be introduced legally. For Gil Robles and the classes he represented, the die had been cast. As Paul Preston notes: "December 1935 and February 1936 revealed that the end was more important than the means. Once convinced that the legal road to corporativism was blocked, he did everything possible to help those who were committed to violence. He had already made two crucial contributions to the success of the 1936 rising. The first, of which he was later to boast, was the creation of mass right wing militancy. The other was the undermining of Socialist faith in the possibilities of bourgeois democracy."[10]

Four days after the elections, on 20 February, the rightists met to begin finalizing their conspiratorial plans. They agreed to embark on a strategy of tension that would culminate in a military uprising and the overthrow of the bourgeois liberal regime.

From February, events rumbled towards their climax on 19 July. Unemployment continued to rise and the agrarian reforms were deliberately ignored by the landed oligarchy.

---

9 Peirats, *La CNT*, op.cit., Vol. I. Ch. 6.
10 Paul Preston, *The Coming of the Spanish Civil War*, London, 1978, p. 178.

From 20 February until 19 July, there was a period of latent civil war throughout much of the country; there were an estimated 113 general strikes and 228 partial stoppages; 1,287 people were wounded in clashes with the security forces or political confrontations, and 269 people killed. There were 213 recorded assassinations, or attempted assassinations, the majority of them carried out by gunmen of the Falange Española, the Spanish fascist organization called into being by a desperate and cornered agrarian capitalist class. In the town of Yeste, in Albacete, for example, seventeen peasants were killed and a similar number wounded defending their land against the Civil Guard who had been ordered to clear it for the building of a reservoir. Land seizures by landless peasants also increased. In Madrid there was a major strike of building workers organized by the CNT and supported by the UGT. This strike, which began with 40,000 workers and soon rose to over 100,000, gave an enormous boost to the CNT unions in Madrid, at the expense of the UGT.

Against this tense background the Fifth Extraordinary Congress of the CNT was held in Zaragoza on 1 May, 1936. It was to be the last regular CNT Congress to meet on Spanish soil until 1977. Attending were 649 delegates representing 982 unions, with a combined membership of 550,595, including the opposition *treintista* unions who had been invited along in an attempt to resolve the differences within the Confederation. There had been a considerable drop in membership, particularly in Catalonia where membership had been dropping steadily since its all-time high of 321,394 in August 1931. The Andalucian Regional was the majority delegation representing 156,000 workers. Close behind them came the Catalans (140,000), the Levante (50,000), Centre (39,000), Aragón (35,000), Galicia (23,000), and Asturias (22,731).

Items on the agenda included agrarian reform, an inquest on the revolutionary risings of 1933 and the October revolt of 1934, the question of a possible revolutionary alliance with the Socialist UGT union, and the drawing up of a thorough and clear statement of the principles and aims of Libertarian Communism as the objective of the CNT.

García Oliver, speaking as a delegate from the Barcelona Weaving and Textile Union, gave his view of the controversial issues on the agenda, one which presumably reflected the view of the Nosotros group and the Defense Committees of the CNT, as well as his own union branch:

"Yesterday we stated that the revolution was feasible and we set out the reasons making our victory, the victory of Libertarian Communism, a possibility. Now again we say, as we did in 1931, that the revolution can be made. But in those days the CNT was the only force. Then there were superior circumstances of a revolutionary nature that have not recurred since. Today there is a strong state, disciplined troops, an arrogant bourgeoisie, etc. And although revolution is possible, and we are confident of it, it is no longer the same as in the days of 1931... Today the revolution is shared with other forces and at this very Congress we must examine the possibility of joint action with the UGT."

He then moved on to discuss the alleged influence of the FAI on the CNT:

"Another issued raised, though it too cannot furnish any reason (for a split) is the question of the *trabazón* (the special relationship between the CNT and FAI in matters relating to defense and solidarity). The thinking of the Opposition unions on this point is shared by many within the CNT—but they do not break away from the CNT on account of it. The union I myself represent will be proposing a new system of structuring the prisoners' aid committees by union. The CNT has not played second fiddle to the FAI. Quite the contrary. The anarchist groups have served the CNT as the instruments of its struggle. But there has been no interference. Can one make an issue out of the fact when today what is being advocated is alliance with the Socialists who, when all is said and done, stand for a quite different way of thinking? It is a question of interpretation of doctrines, a question of majorities and minorities...

"I said earlier that during the squabble between the Opposition and the CNT we used all sorts of weapons to secure victory. But only in an individual capacity. Collectively we were defeated. When we sought to foist upon *Solidaridad Obrera*, directors whom we preferred, we picked up only a handful of votes. But we did not announce any split. We went on fighting, zealously. And we went to the 1931 Congress. There, too, we were defeated, but we were not wiped out in terms of the votes: by then we had support. We went later to the Calle de Cabanas Plenum and this time we won, and within four days the *treintista* manifesto had appeared.

"Comrades, minorities always win through when they have right on their side. Let everyone learn from us. Let everybody strive to win over the majority as we do strive. Anyone who has right on his side yet does not win through...it is because he lacks energy. Struggle wins, but let the agreements worked out at the organization's gatherings be respected by one and all. Let observance of them be the norm. But let us all remain within the Confederation."[11]

Reformists and "planners" alike saw the resolutions agreed by the Zaragoza Congress as a victory for the revolutionary wing of the anarchist movement. Cesar M. Lorenzo, described it as "the total triumph of the FAI." Horacio Prieto (Lorenzo's father), a one-time "pure" anarchist who had gone full circle to become one of the most outstanding representatives of confederal reformism, was virulently opposed to what he described as the "ultras" of both wings. Piqued by Congress' adoption of the Puente-inspired resolution on Libertarian Communism against his recommendations—a resolution that he described as the libertarian movement enveloping itself in "a universe of dreams"—this "ultra" of the mythic center (also, incidentally, a FAI affiliate) resigned as National Secretary of the CNT.[12] FAI Peninsular Secretary de Santillán, frustrated

---

11 Gómez Casas, op.cit., p. 213.

12 César M. Lorenzo, *Les anarchistes espagnoles et le pouvoir,* Paris, 1969, pp. 92–93. This was a reference to the resolution that attempted to spell out a clear definition of Libertarian Communism. Horacio Martínez Prieto, a building worker who joined the CNT late in life because he considered himself a "pure" anarchist, was to become the architect of governmental collaboration. His rise to prominence began and ended with the Republic: in 1932, a year in which he visited Russia, he was editor of the paper *CNT*, by 1934 he was vice-secretary of the National Committee of the CNT, and National Secretary by 1936. On his return from Bilbao in September 1936, where he had been the CNT representative of the Vizcayan Provincial Defense Committee, he orchestrated a sustained campaign to ensure the CNT joined the Republican government. Following various national plenums of Regionals, including one in October that he summoned on his own authority, he was awarded powers to negotiate CNT participation in government with Azaña and Caballero. In November 1936, he represented the FAI Peninsular Committee at the Barcelona Assembly, which confirmed CNT-FAI participation in government. Denounced that same month as a

perhaps at Congress passing over his own minutely detailed economic plan, described it as being "insufficient for a modern economic state."[13]

---

traitor during a national regional of plenums, he stepped down as National Secretary. The following month, he was appointed Director General of Trade alongside former *treintista* Juan López. In December 1937, he headed the CNT delegation to an extraordinary congress of the AIT where he justified the CNT's governmentalism. By April 1938, he was a CNT under-secretary for health in the Negrín Cabinet. At the end of the year he was fully committed to the FAI becoming a political party ("Estudio Polemico," *Timón*, Barcelona, September, 1938, p. 2) and was also urging that negotiations be opened with Franco.

13 "Comunismo y anarquismo," *Tiempos Nuevos*, 6.6.1936.

22

19 July 1936

A rightist coup was imminent. Precise information as to the date of the military rising had been obtained as early as 13 July by CNT-FAI Defense Committee informants in the barracks. The anti-fascist initiative was taken by the Confederal Defense Committee, which began to speed up its plans to resist the military, but their work was deliberately obstructed by a governmental decree on 14 July that ordered the closure of all CNT Locals, a gesture intended, primarily, to appease the right.[1]

On 16 July, the Catalan CNT convened a Regional Plenum to finalize resistance plans. That same morning, the Generalitat requested a meeting with representatives of the Regional Committees of the CNT and FAI to discuss collaboration against the approaching "fascist danger." A special five-man committee was appointed to liaise with the Generalitat, now presided over by Lluis Companys: de Santillán, Oliver, and Ascaso representing the FAI; Durruti and Asens representing the CNT.[2] The anarchists again pressed Companys to keep his part of the bargain struck at the beginning of the year and give them at least enough arms for a 1,000 men. The reply was the Generalitat had none to give. Throughout this period, the armed CNT-FAI Defense Committee patrols on the streets were being arrested and charged with illegal possession of arms.

In spite of the sustained harassment of the anarchists by both the Central and Catalan governments, the discussions with the Generalitat led to an agreement that the CNT and FAI would

---

1 Hobsbawm states the call for resistance came from the Republican government but for the anarchists, "the call came from a body the movement had always refused, on principle, to recognise." op.cit., p. 91.
2 De Santillán, *La revolución y la guerra en España*, p. 34.

collaborate with the Catalan government and all other parties and organizations prepared to confront fascism.[3]

The fact of the matter was that, in spite of the by-now irrefutable evidence that advanced preparations for a military rising were under way, neither Companys nor Prime Minister Casares Quiroga trusted the anarcho-syndicalist CNT, and refused to consider arming a mass labor union whose stated objective was social revolution. The prospect of unleashing a social revolution by arming the people was more catastrophic than the alternative scenario of a military coup and fascism. The slogan of reaction was, at least, the defense of tradition, family, and property! Barcelona police chief Federico Escofet was quite prepared to arm the UGT, but, as he explained:

"To arm the CNT represented an immediate or later danger for the Republican regime in Catalonia—of equal danger for its existence as the military rebellion... Companys and I agreed on the necessity of not distributing the arms...because the CNT-FAI was the dominant force. These armed elements, who undoubtedly would provide invaluable assistance in the struggle against the rebels, could also endanger the existence of the Republic and the government of the Generalitat."[4]

The Regional CNT Defense Committee of Catalonia, based in the working class suburb of Pueblo Nuevo in Barcelona, knew full well it could expect no help from outside sources and had already begun to procure its own arms. On 17 July, militants from the transport workers section of the CNT (many of whom were later to form the core of what became known as the "Friends of Durruti" group), stormed two ships anchored in the port and removed around 150 rifles and a dozen or so handguns. The Confederal Defense Committee organized raids on armories and gun shops, while antique and dilapidated rifles and revolvers, as well as the more modern 300 Winchesters discarded by the defeated Esquerra in the wake of the October 1934 rising, appeared from their hiding places.

The Regional Defense Committee of the CNT and the Liaison Commission of the Anarchist Groups, which included all the members of the Nosotros group, Ascaso, Durruti,

3   Ibid. pp. 34–35.
4   Federico Escofet, *De una derrota a una victoria*, Barcelona, 1984, p. 231.

Oliver, Jover and Aurelio Fernández, were fully prepared for
the struggle that they knew would soon take place in the streets
of the cities. The theorists, on the other hand, were noticeable
by their absence.[5] A detailed contingency plan was ready to go
into operation immediately after they received the signal that
the military putsch had been launched. The Nosotros group
were not revolutionary strategists who directed operations from
behind, but anarchists who led by inspiration and example.
To ensure ease of communication with the confederal defense
cadres at their designated strategic locations around the city,
they had prepared and fitted two trucks as mobile headquarters
that could move with the fighting.

On the afternoon of Friday 17 July, the Peninsular
Committee, the Regional Committee of Catalonia, and the
local Federation of Anarchist Groups (FAI), together with the
Local Federation and Regional Committee of the Libertarian
Youth Organization (JJ.LL.-FIJL) issued a statement that broke
the first news to the public that the army had finally risen in
Morocco:

"The fascist danger is no longer a threat, but a bloody reality...
A section of the army has risen in arms against the people in
an attempt to impose on us the most atrocious tyranny. This
is no time for vacillation. Our agreements must now be put
into practice. In each locality, the anarchist and Libertarian
Youth groups will operate in the closest possible contact with
the responsible committees of the CNT. Confrontations with
the anti-fascist forces must be avoided, whoever they may be:
the categorical imperative of the hour is to defeat militaristic,
clerical, and aristocratic fascism. Do not lose contact, which
has to be permanent, with the Specific organization (FAI),
both regional and national. Long live the Revolution! Death
to Fascism!"[6]

At 9pm on Saturday evening, the eve of the rebellion on
the mainland, the CNT-FAI liaison committee met again with

5 According to García Oliver, neither de Santillán, Montseny, Felipe Alaiz,
Carbó, "nor any of those who, at meetings and assemblies set their caps at the
leadership of the CNT-FAI, which was tacitly in the care of Ascaso, Oliver, and
Durruti. They regarded themselves as the cream of the intelligentsia and this,
it seems, exempted them from having to fight in the streets." Oliver, op.cit.,
p. 176.
6 *Solidaridad Obrera*, 19.7.1936.

President Companys to discuss the situation. Again Companys insisted that the only arms at the disposal of the Generalitat were those of the Assault Guards and the Mossos de Esquadra, the defense groups of the Generalitat. An hour later, the CNT and FAI held a joint meeting to brief the militants that the only arms they were likely to get would be those they seized themselves.

When the Barcelona garrison finally moved out of their barracks at 4:30am on the morning of 19 July, they lacked an essential ingredient for success—surprise! Within minutes, factory and ships' sirens wailed their pre-arranged signal across the city to the 300 or so confederal defense cadres on the streets, alerting them that the rising had started. The two mobile command centers rumbled off to their pre-arranged vantage points. The wailing sirens also signalled the passing of power from the backrooms of the Generalitat, Capitanía General and police headquarters to the union locals and local revolutionary committees.

Having successfully isolated and defeated the units from the various barracks, preventing them joining up, the principle strategic objective for the Regional Defense committee, the co-ordinating body of the workers' resistance, was the arsenal at the San Andres barracks. Anarchist sympathizers in the barracks had informed them that 30,000 rifles and ammunition were stored there. If they managed to seize the San Andres arsenal, they could arm the people, crush the rebellion, and Barcelona would be theirs. Anarcho-syndicalist telephone workers already held and successfully defended the main telephone exchange in the Plaza de Catalunya, an important strategic target for the would-be rebels. CNT-FAI control of the Telefónica, which they shared with the UGT, was to contribute much to the durability of the CNT-FAI predominance in Catalonia. As one of the real and symbolic centers of power, it gave the workers' organizations control over internal and external communications, and inhibited the re-assertion of state power. When the Telefónica was finally restored to the Catalan state on the instructions of the CNT-FAI leadership following the bloody "May Days" of 1937, it symbolized the full restoration of state power and the final collapse of the revolution.

Police chief Escofet did everything in his power to prevent the weapons in the San Andres arsenal falling into the hands of the militants. He knew that once the people took possession of those arms the monopoly of coercion, which gave the state its authority, would be broken and state power would collapse. A company of loyal Civil Guard was sent to defend the building, but they arrived too late—the barracks had already been invaded and ransacked by crowds of workers. This was the pivotal event that transformed a military coup into a social revolution, the brief moment when political power shifted from the Generalitat Palace to the union branches and the local revolutionary committees. Many of the security forces who had remained loyal to the Republic began throwing off their uniforms and joined the people in arms.

On the morning of 20 July, Escofet reported to President Companys that the rebellion had been put down, as he had promised. Companys replied acidly that that was all very well but the situation remained chaotic. Armed and uncontrollable mobs were rampaging through the streets. Escofet threw the ball back into the politician's court:

"President, I undertook to dominate the military revolt in Barcelona, and I have done this. But an authority requires the means of coercion to make itself obeyed and these means do not exist today. As a result, there is no authority. And I, my dear President, do not know how to perform miracles...for the moment we are all overcome by the situation, including the leaders of the CNT. The only solution, President, is to contain the situation politically, without minimizing our respective authorities."[7]

The successful spontaneous insurrection of the Barcelona working class, under anarchist inspiration and leadership, had achieved that rarest of exceptions: "a real victory of insurrection over the military in street fighting."[8] With the collapse of the military and rightist rebellion in the city, the regional committees of the CNT, FAI, and FIJL called a meeting on the afternoon of 20 July in their new headquarters in the Casa

---

7   Escofet, op.cit., p. 352.
8   Marx & Engels, *The Class Struggles in France, 1848–1850*, Moscow, 1962, Vol. I, p. 130.

Cambo building in the Via Layetana to assess the situation and to discuss the role they felt they were being called on to play.

Their position was ambiguous to say the least; the state apparatus had collapsed and political power now lay with the spontaneously created and independent revolutionary committees in the factories, neighborhoods, and rural communities, but where did that leave the unions? This question had been debated at length at the Zaragoza Congress earlier that year. Federico Urales had argued, convincingly, that the great unions and the mammoth industrial federations would cease to exist "by reason of the sustained decentralization of the federal compact of solidarity." In effect, the act of revolution spelled death for the old system—including the CNT and FAI as organizations. Urales argued that the producer was involved both in the economic sphere in the workplace and as an administrative-political consumer within the municipality. The assembly being sovereign in work as well as in the municipality, there would be no room for anything separate from and outside these two aspects of daily life—including the CNT!

As Escofet had foreseen, the administrative leadership of the CNT, overtaken by events, had been as surprised as the politicians at the shift in power that had taken place overnight. Having extolled the virtues of the working class throughout their lives as militants—now that its chains were about to be broken and the dream transformed into a reality by a revolutionary process which threatened to make their role superfluous—they began to have second thoughts. In their hearts, they doubted the ability of the people to administer their own lives in their own interests. In spite of all their earlier threats of social revolution in response to the rightist threat— to say nothing of de Santillán's concern with advance planning and revolutionary preparedness—the "influential militants," who met in the Casa Cambo on 20 July 1936, concluded the objective conditions for social revolution were not right. The civil war, although it had triggered the revolutionary situation, would be the chief obstacle to the consolidation of the revolution and would ultimately destroy it.

The higher committees of the CNT-FAI-FIJL in Catalonia saw themselves caught on the horns of a dilemma: social revolution, fascism, or bourgeois democracy. Either they committed themselves to the solutions offered by social revolution, regardless of the difficulties involved in fighting both fascism and international capitalism, or, through fear of fascism (or of the people), they sacrificed their anarchist principles and revolutionary objectives to bolster and become part of the bourgeois state in the hope it would undergo a transition after the defeat of fascism and become a genuinely humane organ of power, operating into the interests of the people. Faced with an imperfect state of affairs and preferring defeat to a possibly Pyrrhic victory, the Catalan anarchist leadership renounced anarchism in the name of expediency, and removed the social transformation of Spain from their agenda.

But what the CNT-FAI leaders failed to grasp was that the decision whether or not to implement Libertarian Communism was not theirs to make. Anarchism was not something that could be transformed from theory into practice by organizational decree. The anarchists had performed their task as pathfinders and shock troops of the revolution. They had implanted the ideas and helped create the necessary environment in which those ideas and practices could be nourished and grow to flower, but it was beyond their brief or abilities to put anarchism into practice; that was a task only the people themselves could perform. The anarchists had reverted once again to their historical role of the "conscious minority," the role they are destined to play in all societies—authoritarian, totalitarian, and libertarian.

What the CNT-FAI leadership had failed to take on board was the fact that spontaneous defensive movement of 19 July had developed a political direction of its own. On their own initiative, without any intervention by the leadership of the unions or political parties, the rank and file militants of the CNT, representing the dominant force within the Barcelona working class, together with other union militants had, with the collapse of state power, superseded their individual partisan identities and had been welded—Catholics, Communists, Socialists, Republicans, and Anarchists—into genuinely popular, non-partisan revolutionary committees wielding physical and moral power in their respective neighborhoods. They were the natural organisms of the revolution itself and the direct expression of popular power.

The assumption that political power in Catalonia had passed to the higher committees of the CNT-FAI was, probably, the principal blunder which was to undermine the revolutionary process. By failing to displace the "legitimate" political element within the state, the military provoked the collapse of State power. It was the people, led by the militants of the defense committees, who had stood firm against the reactionaries while the government had dithered. In doing so, it lost its right to rule. The people now wielded power—in the working class quarters and at the point of product and distribution—not the State or the union leaders who had now· outlived their usefulness to the revolutionary process. A dual power situation existed—diffused popular power against centralized political and union power.

From the first moment, therefore, the higher committees of the CNT-FAI set aside traditional anarcho-syndicalist reliance on the creative spirit of the people and their capacity for self-organization. They blindly disregarded Isaac Puente's warning in *Libertarian Communism* that "there should be no superstructure above the local organization other than that with a specific function which cannot be carried out locally," thereby becoming the unwitting agents in a tragically destructive process. By imposing their leadership from above, these partisan committees suffocated the mushrooming popular autonomous revolutionary centers—the grass-roots factory and local revolutionary committees, the identifying feature of all great revolutions—and prevented them from proving themselves as an efficient and viable means of coordinating communications, defense, and provisioning. They also prevented the local revolutionary committees from integrating with each other to form a regional, provincial, and national federal network that would facilitate the revolutionary task of social and economic reconstruction.

The process by which this occurred involved many complex factors, psychological as well as political. Particularly powerful were the close ties of loyalty and the moral imperatives of solidarity that bound the individual CNT rank and file militants to the Organization, and made them hesitate to express public disagreement with the course of action being pursued by the leadership at a time of crisis. Equally, the sharp break with normal democratic union procedures due to the "circumstances" of war, governmental collaboration, and the need for "antifascist unity" led to the higher committees ruling in the "interests" of the base. Their moral authority became transformed into coercive authority.

Militants from the barrios committees (which had led and co-ordinated the struggle throughout the city), who were sent on behalf of those local committees to the new CNT-FAI headquarters for information and instruction, were arbitrarily co-opted into the centralized union apparatus. Mariano R. Vázquez, "Marianet," the newly appointed CNT Regional Secretary (and FAI member) was one of the leaders principally responsible for this policy:

"Your place is here, not in the Locals" is how he greeted suitable local militants who came in search of news.[9]

Federica Montseny, sent by the revolutionary committee of San Martin district for instructions, was one of those "influential militants" who was catapulted to organizational prominence without any democratic mandate either from her barrio committee or the union she had only recently joined. She was also co-opted into de Santillán's Nervio group, and on to the FAI Peninsular Committee by a similar process that same day.

Mariano Vazquez's appointment as Regional Secretary of the Catalan CNT had been the result of the policy of the revolutionary anarchists refusing positions of responsibility within the union. In the tradition of the Bakuninist members of the "Alliance" who refused all administrative positions in the First International, anarchists tended not to become involved in the administrative or intermediatory functions of the CNT. The reason for this was to avoid the inevitable friction between their role as revolutionaries and union officials. Earlier that year, at the union elections to appoint the Catalan Regional Secretary, Marcos Alcón had received the most votes, but turned it down. In second place came Francesc Esgleas, husband of Federica Montseny. He also turned it down. The third candidate was "Marianet," whose name (according to García Oliver) had been put forward as a "joke" by comrades from the building

9   Abel Paz, *Paradigmo de una revolucion*, Choisy le roi, 1967, p. 144.

workers' union. He was elected to Regional Secretary on the basis of four votes, an indication of the amount of confidence he inspired among his fellow workers.[10]

If Marianet's nomination was a "joke," it was one that was to have tragic consequences for the Confederation. His career as Catalan Regional Secretary and, later, National Secretary of the CNT was, to say the least, damaging. Like Horacio Prieto, whose place he was to take as National Secretary of the CNT later that year, Marianet, the building worker turned administrator, was an example of the lengths to which people in public life will go when they abandon principles for expediency. Like Prieto, he was putty in the hands of Negrín and the Stalinists; he was continually entering into pacts with the UGT and attending pro-government rallies. By 1938, along with Prieto, he was arguing for the opening of negotiations with Franco.

Meanwhile, at the other Confederal nerve center at the premises of the Transport and Metallurgical Union, a messenger arrived from President Companys requesting a meeting with the CNT-FAI Liaison Committee. Everyone had forgotten about Companys and the Generalitat. "Does it still exist?" someone asked.

Marianet, in line with the collaborationist policy formulated by the CNT-FAI leadership, agreed to the meeting. Instead of ordering the dispersal of these visible, but politically ineffective remnants of the Catalan government, he tacitly admitted their symbolic legitimacy. Why the Catalan CNT-FAI agreed to this is a matter for conjecture: perhaps he and his advisers assumed the government was stronger than it actually was. What is clear is that, due to internal doubts and dissensions, they failed to realize how powerful the popular movement was and that their role as union spokesmen was now inimical to the course of the revolution. Marianet insisted on dealing with the Catalan President as though he was negotiating a union contract:

"This interview won't be like previous ones. Before we begged a few pistols, now we will impose the will of the working people."[11]

---

10 Oliver, op.cit., p. 183.
11 Ibid., p. 145.

García Oliver, de Santillán, and Asens, the CNT-FAI Liaison Committee set up days before the rising, were ushered in to Companys' office on the first floor of the Generalitat Palace. They entered as victors: "armed to the teeth... Shabby and soiled by dust and smoke" to listen to Companys honeyed speech. The only account of this speech is that given by García Oliver:

"'Before I begin,' stated Companys, 'I must say that the CNT and FAI have not received the treatment which they merit by virtue of their true importance... I have found myself obliged to confront and persecute you. You are now masters of the city and Catalonia, for you alone have defeated the fascist soldiery...the fact is that today, you who were subject to harassment up until yesterday, have seen off the fascists and the military. Knowing, then, who and what you are, I can but address you in tones of utmost sincerity. You have won and everything lies at your feet; if you have any need of me, or no longer want me as President of Catalonia, just say the word and I shall become just another foot soldier in the struggle against fascism. I, along with the men of my party, my name, and my prestige, may be of use in the struggle which has ended so felicitously in this city today... You may rely upon me and my loyalty as a man and a politician convinced that today has been the demise of a whole dishonorable past, as a man who honestly wishes to see Catalonia march on the van of the most socially progressive countries.'"[12]

Companys was an artful and skillful politician. He knew the anarchist leadership of old and how to turn their political naiveté to his own advantage to prevent the nascent revolution from consolidating itself. His objective was to recover political power, re-assert the authority of the Generalitat on the streets of the capital, and restore economic normality. The only way to do this was to present his proposals to the anarchists in such a way that they stressed positive, generally held cultural and human values—democracy, social harmony, and anti-fascism. He knew these would provide a basis for a provisional power-sharing arrangement with the CNT-FAI leaders. Acting on Rousseau's dictum that "The agreement of two particular

12 *Solidaridad Obrera*, 19.7.1937.

interests is formed by opposition to a third," he appreciated the need for a military victory over the "common enemy," fascism, which was in itself a sufficiently unifying principle to neutralize the revolutionary demands of the "conscious minority." This would allow him to keep the state bureaucracy intact and provide the necessary breathing space until he could re-introduce the concept of hierarchy.

Anarchist dominance in the region also provided Companys with a useful lever for ensuring Catalan autonomy against possible encroachments on provincial sovereignty by the central government. He reproached Madrid obliquely: "Betrayed by the normal guardians of law and order, we have turned to the proletariat for protection." Coyly, he suggested to the CNT-FAI Liaison committee that under his chairmanship the CNT and FAI, together with all the antifascist parties, should set up "an organ capable of pursuing the revolutionary struggle until victory is assured." This ad hoc body, a bourgeois government in embryo, was to become known as the Central Committee of Antifascist Militias (CCMA), and was decreed into existence by the Generalitat government.

After preliminary discussions with the bourgeois and Marxist politicians thoughtfully assembled by Companys, García Oliver informed them they would relay the CCMA's committee proposals to the Regional Committees of the CNT and FAI. They would have their reply in due course. To the already compromised CNT-FAI leadership, there is little doubt that Companys' skillful maneuvering would have its desired effect. The battle-hardened militants, thrown off balance by the flattery and eulogies of their old enemies, had gone into the Generalitat Palace as victors; they emerged vanquished.

When the CNT-FAI Liaison Committee returned to report Companys' proposals to Marianet, the latter informed them that in anticipation of such a move he had convened a "meeting of militants" for that same afternoon. During the course of the discussion it was suggested that the options open to the "responsible committees" were either to go all out for Libertarian Communism, which would be, according to Federica Montseny, tantamount to imposing an anarchist dictatorship.

Pending the decision of a plenum of local CNT unions and FAI groups, which was to be convened as soon as possible, Marianet and the others agreed to continue negotiations with Companys. The wily Catalan president was contacted by telephone and informed of the Regional Committee's acceptance, in principle, of the proposals concerning the Antifascist Militias Committee of Catalonia—pending, of course, ratification by a plenum of local CNT unions and FAI groups, which would be convened as soon as possible.

Companys' heart must have soared when he heard the news. He knew that having permitted the Generalitat to remain intact and voluntarily committing themselves to collaborating with it, the CNT-FAI leaders, and the organizations they represented, would be bound to the institution of government that they themselves sanctioned. It was only a matter of time. "The anarchist masses will not," he observed, "oppose the common sense of their chiefs."[13]

In the meantime, Durruti, García Oliver, and Aurelio Fernández were empowered by the Regional Committee to continue their discussions as the official Liaison Committee to ensure that should the plenary meeting agree to the setting up of the Militias Committee, it would swing into operation promptly and smoothly. They returned to the Generalitat Palace that same evening to begin provisional discussions with the Catalan politicians—Josep Tarradellas, Artemi Aiguadér and Jaume Miravitlles of the Esquerra, Ramón Peypoch of Catalan Action, Joan Comorera of the Socialist Union of Catalonia, Rafael Vidiella of the UGT and PSOE, and Julián Gorkin of the POUM. The Estat Català was disbarred from participating on the grounds that its leader, Dencàs, was a fascist sympathizer who had fled to Italy, and that the interests of the region were represented by the Generalitat.

The following day, 21 July, the Regional Committee of the CNT held its hastily summoned "extraordinary" assembly of Catalan unions. José Peirats argues this was not, in fact, a properly constituted plenum of unions with a published agenda to be discussed in a regular way by mandated union representatives; it was, rather, an informal gathering of militants at Regional Committee level who, present in a personal capacity, had no

mandate or authority to decide on the issues in question.[14]
More than a month was to pass before a regular plenum of the
Catalan CNT unions was to be held.

The "official" account of the "extraordinary" assembly was
provided later by Marianet:

"On 21 July, 1936, Barcelona was the venue for a Regional
Plenum of the Local Federations and Sub-Regionals called by the
Regional Committee of Catalonia. The situation was considered
and it was unanimously decided not to mention Libertarian
Communism until such time as we had captured that part of
Spain that was in the hands of the rebels. Consequently, the
plenum resolved not to press on with totalitarian achievements,
for we are facing a problem: imposing a dictatorship—wiping
out all the guards and activists from the political parties who
had played their part on the victory over the rebels on 19 and
20 July; a dictatorship which, in any event, would be crushed
from without even if it succeeded within. The plenum, with
the exception of the Regional Federation of Bajo Llobregat,
opted for collaboration with the other political parties and
organizations in setting up the Antifascist Militias Committee.
On the decision of this plenum the CNT and FAI sent their
representatives to it."[15]

According to García Oliver, the delegate from Bajo Llobregat
was the only one to point out that the creation of the Militias
Committee would be an obstacle in the path of the revolutionary
process. Because it was only a provisional agreement, pending
the decision of the plenum, they proposed that the CNT
and FAI withdraw their representatives and press on with the
revolution and the introduction of Libertarian Communism in
line with the ideological objectives of the organization. They
asked that one of the CNT-FAI representatives on the Militias
Committee report to the plenum as to its compatibility with
the revolutionary aspirations of the CNT and FAI.[16]

14 *Noir et Rouge*, No. 36, Paris, December 1967.
15 *Report from the National Committee of the CNT to the AIT/IWMA Conference*,
December 1937.
16 The question of winding up the Militias Committee and withdrawing from
its various subsidiary organs came up for discussion a few weeks later during
a Regional Plenum of the Anarchist Groups of Catalonia (Sitges, 21.8.1938).
The question was no longer being debated as a matter of principle, but
as a ploy to force the withdrawal of the POUM and other minor Marxist

García Oliver claims that, although a member of the Militias Committee, he agreed with the Bajo Llobregat analysis that "all we had really done was hamper the progress of the social revolution for which we had always campaigned." He likened the Committee to a "second-class police commissariat" and urged that the provisional decision to collaborate with it should be reversed:

."The time had come for us...to see through what we had begun on 18 July, dismantling the Militias Committee and forcing the pace in such a way that for the first time in history the anarcho-syndicalist unions would 'go for broke,' that is, go for the maximum anarchist objective—the organization of a Libertarian Communist lifestyle throughout Spain."[17]

Montseny spoke next. She declared that her conscience as an anarchist would not permit her to countenance anarchists forcing the pace of events or "going for broke." For her, that implied the creation of what she described as "an anarchist dictatorship." They should agree to remain inside the Militias Committee in the meantime, but should withdraw "just as soon as the rebel military were defeated, so as to devote ourselves once again to the task of anarchist organization and propaganda."

Diego Abad de Santillán, Peninsular Secretary and FAI representative on the Militias Committee, also favored remaining within that body and continuing to collaborate with other political parties in the antifascist struggle. His argument showed even less faith in the constructive capacity of the workers than Montseny. Amazingly (for a self-styled revolutionary) it revolved around the fear that if the movement did decide to "go for broke" it would pose a threat to all the

and Catalanist parties from the Committee. (*Acta del pleno regional de grupos anarquistas de Catalunya celebrado en Barcelona el 21 de agosto de 1936*.) By ensuring POUM representation, Companys was playing a complicated double, perhaps even triple, game. According to Maximo García Venero, Companys summoned leading POUM members, including Julián Gorkin, and told them "If you do not help me to contain the anarchists I have made up my mind to resign the presidency. The POUM representatives managed to have themselves issued several dozen machine guns, numerous rifles, and ammunition. And, as was only logical, they were recognized as a force with a right to be heard and represented in Catalan life." Maximo García Venero, *Historia del nacionalismo Catalan*, Vol. II, Madrid, 1967, pp. 431–432.
17 Oliver, op.cit., p. 186.

vested interests of capitalism, and, lacking legitimacy in the eyes of international law, would provoke immediate foreign intervention. British warships were already in the harbor, "showing the flag" in a cryptic demonstration of force that the Western democracies would not tolerate revolution. In the face of this threat, he urged that, in the meantime, all mention of Libertarian Communism should be shelved.

Marianet claimed that membership of the Militias Committee would in no way prejudge "our governing from the streets," and not commit the Organization "to dictatorial practices, as would be the case if the CNT were to go for broke."

Winding up the debate, Oliver pointed out that the question of dictatorship had been raised by Federica Montseny. She had been the first to suggest that "going for broke" was "tantamount to installing an anarchist dictatorship which would be as evil as any other." "Since mention has been made of dictatorship," Oliver added:

"Let it be said that none of the ones we have known thus far shared the same character. Nor have tyrannies always had the same meaning. True, there have been tyrannies through imposition upon the people. But there have been tyrannies elected by the people.

"Of all the varieties of dictatorship known, none has yet been enforced through the concerted action of labor unions. And if these labor unions are anarchist in outlook and their militants schooled, like us, in an anarchist ethic, to presuppose that we should resort to the same acts as the Marxists, for instance, is tantamount to saying that anarchism and Marxism are, basically, the same ideology, since they produce identical fruits. Such simplism I cannot accept. And let me say that syndicalism [anarcho-syndicalism], in Spain and worldwide, arose out of an act of affirmation of its constructive values *vis á vis* the history of mankind, because without that demonstration of the ability to build a free socialism, the future would remain the playground of the political formulae thrown up by the French Revolution beginning with a plurality of parties and ending with just one."

The issue was put to the vote. García Oliver proposed Libertarian Communism as an immediate objective—"going for broke." De Santillán, for the FAI, moved that Libertarian Communism be waived as an immediate objective, and participation in the Militias Committee be approved. With the exception of the district federation of Bajo Llobregat, who supported García Oliver, the decision to abandon Libertarian Communism was carried.

In spite of the overwhelming vote against the implementation of Libertarian Communism at this plenum, García Oliver claims he refused to accept the decision. The delegates, summoned in haste and unaware of the business in hand, had rejected the fundamental principles of the CNT without reference back to the membership. He noted, wryly, that the people who had pushed the reformist line had been *faistas* not *treintistas* as Broué and Temime pointed out:[18]

"The *treintistas* had certainly not taken part in the discussion, let alone adopted a stance... Faced with a choice between social revolution and the Militias Committee the organization had chosen the later. Time alone would tell who was right... the majority at the plenum, with de Santillán; Marianet; and Federica and her group of anti-syndicalist anarchists, such as Eusebio Carbó, Felipe Alaiz, García Birlán, Fidel Miró, José Peirats, and others...or the Bajo Llobregat district, which joined with me in arguing the need to press ahead with the social revolution, in a set of circumstances that had never seemed so promising. By their attitude, these self-styled anarchists had bankrupted the FAI as such, it having been set up for the specific purpose of neutralizing the reformist syndicalists inside the CNT."[19]

The crucial nature of this decision, which was to divert the course of the revolution, cannot be stressed strongly enough. It was, in effect, an admission by the CNT-FAI leadership that the ideas they had held concerning the transition from a statist and capitalist society to a Libertarian Communist one were simply not practical due to the "circumstances" of war. Not only did they abandon anarchism, but, by negotiating with

---

18 "[However] the FAI ideology had taken a step backward; the CNT in February had not given the cue to boycott the elections, and the restored *Treintistas* won acceptance for their point of view more than once in the weeks in the weeks that followed." Broué and Temime, op.cit., p. 57.
19 Oliver, op.cit., p. 186.

politicians and representatives of the state without the express consent of the membership, they acted contrary to the union constitution. This reflected a long-standing weakness within the CNT-FAI. Because there was no paid union apparatus it was assumed that "leaderism" was not a problem. This was not the case. The deference of the broad mass of the CNT to the "natural" leaders who had won the workers' trust by their personal sacrifice and commitment to the "idea" led directly to the creation of the "fixed and constant authority" that Bakunin had warned about and had turned well-meaning anarchists into charlatans.

That evening, García Oliver convened a meeting of the Nosotros group together with a number of selected comrades to propose a seizure of the symbolic centers of government in the city by anarchist columns led by Durruti. Durruti, who had been unusually silent during the debate in the plenum that afternoon, had not supported Oliver's motion. For him, the liberation of the 30,000 CNT militants believed captured in rebel-held Zaragoza had priority over everything else.

"García Oliver's argument, here and during the plenum, strikes me as splendid," stated Durruti. "His plan for a coup is perfect. But this does not seem to me the opportune moment. My feeling is that it should be put off until after the capture of Zaragoza, which cannot take more that ten days. In the meantime, I must insist that we shelve these plans until Zaragoza has been taken. At present, with only Catalonia as a base, we would be reduced to the most minimal geographic area."[20]

A jubilant Joan Peiró later noted that anarchism, for the first time, had adapted itself "to history":

"Until July 1936, the tactics of anarchism consisted in remaining on the periphery of the State and from there harassing it and its institutions. The tactics of anarchism in the first half of the nineteenth century, however, consisted of the contrary. Proudhon, for example, fought the State and its institutions from his seat in the French Chamber of Deputies... Anarchism will have to contribute to the economic

---

20 Oliver, op.cit., p. 190.

reconstruction of Spain...to win the war this will involve much closer collaboration than is presently the case."[21]

García Oliver's principled stand against collaboration with the bourgeois parties was short-lived. Working on the "realistic" principle of joining those you have been unable to beat, he accepted the nomination endorsing his membership of the Militias Committee along with the other anarchist representatives—Marcos Alcón, José Asens, Aurelio Fernández, and Diego Abad de Santillán.

By its very nature, the Militias Committee was a compromise, an artificial political solution, an officially sanctioned appendage of the Generalitat government, with each party pursuing divergent and contradictory objectives. Its legitimization of party politics led to a renewed power struggle among the factions in an attempt to boost membership and influence at the expense of the others. The only real area of agreement between the Republican and Socialist factions within the Militias Committee was the ultimate elimination of anarchist influence. It also drew the CNT-FAI leadership inexorably into the State apparatus, until then its principal enemy, and led to the steady erosion of anarchist influence and credibility.

Justifying the irrevocable consequences of his action in joining the artificial and hybrid creation that was the Militias Committee, Oliver later expressed his ambivalence toward the "extraordinary" plenum of local and district committees which had taken the decision to abandon anarchist principles and collaborate with the political parties.

"The CNT and the FAI opted for collaboration and democracy, eschewing the revolutionary totalitarianism which simply had to have led to the revolution's being strangled by the confederal and anarchist dictatorship. They trusted in the word and person of a Catalan democrat, and retained and supported Companys in the office of President of the Generalitat; they accepted the Militias Committee and worked out a system of representation proportionate with numbers which, although not fair...[in that] the UGT and the Socialist Party, minority groups in Catalonia, were assigned an equal number of

21 "Estado, anarquismo y la historia," Juan Peiró, *Timón*, Barcelona, October, 1938, pp. 69–70.

positions with the triumphant CNT and anarchists…implied sacrifice calculated to lure dictatorially inclined parties along the path of loyal collaboration which might not be jeopardized by suicidal competition."[22]

The Central Committee of Antifascist Militias, which was to concern itself almost exclusively with security and military matters, met for the first time that same night, 21 July, in the Maritime Museum, where it established its permanent headquarters. The CNT agreed to parity with the other parties which were much less numerically strong. The UGT, for example, was minuscule in Catalonia in July 1936 with only 12,000 members, but it received the same number of seats as the CNT with its 350,000 members. Companys' Esquerra Republicana also received parity with the two unions. García Oliver points out, however, that this decision had little to do with solidarity or generosity, but pragmatic belief that a compromise of this nature in Catalonia would secure similar concessions in other regions such as Madrid where the CNT was in the minority. The Militias Committee was broken down as follows: CNT–3; UGT–3; Esquerra Republicana (Companys' party)–3; FAI–2; Acció Catalana–1; POUM–1; PSOE (Socialist Party)–1; Unión de Rabassaires (Catalan peasants' party)–1. The Generalitat was represented by a commissioner with a military adviser.[23]

Other important administrative organs, such as the Supplies Committee, the Investigation Commission, the New Unified School Council, the Council of the Economy, the Revolutionary Tribunals, etc., were organized on a similar basis with union, party, and FAI representation.

The CNT-FAI leaders saw the role of the Militias Committee as "establishing revolutionary order in the rearguard, the recruiting, organization, and training of combat troops and officers…the provision of food and clothes, the organization of the economy, legislation, the administration of justice…the

22 "El Comité Central de Milicias Antifascistas de Catalonia," *Solidaridad Obrera*, 18.8.1937.
23 This was the only meeting of the Militias Committee that Durruti attended as a CNT delegate. Perhaps he also sensed the contradictions that existed between the governmental role of the Militias Committee and the local organs of the social revolution.

setting up of war industries, propaganda, relations with the Madrid government, land cultivation, health, and the defense of coasts and frontiers. We had to organize the payment of militias, their families, and the widows of combatants, in fact to tens of thousands of people. We were faced with tasks which in any governmental system would require a massive bureaucracy. The Militias Committee was the war, interior, and foreign ministries rolled into one... The Committee was the most legitimate expression of the power of the people."[24]

President Azaña was horrified by Companys' accommodation with the CNT-FAI. He described it, despairingly, as a plot to abolish the Spanish State. Companys had, however, no other option short of forming Generalitat militias, as Communist Joan Comorera had suggested, to challenge the CNT-FAI and POUM for control of the streets.[25] The Republican forces remaining in Catalonia amounted to no more than 5,000 men of the police and security forces—and in the revolutionary euphoria of those early July days even these could not be relied upon to support the Generalitat. The regular army had been disbanded by the Madrid government on the morning on 19 July and the soldiers had dispersed, some fleeing to join the rebels, some returning home while, others joined the newly formed workers' militias. The 40,000 or so anarcho-syndicalist militants, on the other hand, were organized and well-armed with the weapons taken from the San Andres barracks and from the defeated soldiers; they also controlled the communications and transport infrastructure of the whole region.

---

24 De Santillán, op.cit., p. 169.
25 Manuel Benavides, *Guerra y Revolucion en Catalunya*, Mexico, 1946, p. 190.

23

The FAI Turned Upside Down

From 21 July onward, the FAI, led by Diego Abad de Santillán, ceased to operate as an independent entity. The *trabazón* and the Civil War had fused both organizations into an entity known as the CNT-FAI. However, the sharing of power with the other political parties, first through the Militias Committee, then, later, through the Generalitat and central governments, also meant the sharing of values. It was not long before the bourgeois utilitarian strategy of expediency displaced traditional anarchist concern for the values of social justice.

From 21 July onwards, as we have seen, social revolution was removed from the agenda of the joint CNT-FAI committees. The revolutionary events that were, by that time, moving into top gear in industry and in the countryside, particularly in Aragón, were ignored. Other than calling off the general strike declared on 19 July, the higher committees provided no guidelines for the militants apart from urging for a military victory against fascism "at any price." The "price" was the formal renunciation of anarchist principles. On 27 July, *faista* and Catalan Regional Secretary Mariano Vázquez met the British consul in Barcelona to promise them that the CNT would provide guards to ensure that the workers would not socialize eighty-seven companies in which Britain expressed an interest. The CNT-FAI leadership gave similar assurances to the representatives of other nations that their industrial and commercial interests would also be protected.

Having taken the unilateral decision to abandon Libertarian Communism as the immediate objective of the

CNT-FAI, the leadership had to convince the broad base of the membership—and the "conscious minority"—that the ideals nourished by three generations of activists (ideals for which countless militants had died, been tortured, or spent long years in prison), could not be applied in practice against a backdrop of civil war and the hostility of international capitalism. The dilemma, as they presented it, was war or revolution.

The first Regional Plenum of the Catalan CNT took place on 9 August. There was no agenda to be discussed and either accepted or rejected by the general assembly; it was, rather, an outlining of the reasons for the decisions taken to date and the blunt statement that the policy of the CNT-FAI was now "antifascist unity," not Libertarian Communism.

The revolution, however, was developing along very different lines in the rural areas of neighboring Aragón. While the CNT-FAI leaders in Catalonia were urging their members to give precedence to the war against fascism over class war, as though they were in some way different, the rural workers of Aragón were pressing ahead with the revolution and expressing their anger and discontent openly, subjecting the Barcelona-based leaders to embarrassing public criticism.

The revolutionary mood of the workers was expressed during a local general assembly of unions at Valderrobes in Teruel province:

"We have said it everywhere, including in the regional assembly in Caspe—we must not forget what happened to our anarchist comrades in Russia... 'I do not know whether or not Aragón is in a position to implement Libertarian Communism,' said one delegate, 'Nor do I know if the time has arrived to do away forever with the previous outmoded system. What I do know is that throughout Upper and Lower Aragón, by unanimous desire and free will, communitarian life is being organized within the greatest possible liberty. And all this without any talk of Libertarian Communism.'

"We would never have believed that it would be the very anarchist daily *Tierra y Libertad*, which would attempt to douse Aragón in cold water, as occurred during the general assembly in Caspe with comrade Marianet. It is easy [to say] that the confederal members of Aragón, Rioja, and Navarre should not forget confederal tactics; what we have not forgotten, nor can we forget, is that we are living a reality which no one can deny… In Spain it is possible to establish liberty and justice, and we firmly believe it is time to demonstrate this. This is what we are doing, neither more nor less."[1]

The arguments of the war and the threat of international intervention carried the day for the CNT-FAI leadership in the argument over revolution. There were three distinct points of view within the movement on the question of war and revolution. Out of the two million or so members of the CNT, perhaps only 300,000 or so might have described themselves as conscious anarchists or anarcho-syndicalists. Most of these believed the war would be over in a matter of weeks. After all, a few days had been sufficient to rout the army in Barcelona, Madrid, Valencia, and other industrial centers. They were enemies of collaboration and continued to believe in Libertarian Communism as a matter of principle, but— either out of deference to the CNT-FAI leadership or simply resigning themselves to the "force of circumstances" and requirements of the war argument—decided to forego it as a short term objective.

The CNT-FAI leaders, on the other hand, anticipated a lengthy war and opposed implementing Libertarian Communism until it had been won. To this end they committed themselves to maintaining public order, restoring production, and reassuring their bourgeois allies and international capitalism alike that they had nothing to fear from the anarchists. In the name of "antifascist unity," they opted for compromise and accommodation with the bourgeois and Marxist parties, but their strategic reasons were to prevent a victorious but exhausted CNT being overwhelmed by another political force, which had been more sparing with its resources. It was an ultimately corrupting strategy that soon absorbed all their energies, separated principles from practice, distanced the movement from its anarcho-syndicalistic constitution, removed the decision-making process from the rank and file, and transformed what had been a great working class instrument into just another oligarchic reformist socialist institution.

---

1   *Solidaridad Obrera*, 9.10.1936, p. 3.

"National unity," the rallying cry of statists through the ages, was the balm which soothed the painful memories and experiences of class collaboration over the previous fifty years. Political inexperience and naiveté as to the nature and mechanics of power politics, with its distinction between private and public morality, led the CNT-FAI leaders, in a spirit of forgiveness and in the name of anti-fascist solidarity, to overlook the systematically repressive role played by the Socialists and Nationalists under the Primo de Rivera dictatorship and in the early years of the Second Republic, its anti-libertarian legislation and the more recent bloody and unnecessary suppression of the peasants of Casas Viejas. The world of politics demanded the nature of Machiavelli's *The Prince*. It was a world for which the CNT-FAI leaders were unsuited and unprepared. Although they were "lions" who could "frighten the wolves," they had none of the fox's knowledge of the "traps and snares" of political life. As Machiavelli observed, "Those who simply hold to the nature of the lion do not understand their business."[2] It did not take them too long to "understand" the business, but by that time their business was sustaining the State, not overthrowing it.

The third body of option was that held by the "conscious minority" of articulate so-called "uncontrollable" anarchists who anticipated a lengthy war, but held that war and revolution were inseparable. Only a libertarian revolution could finally destroy fascism because to do so meant destroying the State, since fascism was only the State in a particular mode of operation: all States turn to fascism when the threat to power and privilege that the State protects and embodies becomes sufficiently menacing. Fascism occurs when privilege can no longer be secured by voluntary means; it is, in other words, enforced class collaboration, as opposed to the voluntary class collaboration of liberal democracy. The militants who held this view, however, were the most active and committed ones who had gone off to fight with the militia columns of Aragón and Levante in the early days of July and August. Isolated at the front, they had little chance of their views being published in the leadership-controlled confederal media or in the general assemblies. It was, therefore, very much a vanguard versus

2   Machiavelli, *The Prince*, Ch. XVIII.

rearguard debate; the activists at the front urging revolution
in the rear, while those in the rear (the administrators and
"leaders," supported by a fatalistically resigned majority),
urged war.

The final collapse into oligarchy was rapid. By late
September 1936, the Peninsular Committee of the FAI began
to assert its organizational authority over the affiliated groups.
In a numbered, but undated, first circular to the regional
federations and groups, the Peninsular Committee informed
its affiliates of the need to restructure the organization and the
need to recruit new members. The underlying assumption was
that all that was required for final victory was the creation of a
sufficiently large, solid, and cohesive organization:

"We, on this Committee, have seen to it that in all its
activities the specific movement (FAI) has been linked with
the Confederal Organization, establishing a single front that
has kept the ideal which we champion enjoying immensely
high prestige. The feverish activity of the early moments of
the struggle, and the no less intense activity which followed
it, in terms both of the war and of the reconstruction of the
economy, was wholly shared with the Confederal Organization,
the letters, which stand for the Confederal and Specific
movements, binding into one single acronym...

"The battle joined against fascism remains a furious one,
and our primary concern has been, and remains, to mobilize
the wherewithal for its prosecution. Now then, we must bear
it in mind that the greater the organized and cohesive force
we may have, the better our chances of this will be. Likewise,
the reorganization of our cadres and the expansion of our
numbers are matters of urgency. The ethos which the heroism
of our militants has aroused to favorable effect among the
people has to be capitalized upon so as to broaden the scope
of our action. The FAI's influence must reach into every nook
and cranny, and, to this end, it requires numerous and well-
prepared groups. The example of the Regionals, which are
engaged in overhauling their organization must be taken
on board as the model to be imitated, and in this way we
will ensure that the tremendous aura which surrounds our
movement may faithfully reflect our membership. The gaps
torn in our ranks by the shrapnel of murderous fascism have

to be speedily filled by means of honourable replacements for our fallen comrades..."[3]

A short while later, the Catalan press informed the world that the CNT had officially renounced its apolitical stance and was now a full member of the Generalitat government of Catalonia, which had replaced the Militias Committee. The CNT-FAI leaders were now totally caught up in the narrow technical aspects of the war against fascism and had lost all sight of the broader consequences of their actions. De Santillán later reflected on the decision to joint the government: "The Militias Committee guaranteed the supremacy of the people in arms, guaranteed Catalonia's autonomy, guaranteed the purity and legitimacy of war, guaranteed the resurrection of the Spanish pulse and of the Spanish soul: but we were told and it was repeated to us endlessly that as long as we persisted in retaining it, that is, as long as we persisted in propping up the power of the people, weapons would not come to Catalonia, nor would we be granted the foreign currency to obtain them from abroad, nor would we be supplied with the raw materials for our industry. And since losing the war meant losing everything and returning to a state like the one that prevailed in the Spain of Ferdinand VII, and in the conviction that the drive given by us and our people could not vanish completely from the new economic life, we quit the Militias Committee to join the Generalitat government in its Defense Councillorship and the other vital departments of the autonomous government."[4]

On 23 October, the CNT-FAI leaders signed a "Pact of Unity" with the UGT and Stalinist PSUC, bringing control of the spontaneous collectivization process begun by the workers under the control of the State. It was Article 15 of this agreement, however, which showed that the CNT-FAI leadership were prepared to act ruthlessly against the "conscious minority" of anarchists who insisted on pushing revolutionary class war policies against their own recommendations. "We are agreed upon common action to stamp out the harmful activities of uncontrollable groups which, out of lack of understanding or malice, pose a threat to the implementation of this program.[5]

---

3 Peirats, op.cit., Vol. II, pp. 242–244.
4 De Santillán, *Por que perdimos la guerra*, op.cit.
5 *Diario Oficial de la Generalitat de Catalonia*, 11.10.1936.

Two days later, on 25 October, the FAI Peninsular Committee issued a third notice to the Regional Committees, Local Federations and groups. It provides a telling insight into the now scarcely-concealed authoritarian thinking of the Peninsular Committee:

"Motives for Intervention: Due to the imperious nature of the circumstances in which we have been placed by the fascist revolt and the struggle we have committed ourselves in order to crush it, and being unable to speedily and fully realize our ideal aspirations, due to our having to accept collaboration with other sectors, to the purpose and effect of winning the war, so as to contribute for the duration of that war to the maintenance of the liaison and collaboration of antagonistic political parties, and because the people's frame of mind called for this, we have come out in favour of intervention in organisms of an official nature which we first seek to modify by infusing them with the revolutionary tenor which our inclusion within them demanded...

"Our pressing and crucial mission: Unless we want our hopes for a free society dashed, and if, as is the case, we aim to have our say in the life of the collectivity, we need to have an organism encapsulating those concepts which are the condensation of a splendid corpus of teaching and which we have so steadfastly clung to and enriched for their realization.

"The unions, having become hybrid agencies from the political viewpoint, as a result of the circumstances noted earlier, cannot stamp upon their activities anything except the professional function allotted to them; and there necessarily must be a driving force producing the fabulous amount of energy required to shift them in the direction which best suits the preoccupations of mankind with renewal and emancipation. The driving force to which we refer cannot but be the Specific Organization [the FAI].

"The FAI, an organism whose popular status has grown immeasurably, has, as necessarily it must have, an obligation to encompass the membership in keeping with this status and this favorable standing which the Spanish people has awarded it.

"The expansion of the membership of our organization must be immediate. Our activity in respect of the training of recruits must be so boosted that this is achieved in minimum time. As the acceleration of this recruiting drive may raise serious drawbacks due to the infiltration of persons who would previously not have been granted admission, we can, for the purposes of their adoption, employ the procedure which enables us to make our choice of them once we have them under supervision. This procedure may consist of recruiting them in such a way that, until such time as we are assured of their purity, they are kept in the dark concerning the full activities of the organization.

"We will have to overhaul the current format of our organization: Our organization on the basis of small affinity groups has produced splendid results in the heroic days of clandestinity and during those times when, without their being clandestine, people's obtuseness denied it recognition of the value which resided within it, reducing its influence to that enjoyed by its organisms alone.

"The present moment, which ushers in a new era for our movement, an era when our activities will expand considerably, compels a broad expansion of the base and the mobilization of a large number of militants who may deploy their organizing abilities in order to effect the transformation which we have for so long thought. We must seek out the unknown comrades with ability, who live amid anonymity so that they may work alongside those already distinguished in the tasks which have been but outlines. The trade union organization, our beloved CNT, may be an inexhaustible quarry of militants from which we may take whom our anarchist movement requires."[6]

On 4 November, the logic of collaborationism pursued by the leadership of the Spanish anarchist movement reached its inevitable conclusion. Following a sustained campaign by CNT National Secretary Horacio Prieto, the CNT joined Largo Caballero's Popular Front government. Caballero's new cabinet included four libertarians: two from the reformist unionist tendency of the CNT—Joan Peiró and Juan López— and two anarchists—García Oliver and Federica Montseny of the FAI Peninsular Committee. If the news was met with dismay by rank and file and militia papers such as *Linea del Fuego*, it was defended with bland self-assurance by *Solidaridad Obrera*, who acclaimed it as "one of the most momentous events in

---

6   De Santillán, op.cit., pp. 244–245.

this country's political history."[7] For the "influential" militants
of the CNT and FAI, their preemptive fusion with the State
apparatus to prevent "the revolution deviating from its course"
meant the State no longer represented a source of class division
or oppression.

For liberal historians such as Raymond Carr, the "anarchists"
had no alternative in practice:

"Their theory could not embrace the circumstances in
which they found themselves. The anarcho-syndicalists, always
afflicted with a peculiar brand of revolutionary optimism,
had assumed they would be the only power on the morrow
of the victory of the revolution. The revolution that anarcho-
syndicalists had planned as their own work was handed to
them in July, suddenly, as a reaction of a right wing coup
against a bourgeois democratic government... Powerful in
Barcelona and elsewhere in Catalonia, they were clearly not a
predominant force in the Republic as a whole; if they sought
to force through 'their' revolution they would not merely fail,
but would, by a dictatorship, outrage libertarian principles
as such and weaken the war effort against 'fascism' which, if
it triumphed, would destroy both liberal democracy and the
CNT alike. Anarcho-syndicalism had not developed, because
it had never contemplated the political strategy of a wartime
alliance of bourgeois democrats and workers' organizations
against a counter-revolutionary right."[8]

Carr is perfectly correct in his assessment here, but it was
not the "anarchists" who had no alternative in practice—they
had and were proving it with growing success to the enormous
dismay of authoritarians of every color and hue—it was the
leadership who had "no alternative in practice." Administrative
power had altered their view of the world to such an extent
that they had ceased to act as anarchists. By assuming
the responsibilities of government, irrespective of how
"revolutionary," "progressive," or antifascist that government
might or might not have been, they had ceased to be an
independent force. They had voluntarily bound themselves
to the State and gone against their own beliefs, values, and

---

7   *Solidaridad Obrera*, 4.11.1936.
8   Carr, op.cit., p. 112.

priorities. They had undergone what sociologists describe as "the agentic shift," i.e., from being champions of freedom, defenders of the revolution, and opponents of the authority system, to being agents of that system, not only responsible to it rather than their own membership, but committed to it.

As the softening-up campaign intensified, an increasing number of rank and file anarchist militants began to express their concern more publicly at the unashamedly collaborationist line being taken by the "notables" of the Regional and National Committees of the CNT-FAI. The language of coercive authority began to creep into CNT-FAI official communiqués—words redolent of morality, responsibility, duty, etc.—all concerned with suborning the conflictive interests of the individual to organic authority.

Press censorship, loyalty to the organization, and the combined external threat from the bourgeois, Marxist, and fascist camps means there is little documentary evidence to support this thesis to gauge how widely felt or profound this crisis of confidence was at the time. The anarchist leaders' entry into the Caballero government permitted that government to transfer safely to Valencia, without the risk of a popular anarchist movement taking over the administration of the capital. Safely ensconced in Valencia, the government began with a will to systematically strip away the revolutionary achievements of the people. Its first task was to recover its lost powers from the mainly autonomous regions and local committees. This heightened tension considerably between the leadership and the base by the end of November 1936. Frustration with the total disinterest and lack of contact with the mass of "anonymous activists" of the Catalan leadership became so intense that, at one stage, the Defense Committees of the Barcelona CNT apparently suggested deposing Mariano Vázquez from the regional secretaryship.[9]

In an attempt to reduce the obviously growing dissension, Alejandro Gilabert, Secretary of the Barcelona Local Federation of Anarchist Groups (FAI), issued an Orwellian warning to the more vociferous critics of governmental collaboration among the membership, the so-called "uncontrollables," by casting doubt on their integrity:

---

9   Marcos Alcón, "Recordando el 19 de Julio de 1936," *Espoir*, 20.7.1975, p. 3.

"Some enemies of anarchism, posing as comrades, are now busily talking to us of principles, tactics, and ideas. They take the view that anarchism has deviated from its normal course by dallying with the bourgeoisie and reneging upon its anti-statist principles.

"These criticisms are not prompted by very healthy intentions. They have a double motive which needs to be exposed. Naturally, anarchism in Spain has undergone a change of course. It has amended all of its negative content. When anarchism was still a movement of permanent opposition, it was only to be expected that it should deny all that was established. But we in Spain are facing special circumstances. Here, we have ceased to offer opposition so as to become a decisive force. Instead of denying, anarchism has to realize. The ones who realize will be the ones who win.

"A negative stance, the classic posture of international anarchism, cannot be expected of us Spaniards. The times are too serious for us to waste time looking outwards. Is there any positive example, any effective precedent in the outside world that we can take as our guide? International anarchism carries very little weight when it comes to prescribing guidelines for Spanish anarchism. We have to say with pride that Spain must serve as the example for the world's anarchists…

"We anarchists have an obligation and a duty to criticize and to direct the war against fascism and the revolution against capitalism, not merely from below, from the grassroots, but also by assuming positions of responsibility in the organs governing the destinies of the nation.

"Those who criticize the stance of the anarchists are covert enemies, agents of the bourgeoisie, individuals who do not get much satisfaction from the libertarian influence weighing upon the Spanish people. This is anarchism's time and we have to accept the struggle with all its consequences, shouldering the full responsibility for these decisive times!"[10]

The justification of the collaborationist theory of the leadership of the CNT and FAI failed to convince many anarchists inside or outside Spain. The foreign anarchists were not subject to the censorship imposed on the Confederal press.

10 Alejandro Gilabert, "La hora del anarquismo," *La Protesta*, Buenos Aires. Quoted in *Las pendientes resbalizadas*, Montevideo, 1939, pp. 85–86.

Writing in the French anarchist press, Sébastian Faure mildly
rebuked the CNT-FAI on three main points: participation
was not unanimously approved—a sizeable minority
opposed it, therefore the unity and the moral strength of the
movement had been damaged; political parties had gained
in influence through government participation, and notions
of direct action and class struggle had been weakened; and,
finally, the federalism of the anarchist movement had been
damaged through cooperation with a centralist, authoritarian
government. Compared to the hostile comments being
published in *Le Combat Syndicaliste*, the French anarchist paper
Terre Libre, and André Proudhommeaux's *L'Espagne Nouvelle*,
Faure's devastatingly lucid observations were conciliatory:

"If reality contradicts principles, then these principles must
be mistaken, in which case we must lose no time abandoning
them; we should be honest enough to admit their falseness in
public and we should have virtue enough to devote as much
ardor to combating them as being active against them as
formerly we did in their defense. Similarly, we should strive
forthwith to seek out more solid, more just and less fallible
principles. If, on the other hand, the principles upon which
our ideology and tactics depend still hold, regardless of the
circumstances, and are as valid today as ever they were, then
we should keep faith with them. To depart, even for a short
space of time in exceptional circumstances, from the line our
principles indicate we should adopt is to commit a grave error,
a dangerous error of judgement. To persist in this error is to
commit a grievous mistake, the consequences of which lead
on to the temporary jettisoning of principles and, through
concession after concession, to the absolute final abandonment
of principle. Once again, this is the mechanism, the slippery
slope which can lead far astray."[11]

The anarchist ministers soon discovered their powers to
influence events in Cabinet were non-existent. The Socialists
controlled the six most important ministries—War, State,
Housing, Labor, Interior, and the Presidency. The CNT and
FAI had to settle for four—Industry (Joan Peiró), Trade
(Juan López), Justice (García Oliver), and Health (Federica

---

11 Sebastian Faure, "La pointe fatale," *Le Libertaire*, No. 559, 22.7.1937.

Montseny). Largo Caballero, the enemy of the CNT, retained supreme executive power through his control of the War Council.[12]

12 Caballero's first offer of a ministry without portfolio was accepted in principle by the National Committee of the CNT headed by David Antona, acting general secretary following Horacio Prieto's resignation. This provisional (and secret) decision (which had designated Antonio Moreno as the ministerial candidate) was rejected by a National Plenum of the CNT (i.e. the base) on 3 September. By this time, however, the Catalan Regional Committee of the CNT had agreed to participate in the Generalidad government, but had gone without the luxury of referring back to representatives of the rank and file. An alternative suggestion was made that a national government be formed by the two main trade union bodies—the CNT and UGT and presided over by Largo Caballero. By the second week in September, Horacio Prieto had managed to return to Madrid from the Basque country, where he had been cut off by the rising. He reassumed the role of General Secretary and reasserted his considerable influence over the National Committee. At a meeting in Valencia, he openly criticized the anti-collaborationist decision of the National Plenum and openly advocated CNT participation, provided it had several ministries of note. He was supported by the Levante Regional Committee. The CNT National Committee was no longer repudiating involvement in politics as a matter of principle, it was merely haggling over the price. A CNT-FAI think tank, consisting of Juan López for Levante, Federica Montseny for Catalonia, and Aurelio Fernández for the Asturias, came up with proposals for a National Defense Council consisting of five delegates from the CNT, five from the UGT and four Republicans, headed by Largo Caballero with Manuel Azaña as President. Horacio Prieto convened a further two National Plenums before the earlier decision was finally revoked, one on 28 September and another on 18 October. It was at the latter that the decision, in principle, was taken to join the central government. It was left to Horacio Prieto to handle the details. Prieto proposed the names of Juan López and Joan Peiró, both former *treintistas*, and Federica Montseny and García Oliver as "radical members of the movement in their capacity as FAI militants." (Juan Gómez Casas, *La FAI*, op.cit., p. 235.) Prieto also offered Pestaña a governmental portfolio on the condition he abandon the Partido Sindicalista, but he rejected the offer, quite logically, on the grounds that it was for the CNT to abandon its position, having abandoned its principles. Pestaña commented, somewhat wryly, on the appointment of the anarchist ministers: "They have offered them nominal portfolios without any executive value at this moment in time in order to prevent them creating greater problems. What can García Oliver do in the Ministry of Justice? And what can Federica do in a Ministry of Health, which does not exist? What industry is Peiró going to lead if the only one there is is of war, and that is controlled by Largo Caballero? Apart from the fact that Juan López knows nothing of commerce, the truth is that, although he knows a lot about industry, neither can he achieve a great deal, because all foreign purchases, war material above all else, also comes under the control of the Chief of State. They have gone in as peasants, to give all with nothing in return, other than perhaps personal vanity." (De Lera, op.cit., p. 335.) There is considerable confusion surrounding Prieto's re-appointment as CNT National Secretary, having resigned on a matter of principle at the Zaragoza Congress in May that year. According to his son-in-law (César Lorenzo, op.cit., p. 221), he was re-instated by a "reunion of

By January 1937, Caballero had broken the power of the autonomous regions and converted their administrations into regional sub-governments under central control. His next main task was to restore the monopoly of violence to the State by stabilizing the revolutionary forces and demobilizing or incorporating the predominantly anarchist-controlled militias into regular military units. Militia units not prepared to accept militarization thereby converting to regular army formations, were refused weapons, provisions, and pay. "Uncontrollable" rank and file militants, who openly questioned the policies of the higher committees, were criminalized. The CNT and FAI leadership openly backed the government against their own militants and refused to support the militia columns' urgent requests for men, provisions, and munitions.[13] At a meeting

---

militants" in June, pending a national referendum. This referendum appears never to have taken place. The "reunion of militants," whoever they might have been, operated in a manifestly undemocratic way. Just weeks earlier the Zaragoza Congress had established clear norms for office holders (only one year at a time and no second re-election). Also, one could ask what Prieto held with regard to the resolutions concerning Libertarian Communism which had been approved by the rank and file at the Zaragoza Congress, resolutions which he clearly disagreed with, having chosen to resign over them.

13 On 4 October 1936, FAI members Dionisio Eroles and Aurelio Fernández were appointed executive members of the Council of Safety, a body set up under the aegis of the Generalitat to "unify" the various security services. Three weeks later, on 23 October, the obsession of the CNT-FAI leadership with "antifascist unity" widened still further with the signing of the "Pact of Unity" between the CNT and FAI and the PSUC in Catalonia. Article 2 of this agreement stated that, although they supported collectivization "of everything which may be essential in the interests of the war," the Council's understanding was that "this collectivization would fail to produce the desired results unless overseen and orchestrated by a body genuinely representative of the 'collectivity,'" in this instance the Generalitat Council. "With regard to small industry, we do not advocate collectivization here, except in cases of sedition by owners or of urgent war needs. Wheresoever small industries may be collectivized on grounds of war needs, the expropriated owners are to be compensated in such a way as to ensure their livelihoods… In the event of collectivization of foreign undertakings, a compensation formula shall be agreed which is equal to the total capital. We advocate a single command to orchestrate the actions of every combat unit, the introduction of a conscript militia and its conversion into a great People's Army, and the strengthening of discipline…" Article 15, however, showed just how far down the road of bureaucratic conservatism this once great libertarian organization had gone: "We are agreed upon common action to stamp out the harmful activities of uncontrollable groups, which, out of lack of understanding or malice, pose a threat to the implementation of this program."

called by the CNT-FAI in Valencia on 4 December to rally
support for militarization, García Oliver declared:

"No matter which organization the workers belong to, they
must employ the same methods the enemy uses in order to
win."

The distance between the base and the leadership widened
still further. As Faure had foreseen, one concession led to
another until the "notables" had been transformed into the
pliable and willing agents of the State. Through their obsession
with an illusory antifascist unity with bourgeois Liberal and
Marxist parties, the CNT and FAI leadership had become
totally compromised and prepared the scenario for the final
coup de grace—the "May Days" of 1937.

The apogee of reformist process came in May 1937 in
Barcelona when the CNT and FAI leadership ordered their
own militants to lay down the arms they had taken up in the
face of a campaign of provocation sustained by the PSUC and
the Catalan nationalists since early January. This proved to be
the key event that brought down the government of Largo
Caballero, the CNT-FAI leadership's sole ally in a predominantly
pro-Communist cabinet. It finally broke the tremendous moral
influence of the CNT-FAI in its main stronghold—Catalonia.
The way was now open for the pro-Russian government of
Juan Negrín to destroy what was perhaps the most positive
achievement of the revolution—the anarchist-dominated
Council of Aragón.

The overt hostility of the new Negrín administration to the
FAI led to a major crisis for the anarchist organization in June
1937. Negrín's newly appointed Minister of Justice, Manuel
Irujo, hit upon a legalistic line of attack against the anarchist
organization. Because the FAI was an organization which had
not been registered prior to February 1936 (in fact it had never
been registered, hence its misrepresentation as a "secret"
organization), Irujo ruled it could not retain its representation
on the Popular Tribunals. An organization not subject to
legislation and a declared enemy of state power could hardly
be permitted to share in the running of the state apparatus, a
share provided by the FAI's symbiotic relationship to the CNT.

The CNT National Committee complained bitterly about this decision. They also expressed concern about the creation of Special Tribunals, purportedly set up to try cases of espionage and high treason, but whose definition of such offences was so vague that it gave the police draconian power to quash all alleged anti-government activities. These Star Chamber courts were tailor-made for the repression of "uncontrollable" elements within the POUM and CNT.

Faced with the "consequences" of clandestinity, i.e. becoming a legally "non-existent" body, which meant losing representation on all official bodies, the Peninsular Committee of the FAI convened an urgent National Plenum in Valencia to discuss its legal position in relation to the State and to consider proposals to "overhaul" the ideological principles that had inspired it throughout its ten year existence and become a legally registered organization. The Plenum, which opened on 4 July, lasted four days. The proposals for reorganization, submitted at the end of this Plenum to a referendum of Regional Plenums, were of historic importance for the Spanish anarchist movement. From a federal body of local autonomous affinity groups, into which members were co-opted, the FAI was to be transformed into a centrally coordinated political organization open to anyone who wished to join and was prepared to cooperate with it.

The May events provided the FAI leaders with the justification they needed for a tightening of organizational discipline and for insisting on greater firmness of control. On 17 July, following an intensive propaganda recruitment drive, with meetings in Madrid, Cartagena, and Castellón, the anarchist and anarcho-syndicalist press published the following communiqué from the FAI's Peninsular Committee:

"Workers of Spain: The FAI, which has at all times battled for your emancipation, which has been in the van of the struggle for your revolution, which has as its motto in this war against fascism and the international bourgeoisie, the winning of the effective freedom of the proletarian class, opens its door to you.

"Every revolutionary who fights for freedom against a past of exploitation and calumny, against any attempt at repression and dictatorship, has an honored place. The FAI, an organization which resolved at its latest historic plenum held in Valencia to broaden its ranks so as to make our well-tried Federation the instrument of the revolutionary libertarian proletariat... The FAI is not becoming yet another political party and does not abjure its goals nor forswear its methods; it only makes its stand *vis à vis* the reality of the Spain which shapes the new world, which sheds her finest sons' unselfish blood, which seeks to make a reality of a system of intercourse apt to its libertarian existence and calls upon all true revolutionaries to carry forward this liberating enterprise.

"Our FAI seeks the victory of the people, of the proletariat and not the victory of any faction. It seeks the revolution with and for the proletariat. Let those who are with the Spanish revolution, which is the revolution for freedom, swell our ranks. Together, in a mighty iron bloc, we shall march on to victory and, together with the FAI, we shall crush the reaction."[14]

Shortly after, the Secretary of the FAI Peninsular Committee announced that the national membership of the organization stood at 160,000.

Alejandro Gilabert of the FAI spelled out what the reorganization would mean in an interview in *Solidaridad Obrera*:

"Question: In what circumstances does the anarchist movement stand at present?

"Answer: Iberian anarchism finds itself, at present, in a position to wield and to lay claim to the leadership of the revolution being lived and acted out by our people: for this reason, the FAI has agreed to equip itself with a new organizational structure, admitting all persons of libertarian inclinations into its ranks.

"Question: What are the implications of the FAI's new structure?

"Answer: In political terms, it will produce a real revolution. Because, before a month is out, the FAI will be the most powerful revolutionary movement in Spain, not to mention its thousands of members in Portugal, France, and the USA. For, as you must be aware, the Portuguese Anarchist Union, the Federation of Spanish Speaking Anarchist groups in France,

---

14 Peirats, op.cit., Vol. II. Ch. 24.

and the Federation of Spanish Speaking Anarchist groups in the USA are also affiliated to the FAI.

"Question: How many members has the FAI in Barcelona?

"Answer: With the new format, the FAI will have upwards of 30,000 members in Barcelona alone, for it now turns out that a huge mass of anarchists were not hitherto affiliated to the FAI, even though they spoke on its behalf from time to time.

"Question: Does the new format it has adopted imply that the FAI has turned itself into a new political party?

"Answer: It will be a revolutionary party, or a specific organization that will suffuse public life so as to provide the proletariat with an instrument to orchestrate its revolutionary feats, driving the revolution forward from all of the popular organisms.

"Question: How will the FAI operate in the light of its new format?

"Answer: According to the new approach, the FAI will do everything possible to ensure that our revolution may not be the expression of any totalitarian creed, but rather the creature of all the popular antifascist sectors with any influence upon political and social life. As anarchists, we are the foes of any totalitarian form of government, and the FAI in its new phase of political activity will deploy all of its resources to avert the disfiguration or strangulation of the Iberian revolution by any party dictatorship.

"Question: Is the FAI giving up on the introduction of Libertarian Communism?

"Answer: We, the anarchists within the discipline of the FAI, want the future of Iberia to be the product of the concerted action of all those sectors who are at one on the creation of a society without class privileges, wherein the organisms of labor, administration, and intercourse may be the principal factor in furnishing our country, by means of federal practices, with the channel that will meet the needs of her different regions, for this is the political, social, and revolutionary import of the FAI's new structure according to the agreements reached at the Peninsular Plenum which our organization held in Valencia during the first days of July."[15]

---

15 *Solidaridad Obrera*, 10.8.1937.

The Peninsular Committee's proposals that the FAI should become a legally registered political body in order to defend itself and build up a mass anarchist organization met with a hostile reception from a sizeable minority of those who had remained affiliated to the organization. Feelings ran particularly high in Catalonia where, during a Regional Plenum of groups on 5–7 August, angry clashes broke out between supporters of the reorganization and those who saw it as a highly dangerous venture which ran directly contrary to the fundamental aims and principles of anarchism. A split was threatened. Dissent had focused on the section of the resolution which stated: "in contrast to our inhibitionist stance of the past, it is the duty of all anarchists to take a place in whatever public institutions may serve to consolidate and to bolster the new state of affairs." The militants took this as a clear commitment to political intervention in government and official institutions.

The proposal that FAI personnel delegated to public offices would be obliged to carry out all missions entrusted to them and to report back on their tasks and their work to the committees also caused emotions to run high. "Any FAI affiliate," the resolution added, "who may be assigned to take up any public office—regardless of the nature of that office—shall be liable to be disowned or dismissed from that office just as soon as the organization's appropriate organs may so determine; and the committees shall have an obligation to report back on such instances also."

Equally worrying was the fact that the tried and tested affinity group structure, which had been the core of organized anarchism in Spain since the days of the First International, was being abandoned, and membership of the FAI was to be thrown open to the vaguely defined "like-minded individuals or militants." Neither was there any reference in the resolution either reaffirming anarchist principles or denouncing the State. The only reference to anarchism was the brief statement: "As anarchists, we are the foes of dictatorship, whether they be the dictatorship of castle or party; we are the foes of the totalitarian form of government and we believe that the future of our people will be the result of the concerted actions of all those sectors which collaborate in the creation of a society without privileges, wherein the organisms of labor, administration, and intercourse may be the principal factors in furnishing Spain, by means of federal practices, with the channel that will meet the needs of the different regions."[16]

In spite of the angry denunciations of the betrayal of anarchist principles, majority feeling at the Plenum was to accept the new format in its entirety. But, given the size of the minority opposed, there was a serious threat to the unity of the movement. A working party was set up to seek a compromise formula that might reconcile the opposing views. The working party drafted a proposition that was eventually approved by all the groups from Catalonia attending the Plenum:

"Being persuaded that cordiality between members of the anarchist communion is inescapably necessary, we hereby state... That with regard to the result of deliberations held on whether to grant or withhold approval from the proposition drawn up by the Peninsular Plenum, and given that a majority pronounced in favor of it, said proposition is taken as approved: but it being recognized that there has also been great opposition to that proposition, so much so as to degenerate into blatant threat of splitting, it is to be left up to the groups who do not accept it to go on as they have hitherto, but bearing in mind that their decisions of an organizational nature will carry the numerical weight appropriate to the size of their membership."[17]

The following week, 14 August, a plenum of delegates from the Barcelona groups agreed that the Local Federation's Secretariat would call upon each ward separately to appoint the reorganizing commission of the groups. It was also agreed to respect the autonomy of the affinity groups not in agreement with the new structure. These groups were to remain outside the new structure but would have organizational representation at the plenums and congresses.

Although membership of the FAI rocketed, a significant number of groups refused to cooperate with the proposed restructuring of the organization, and a stalemate ensued. FAI spokesman Alejandro Gilabert sought to allay the fears of the

---

16 Ibid.
17 Ibid., 12.10.1937.

opposition groups in an article in *Solidaridad Obrera* entitled "Comrades, the FAI!":

"It is not out of place to dwell upon the matter. No anarchist should cease to think of the FAI as his own organization. I have said, and reiterated on many occasions, that a large number of anarchists are not organized in the FAI, oblivious of the enormous harm they do the libertarian movement by this attitude. It is not enough to be a militant of the CNT...the anarchist must pursue specifically libertarian activities under the aegis and discipline of his own organization.

"Those comrades who believe that the CNT represents anarchism are sorely mistaken. The CNT is a mass organization which defends the moral and economic interests of the workers, but it is not a specifically anarchist organization, though its objective is Libertarian Communism. Let it be said once and for all, it is the FAI which represents anarchism. It is true there have been innumerable circumstances that forced many anarchists to hold back somewhat from the FAI, but it is no less true that those circumstances have been overcome and beaten. Today there is a place in the FAI for all libertarian elements. The new organizational format with which the FAI has endowed itself offers the movement greater breadth and affords each militant somewhere to be active to some effect."

The "Friends of Durruti," an important group of rank and file activists originating from the Durruti Column, provided the most perceptive analysis of what the changes in the FAI structure meant. Since the early Spring of 1937, when their paper, *El Amigo del Pueblo*, first appeared, this "conscious minority" had been the only organized section within the movement to publicly challenge the ever-deepening embroilment of the CNT-FAI "administrators" in collaboration, and urge a return to the revolutionary spirit of the summer of 1936. The "Friends of Durruti" saw the real purpose behind the changes that would only benefit self-serving elitists—to justify and perpetuate collaboration. The CNT-FAI leadership had gone so far down the governmental road that the situational etiquette of the working relationship they had established with state functionaries meant they had now become part of the authority system which, as anarchists, they had previously repudiated. They had become part of the problem. To withdraw from government now would be a public admission that their repudiation of Libertarian Communism and all their actions to date had been destructive and negative. The sequential dynamic of their position left them with no choice but to see collaboration through right to the bitter end. If social revolution was to be restored to the agenda it would not come through the official apparatus of the CNT-FAI:

"The real meaning of the decision [of the FAI plenum] is the fact that the band of comrades who recommend this metamorphosis aim, not only to see the FAI possessed of an organization structure similar to that of other sectors, but also, on the basis of this ill-considered step, the intention is to perpetuate the governmental collaboration begun after July. At the very moment when a complete re-assessment of mistakes is called for, the error is compounded and the whole catalog of catastrophes and counter-revolution blessed and absolved.

"The lesson has been in vain. During the course of the past year it has become clear that it is not possible to share revolutionary responsibility with the petite-bourgeoisie and with those parties which, although they claim the label 'Marxist' are self-evidently appendages of the deskocracy. But common sense has yet to have its way in our ranks.

"It has been stated with the utmost clarity that Libertarian Communism is being foresworn for the sake of a rapprochement with antifascist groupings. Excellent! Are these other groupings by some chance forswearing their programs so as to win over the CNT and the FAI...?

"It is truly deplorable that certain comrades with a long history in the anarchist movement have yet to grasp the reason why the anarchist groups have been able to work feats of such colossal importance, which may be equalled, but cannot possibly be outdone. And it defies understanding that, entering once again a period of oppression, there is this wish to tear up the formula which has opened up so many possibilities to the struggles waged by the proletariat of this peninsula.

"But what really disturbs us is the new program that is to take the place of Libertarian Communism. Will the confusion that favors only parvenus and individuals who seek only to 'get on' at the expense of the proletariat prevail? Is the aim that our organization should be a mainstay of bourgeois democracy and of foreign capitalism to boot?

"It appears that this new approach is in line with certain editorials that have appeared in *Solidaridad Obrera*. There is talk of governing. But how to go about governing? Is there to be a repetition of the hybrid arrangements which have been concocted over the past years of counter-revolution? Will there be government arm in arm with the petite-bourgeoisie?

"A few days ago one of the comrades who advocates this new approach stated publicly that we agreed with a certain sentence or notion voiced by Manuel Azaña in his latest address. But can this possibly be said? Azaña spoke of a regime of freedom. But is anyone going to believe that Azaña can assure the working class of a single atom of freedom? And what is this freedom of which Azaña speaks to us? And how are we anarchists going to see eye to eye with one of the biggest tyrants the proletariat has had to put up with?"[18]

By the end of August 1937, with the break up of the Council of Aragón, the last stronghold of anarchist practice, the Spanish revolution, perhaps the most profound and inspiring social experiment in recorded history, was over; the Republican bourgeoisie and the Soviet advisers of the Spanish Communist Party were free from the immediate danger from the enemy within—the Catalan Nationalists had been neutralized, the Socialist Party had been split, and the influence of the "conscious minority" of anarchists had collapsed—but they were too late. Having surrendered their political, military, and economic power to their own leaders, they had seen these leaders acquiesce to the systematic dismantlement of their achievements; the terrorizing, imprisonment, and murder of their militants; and the perversion of their aspirations for a free society out of all identifiable shape. With nothing left to fight for, it was now just a matter of time before the will to resist collapsed, taking with it the Second Republic and that institutional monstrosity which had grown out of what had once been a great working class association—the FAI!

---

18 *El Amigo del Pueblo*, No. 6, 12.8.1937.

Index

234   *We, the Anarchists!*

S

Sagra, Ramón de la 2
Saint Simonism 2
Salvat (Companys' envoy) 168–169
Sanjurjo Sacanell, Gen. José 112, 134–135
Sanz, Ricardo 19, 20, 80, 163, 168
Sastre, Miguel 18
Schapiro, Alexander 58–59, 129, 137
Seguí, Salvador "El Noi del Sucre" 17–18, 20, 21–22, 24
"Seisdedos" 140
Selvas, Juan 124
Sindicato Libre ("Free" Union) 18
Sindicatos de oposición 130
Sirvent, Manuel (CNT National Secretary 1930) 14, 93
Spanish Socialist Party (PSOE) 23, 99, 148, 164, 199
Socialist Union of Catalonia 193
Social Origins of Dictatorship and Democracy 85
El Sol 86
Soldado del Pueblo 174
Soldevilla, Cardinal Archbishop of Zaragoza 22
Solidaridad Obrera 19–20, 23–24, 25, 74, 76, 77, 81, 97, 98, 100–101, 114, 115, 116, 121, 122, 136, 142, 149, 150, 162, 173, 178, 183, 191, 200, 204, 210, 218, 219, 222, 224
Solidaridad Proletaria 27
Solidarios, Los (book) 19
Sousa, Germinal de 101, 166
S*pain* 139
Spain 1808–1975 97
Spain The Unfinished Revolution 40
Spanish Anarchists, The 82
Spanish Civil War, The 40
Spanish Cockpit, The 40
Spanish Labyrinth, The 40
Spanish Republic and the Civil War 1931–1939, The 40
Spanish Tragedy, The 40, 96
Special Tribunals 217
Suberviela, Gregorio 20, 80

Suplemento 30
Supplies Committee 200

T

Tarradellas, Josep 193
Terre Libre 213
Terrorismo en Barcelona 18
Thomas, Hugh 40, 123–124, 148
Tiempos Nuevos 162, 180
Tierra, La 114, 139
Tierra y Libertad 46, 118, 139, 148, 157, 166, 174, 203
Timón 180, 199
Tolstoy, Leo 49
Torhyo, Jacinto 158, 166
Torres Escartín, Rafael 19
Toto, Antonio del 20
Trabal Sanz, José Antonio 167, 169
trabazón 202
Treintista Manifesto 101, 108, 179
Treintistas 80, 109, 128–129, 177, 197, 214

U

UGT (Unión General de Trabajadores) 10, 12, 18, 23–24, 34, 61, 82–83, 94, 115, 121, 136, 138, 147, 160, 177, 182, 190, 193–199, 200, 214
Uleda, Federico 108
Unamuno, Miguel de 92
Un ano de conspiración (antes de la republica) 71
Union of Militants 62
Urales, Federic (Montseny I Carret, Joan and family) 26, 57, 81, 186

V

Vallina, Pedro 99
Vázquez, Mariano Rodríguez, "Marianet" (CNT National Secretary 1936–1939) 14, 189–190, 193–194, 196, 202–203, 211
Velasco, Martínez de 145

Friends of AK Press

AK Press is a worker-run co-operative that publishes and distributes radical books, visual & audio media, and other mind-altering material. We're a dozen people who work long hours for short money, because we believe in what we do. We're anarchists, which is reflected both in the books we publish and in the way we organize our business. All decisions at AK Press are made collectively—from what we publish to what we carry for distribution. All the work, from sweeping the floors to answering the phones, is shared equally.

Currently, AK Press publishes about twenty titles per year. If we had the money, we would publish forty titles in the coming year—new works from new voices, as well as a growing mountain of classic titles that, unfortunately, are being left out of print.

All these projects can come out sooner with your help. With the Friends of AK Press program, you pay a minimum of $25 per month (of course, we welcome larger contributions), for a minimum three month period. All the money received goes directly into our publishing funds. In return, Friends automatically receive (for the duration of their membership), one FREE copy of EVERY new AK Press title (books, dvds, and cds), as they appear. As well, Friends are entitled to a 10% discount on everything featured in the AK Press Distribution Catalog and on our website—thousands of titles from the hundreds of publishers we work with. We also have a program where groups or individuals can sponsor a whole book. Please contact us for details. To become a Friend, go to: http://www.akpress.org.

Also from AK Press

WARD CHURCHILL—Pacifism as Pathology
WARD CHURCHILL—Since Predator Came
CLASS WAR FEDERATION —Unfinished Business
HARRY CLEAVER—Reading Capital Politically
ALEXANDER COCKBURN & JEFFREY ST. CLAIR (eds)—Dime's Worth
of Difference
ALEXANDER COCKBURN & JEFFREY ST. CLAIR (eds)—End Times:
Death of the Fourth Estate
ALEXANDER COCKBURN & JEFFREY ST. CLAIR (eds)—The Politics of
Anti-Semitism
ALEXANDER COCKBURN & JEFFREY ST. CLAIR (eds)—Serpents in
the Garden
DANIEL COHN-BENDIT & GABRIEL COHN-BENDIT—Obsolete
Communism: The Left-Wing Alternative
BENJAMIN DANGL—The Price of Fire
DARK STAR COLLECTIVE —Beneath the Paving Stones
DARK STAR COLLECTIVE —Quiet Rumours: An Anarcha-Feminist
Reader
VOLTAIRINE de CLEYRE—Voltairine de Cleyre Reader
CHRIS DUNCAN—My First Time: A Collection of First Punk Show
Stories
EG SMITH COLLECTIVE—Animal Ingredients A–Z (3rd edition)
HOWARD EHRLICH—Reinventing Anarchy, Again
SIMON FORD—Realization and Suppression of the Situationist
International
JOSHUA FRANK & JEFFREY ST. CLAIR (eds)—Red State Rebels
BENJAMIN FRANKS—Rebel Alliances
YVES FREMION & VOLNY—Orgasms of History: 3000 Years of
Spontaneous Revolt
EMMA GOLDMAN (edited by DAVID PORTER)—Vision on Fire
BERNARD GOLDSTEIN—Five Years in the Warsaw Ghetto
DAVID GRAEBER—Possibilities
DAVID GRAEBER & STEVPHEN SHUKAITIS—Constituent Imagination
DANIEL GUÉRIN—No Gods No Masters: An Anthology of Anarchism
AGUSTIN GUILLAMÓN—The Friends Of Durruti Group, 1937–1939
ANN HANSEN—Direct Action: Memoirs Of An Urban Guerilla
MATT HERN—Everywhere All the Time: A New Deschooling Reader
WILLIAM HERRICK—Jumping the Line
FRED HO—Legacy to Liberation
GEORGY KATSIAFICAS—Subversion of Politics
KATHY KELLY—Other Lands Have Dreams: From Baghdad to Pekin
Prison
JAMES KELMAN—Some Recent Attacks: Essays Cultural And Political
TERENCE KISSACK—Free Comrades
KEN KNABB—Complete Cinematic Works of Guy Debord
KATYA KOMISARUK—Beat the Heat: How to Handle Encounters With
Law Enforcement
PETER KROPOTKIN—The Conquest of Bread
SAUL LANDAU—A Bush & Botox World

CDs
MUMIA ABU JAMAL—All Things Censored Vol.1
JUDI BARI—Who Bombed Judi Bari?
JELLO BIAFRA—Become the Media
JELLO BIAFRA—In the Grip of Official Treason
NOAM CHOMSKY—Case Studies in Hypocrisy
NOAM CHOMSKY—The Imperial Presidency
NOAM CHOMSKY—New War On Terrorism: Fact And Fiction
NOAM CHOMSKY—Propaganda and Control of the Public Mind
NOAM CHOMSKY & CHUMBAWAMBA—For A Free Humanity: For
    Anarchy
CHUMBAWAMBA—A Singsong and A Scrap
WARD CHURCHILL—Doing Time: The Politics of Imprisonment
WARD CHURCHILL—In A Pig's Eye
ANGELA DAVIS—The Prison Industrial Complex
THE EX—1936: The Spanish Revolution
NORMAN FINKELSTEIN—An Issue of Justice
ROBERT FISK—War, Journalism, and the Middle East
FREEDOM ARCHIVES—Chile: Promise of Freedom
FREEDOM ARCHIVES—Prisons on Fire: George Jackson, Attica & Black
    Liberation
FREEDOM ARCHIVES—Robert F. Williams
JAMES KELMAN—Seven Stories
TOM LEONARD—Nora's Place and Other Poems 1965–99
CASEY NEILL—Memory Against Forgetting
GREG PALAST—Live From the Armed Madhouse
UTAH PHILLIPS—I've Got To know
UTAH PHILLIPS—Starlight on the Rails box set
DAVID ROVICS—Behind the Barricades: Best of David Rovics
ARUNDHATI ROY—Come September
HOWARD ZINN—Heroes and Martyrs: Emma Goldman, Sacco &
    Vanzetti, and the Revolutionary Struggle
HOWARD ZINN—A People's History of the United States
HOWARD ZINN—People's History Project Box Set
HOWARD ZINN—Stories Hollywood Never Tells

DVDs
NOAM CHOMSKY—Imperial Grand Strategy
NOAM CHOMSKY—Distorted Morality
STEVEN FISCHLER & JOEL SUCHER—Anarchism in America/Free
    Voice of Labor
ARUNDHATI ROY—Instant-Mix Imperial Democracy
ROZ PAYNE ARCHIVES—What We Want, What We Believe: The Black
    Panther Party Library (4 DVD set)
HOWARD ZINN & ANTHONY ARNOVE (ed.)—Readings from Voices
    of a People's History of the United States